Lecture Notes of the Institute for Computer Sciences, Social Informatics and Telecommunications Engineering 435

More information about this series at https://link.springer.com/bookseries/8197

Eva Brooks · Jeanette Sjöberg ·
Anders Kalsgaard Møller (Eds.)

Design, Learning, and Innovation

6th EAI International Conference, DLI 2021
Virtual Event, December 10–11, 2021
Proceedings

Editors
Eva Brooks ⓘ
Department of Culture and Learning
Aalborg University
Aalborg, Denmark

Jeanette Sjöberg ⓘ
Halmstad University
Halmstad, Sweden

Anders Kalsgaard Møller ⓘ
Aalborg University
Aalborg, Denmark

ISSN 1867-8211   ISSN 1867-822X (electronic)
Lecture Notes of the Institute for Computer Sciences, Social Informatics
and Telecommunications Engineering
ISBN 978-3-031-06674-0   ISBN 978-3-031-06675-7 (eBook)
https://doi.org/10.1007/978-3-031-06675-7

This Springer imprint is published by the registered company Springer Nature Switzerland AG
The registered company address is: Gewerbestrasse 11, 6330 Cham, Switzerland

Preface

We are delighted to introduce the proceedings of the sixth edition of the European Alliance for Innovation (EAI) International Conference on Design, Learning & Innovation (DLI 2021). This conference brought together researchers, designers, educators, and practitioners around the world to share their latest research findings, emerging technologies, and innovative methods in the areas of inclusive and playful designs and learning with digital technologies. The theme for DLI 2021 was "Shifting boundaries to discover novel ways and emerging technologies to realise human needs, ideas, and desires", targeting a conceptualisation of the effects and impact of digital technologies for, in an inclusive and playful way, fostering human beings to realise their needs, ideas and desires.

The technical program of DLI 2021 consisted of 17 full papers included in the four main conference tracks Session 1 – Digital Technologies, Design and Learning; Session 2 – Tools and Models; Session 3 – Artificial Intelligence, Virtual Reality and Augmented Reality in Learning; and Session 4 – Innovative Designs and Learning. These four tracks were chaired by Vitor Carvalho, Camilla Finsterbach Kaup, Ulrike Sperling and Susanne Dau respectively. Their contribution to the discussion related to the sessions was exceptional and created a productive online atmosphere with fruitful and constructive dialogues.

Wendy Keay-Bright, Professor and Director of the Centre for Applied Research in Inclusive Arts and Design (CARIAD) at Cardiff Metropolitan University, Wales, gave an inspirational keynote presentation on, "Crafting the Space: Creating Playful Interactions within Inclusive Design Contexts", which was grounded in her experiences from several years of working closely with end users.

The paper presentations addressed new dimensions and key challenges and provided critical and innovative perspectives of employing digital technologies and games to develop and implement future design, learning and innovation. This was reflected, among other things, by the paper which received the Best Paper Award of DLI 2021 titled "Orchestration Between Computational Thinking and Mathematics" – congratulations to Camilla Finsterbach Kaup from Aalborg University, Denmark, on the award!

The collaboration between the Organizing Committee members was essential for the successful planning and performance of the conference. We sincerely appreciated the coordination with Lenka Lezanska, senior conference manager at the European Alliance for Innovation (EAI), and with the steering chair, Imrich Chlamtac. We are genuinely thankful for support of the Organizing committee team: Anders Kalsgaard Møller (Technical Program Committee Chair), João Martinho Moura (Web Chair), Camilla Finsterbach Kaup and Maja Højslet Schurer (Publicity and Social Media Chairs), Patrik Lilja Skånberg (Workshop and Symposium Chair), Dorina Gnaur (Sponsorship and Exhibit Chair) and Emma Edstrand (Work-in-Progress and Poster Chair).

We also acknowledge the outstanding work by the Technical Program Committee. Last but not least, we are grateful to all the authors who submitted their papers to the DLI 2021 conference.

We strongly believe that the DLI conference provides a fruitful forum for researchers, designers, educators and practitioners to discuss the cross-disciplinary field of digital technology and its implications on design, learning and innovation. We also expect that the future DLI conferences will be as fruitful for knowledge exchange as this year's, as indicated by the contributions presented in this volume.

January 2021

Eva Brooks
Jeanette Sjöberg

Organization

Steering Committee

Imrich Chlamtac   University of Trento, Italy
Eva Brooks   Aalborg University, Denmark

Organizing Committee

General Co-chairs

Jeanette Sjöberg   Halmstad University, Sweden
Eva Brooks   Aalborg University, Denmark

Technical Program Committee Chair

Anders Kalsgaard Møller   Aalborg University, Denmark

Sponsorship and Exhibit Chair

Dorina Gnaur   Aalborg University, Denmark

Workshops and Symposium Chair

Patrik Lilja Skånberg   Halmstad University, Sweden

Publicity and Social Media Chairs

Camilla Finsterbach Kau   Aalborg University, Denmark
Maja Højslet Schurer   Aalborg University, Denmark

Publications Chairs

Eva Brooks   Aalborg University, Denmark
Jeanette Sjöberg   Halmstad University, Sweden

Web Chair

João Martinho Moura   Polytechnic Institute of Cávado and Ave, Portugal

Work-in-Progress and Posters Chair

Emma Edstrand   Halmstad University, Sweden

Technical Program Committee

S. R. Balasundaram	National Institute of Technology, Tiruchirappalli, India
Pedro Beça	University of Aveiro, Portugal
Thomas Bjørner	Aalborg University, Denmark
Anthony Lewis Brooks	Aalborg University, Denmark
Eva Brooks	Aalborg University, Denmark
Ana Amélia Carvalho	University of Coimbra, Portugal
Martin Cooney	Halmstad University, Sweden
Susanne Dau	University College of Northern Denmark, Denmark
Emma Edstrand	Halmstad University, Sweden
Taciana Pontual da Rocha Falcão	Universidade Federal Rural de Pernambuco, Brazil
Dorina Gnaur	Aalborg University, Denmark
Lena Hylving	Halmstad University, Sweden
Henrik Kasch	University College of Southern Denmark, Denmark
Camilla Finsterbach Kaup	Aalborg University, Denmark
Susanne Lindberg	Halmstad University, Sweden
Anders Kalsgaard Møller	Aalborg University, Denmark
Stamatis Papadakis	University of Crete, Greece
Louise Peterson	University of Gothenburg, Sweden
Vitor Sá	Catholic University of Portugal, Portugal
Maja Højslet Schurer	Aalborg University, Denmark
Jeanette Sjöberg	Halmstad University, Sweden
Patrik Lilja Skångberg	Halmstad University, Sweden
Valentina Terzieva	Institute of Information and Communication Technologies, Bulgarian Academy of Sciences, Bulgaria
Michele Della Ventura	Music Academy "Studio Musica", Italy
Pontus Wärnestål	Halmstad University, Sweden

Contents

Innovative Designs and Learning

Digital Technologies, Design and Learning

Digital Technologies, Design and Learning

Jeanette Sjöberg[1] and Eva Brooks[2]

[1] Halmstad University, Kristian IVs väg 3, 30118 Halmstad, Sweden
jeanette.sjoberg@hh.se
[2] Aalborg University, Kroghstræde 3, 9220 Aalborg, Denmark
eb@hum.aau.dk

Abstract. In this first part of the volume, contributions from EAI DLI 2021 elaborates on questions related to how people generally can contribute to the development of enhanced learning by taking active participation in various societal practices, which are personalised designed and includes digital technologies, and which are evaluated separately. Focus is on how digital technologies can add value in various learning scenarios and settings through design.

Keywords: Adaptive Learning Platforms · AI · Design processes · Digitalisation · Evaluation · Learning analytics · Learning environments · Innovation · Personalisation

1 Introduction

1.1 Scope

This first section of the EAI DLI 2021 proceedings is themed "Digital Technologies, Design and Learning" and it focuses on the emergent potentials digital technology might have for enhancing learning.

> The education sector has an opening to provide a more significant objective in communication conditions, appropriate knowledge, and deployment of understanding. Information will be set free and easily accessible; nevertheless, the perspective and understanding of knowledge will be essential to unravelling innovative learning methods [1, p. 32].

The digitalization of society means, among other things, new ways of dealing with everyday life, which often must start from an individual perspective. It will therefore be important to evaluate various aspects of digital technologies in order to find out how they best can contribute to support individual development and personalised learning. How do we design for such digital technologies to be integrated in learning practices? In what ways can we create knowledge through participation and how do we retain these experiences and use them to improve a practice? The four chapters included here raise issues about how digital technologies can be used to develop design processes for learning in various settings and stages of life, where a participatory perspective becomes a crucial aspect for understanding the importance of personalised commitment and individual creation of learning processes in relation to digital technology. Furthermore, they seek to understand how to evaluate user experiences so that they can enrich the design practice of an educational setting. The chapters in different ways contribute to defining various learning practices which includes digital technologies as support for learning, where focus primarily is on the design processes and the evaluation of those. The purpose for evaluation is raised as an important issue, since it contributes to the individual shaping of contemporary learning practices.

The opening contribution in this first section investigates the potential of technology, in the form of a digital platform, in combination with design to support, optimise and develop the performance of Taekwondo athletes. The second contribution presents a study which provides a framework for how accelerated learning about human-centred AI as design practice can be facilitated in small and medium-sized companies by the means of an educational program, as well as accounts for the different perspectives of the participants' experiences. The third contribution includes a systematic literature review on different evaluation methods being used for evaluating Learning Analytics and Learning Analytics Dashboards on Adaptive Learning Platforms, focusing on the purposes for evaluation. Finally, the fourth contribution examines various ways of personalization at the same time, focusing on written, non-interactive narratives, and testing how this affects the reader experience, focusing on how to get an understanding of a person's personality to find stories that fit individual preferences by using a narrative approach.

The following text snippets elaborate from each contribution to further assist readership.

2   Development and Design of an Evaluation Interface for Taekwondo Athletes: First Insights

This paper is authored by Tânia Silva, Nuno Martins, Pedro Cunha, Vítor Carvalho and Filomena Soares, and titled Development and Design of an Evaluation Interface for Taekwondo Athletes: First Insights. This project is integrated in a work team whose focus is the development of the technological and design components, and here the authors discuss the first research phase of the development and analysis of a support interface for Taekwondo athletes, where the first research phase consisted of analysing content related to the importance of design and data structuring in sports. The development of technological solutions to support athletes' training and performance in Taekwondo has been very limited and the aim of this study is therefore to solve the existing gap through the development of an interactive digital platform allowing real time analysis and feedback from the coach to the athlete based on relevant data. Hence, the overall purpose of the study was to explore the potential of technology in combination with design to optimise and develop the performance of Taekwondo athletes. The authors argue that it is possible to promote the theoretical and practical learning of Taekwondo, based on the access to information such as the values of the force applied in the strikes, the calculation of acceleration and speed of the movements performed. Thus, the creation of an appealing and objective interface is relevant, with the intention of reducing the athlete's analysis time and, simultaneously, contributing to the progressive performance of the athlete. The main contribution of this paper clarifies that by exploring and evaluating various sport interfaces (not only Taekwondo), which was the first stage of the project, the authors could identify relevant needs that trigger the necessity of development of a specific platform for Taekwondo athletes, such as: non-existence of evaluation systems for the athletes; absence of a database to store information related to the athletes' training; lack of organisation regarding the learning content of the different techniques of the sport.

3   Multi-disciplinary Learning and Innovation for Professional Design of AI-Powered Services

The paper titled Multi-disciplinary Learning and Innovation for Professional Design of AI-Powered Services by Pontus Wärnestål includes a study where a practical learning and innovation program called AI.m1, that aims to accelerate companies' ability to design human-centred AI-powered services, has been examined through interviews with participating designers, developers, innovation leaders, researchers, AI experts, and company leaders who has completed the learning cycle of the model, which has been iterated in stages. Currently, 15 small and medium sized companies from different sectors have completed the learning cycle. The aim of this study is to provide a framework for how accelerated learning about human-centred AI as design practice can be facilitated in small and medium-sized companies. A second aim of the study is to evaluate the AI.m program experience from three perspectives: the company perspective, researchers' perspective, and the design agency perspective. There is a high complexity of business, service, and user experience design for AI-powered digital platforms, and consequently the author argues that there is a strong need for designers and innovation leaders to be "AI literate" to make better use of AI technologies in human centered services and products. This includes learning how to adapt design and development processes to fit AI-powered services, communication in cross-functional teams, and continuous competency development strategies. Methodologically, 24 semi-structured deep interviews were carried out individually and were analysed qualitatively by service innovation researchers. In addition, auxiliary data (such as written notes, whiteboard photographs and digital collaboration areas that were created during the workshops) were used to complement the interpretation of verbal anecdotes raised in the interviews in the analysis stage. The qualitative analysis provided a set of categories of learning implications organised as a framework of prompts to help organisations develop AI and design capabilities. The study concludes that the AI.m learning cycle and process model has successfully fast-tracked 15 small and medium-sized companies from a variety of sectors in their capability development of using emerging AI technologies in their business and service offerings.

4   Evaluation of Learning Analytics on Adaptive LearningSystems: A work in progress Systematic Review

The paper titled Evaluation of Learning Analytics on Adaptive LearningSystems: A work in progress Systematic Review, authored by Tobias Tretow-Fish and Md. Khalid, addresses issues relating to the relatively new and multi-disciplinary research area of Adaptive Learning (AL). More specifically, the authors claim that there is an absence of a systematic overview of methods for evaluating Learning Analytics (LA) and Learning Analytics Dashboards (LAD) of Adaptive Learning Platforms (ALPs), which is why they sat out to perform a systematic literature review of the field, focusing on the purposes for evaluation due to different methods being used. The aim of the study was to review evaluation methods used for LA and LAD on ALPs. The authors argue that it is interesting to investigate the purpose of applying different methods of evaluation to get a better understanding of which perspectives are being evaluated from as well as how they are being evaluated. In the study, 10 articles and 2 reviews were analysed and synthesised based on methods used in the respective studies. The selection of articles was conducted according to the Preferred Reporting Items for Systematic Reviews and Meta-Analyses (PRISMA), which includes four phases: identification, screening, eligibility, and included. In the analysis, the methods used in the studies were then grouped into five categories (C1-5): C1) evaluation of LA and LAD design and framework, C2) evaluation of performance with LA and LAD, C3) evaluation of adaptivity functions of the system, C4) evaluation of perceived value, and C5) Evaluation of pedagogical and didactic theory/context. The main contribution of this paper clarifies that while there is a relative high representation of evaluations in the C1-C4 categories of methods, which contribute to the design and development of the interaction and interface design features, the C5 category is not represented, which means that the presence of pedagogical and didactic theory in the LA, LAD, and ALPs is lacking. Though traces of pedagogical theory are present none of the studies evaluate its impact.

5   Personality in Personalisation: A User Study with an Interactive Narrative, a Personality Test and a Personalised Short Story

The final contribution in this part of the DLI 2021 section on digital Technologies, design and learning is authored by Waltteri Nybom and Mick Grierson and titled Personality in Personalisation: A User Study with an Interactive Narrative, a Personality Test and a Personalised Short Story. The paper focuses on how to get an understanding of a person's personality in order to find stories that fit individual preferences by using a narrative approach. In this study, which was developed to explore the use of a psychological frameworks for the personalisation of narratives, users are presented with an interactive narrative designed to capture their personality using the five-factor model (FFM) and the Need for Affect (NFA), and then personalises a narrative to match with their personality scores. Hence, the study seeks to consider various ways of personalization at the same time, focusing on written, non-interactive narratives, and testing how this affects the reader experience. The study consists of 59 participants (17 women, 36 men), volunteers of all ages above 18 who were found by posting about the study on internet discussion boards on interactive narratives and other relevant topics. The study consists of three sections: an interactive narrative specifically written for this study which uses a 2nd person perspective where the user assumes the role of the protagonist and makes choices that determine what the protagonist does and how the plot advances; a personality test consisting of a 10-item FFM questionnaire and a 10-item NFA questionnaire; and a personalised short story written for the experiment and personalised for the participants. The findings show that the personalisation appeared to work well, especially regarding the issue of relating with the protagonist. It was also found that extraverted people appear to prefer reading narratives with less formal language, and introverts prefer narratives with more formal language, something that does not appear to have been tested before.

6 Epilogue and Acknowledgements

This first section on Digital Technologies, Design and Learning, introduces four contributions to promote readership of each full paper that are presented in the following chapters. In doing so, the authors of this chapter acknowledge the contribution to this section/volume by each author whose original work was presented in the EAI DLI 2021 events online December 2, 2021.

Reference

1. Qureshi, M. I., Khan, N., Raza, H., Imran, A., Ismail, F.: Digital technologies in education 4.0. does it enhance the effectiveness of learning? A systematic literature review. Int. J. Interact. Mob. Technol. **15**(4), 31-47 (2021)

Development and Design of an Evaluation Interface for Taekwondo Athletes: First Insights

Tânia Silva[1], Nuno Martins[2] (ID), Pedro Cunha[3] (ID), Vítor Carvalho[3,4](✉) (ID), and Filomena Soares[3] (ID)

[1] School of Design, IPCA, 4750-810 Barcelos, Portugal
[2] Research Institute for Design, Media and Culture, School of Design, Polytechnic Institute of Cavado and Ave, 4750-810 Barcelos, Portugal
[3] Algoritmi R&D, School of Engineering, University of Minho, 4800-058 Guimarães, Portugal
vcarvalho@ipca.pt
[4] 2Ai-School of Technology, IPCA, 4750-810 Barcelos, Portugal

Abstract. This paper focuses on the first research phase of the development and analysis of a support interface for Taekwondo athletes. This study aims to solve the existing gap in the time of analysis and feedback from the coach to the athlete. Through the creation of a platform supported by a system based on deep learning, it is intended to design a user interface that promotes the physical and theoretical development of the various athletes of this sport. Therefore, it became fundamental to perform the analysis of standard structures in which statistics and data concerning the athlete are often presented in a digital context. The first research phase consisted of analyzing content related to the importance of design and data structuring in sports. Consequently, the study and evaluation of similar applications began to understand the various tools and graphical user interfaces used to enhance and stimulate the performance of athletes. Since there is not a great diversity of applications inherent to Taekwondo, the research was extended to platforms of other sports categories, namely: Fitbit, HomeCourt and Strava. Based on the study undertaken there were identified relevant needs that trigger the necessity of development of a specific platform for Taekwondo athletes.

Keywords: Design process · UI/UX design · Taekwondo

1 Introduction

In the last years, the number of Taekwondo practitioners in Portugal has registered a continuous increase presenting in 2020 an increment of more than a thousand federated athletes [1]. This martial art, traditional from Korea, emerged in the 20th century and resulted from the combination of techniques from other disciplines such as Kung Fu and Karate.

In Taekwondo the development of technological solutions to support athletes' training and performance has been practically nonexistent. Data and evaluations are performed manually, which results in several limitations, namely:

E. Brooks et al. (Eds.): DLI 2021, LNICST 435, pp. 7–20, 2022.
https://doi.org/10.1007/978-3-031-06675-7_1

- Inaccurate and low-fidelity performance evaluations;
- Delay in identifying difficulties experienced by the athlete;
- Difficulty in clarifying errors;
- and, slowdown in the athlete's evolution and progress.

Thus, this study aims to respond to this gap through the development of an interactive digital platform, where the coach and the athlete can monitor and analyze, in real time, a set of relevant data for the evaluation of the athlete, specifically force, speed and acceleration. In this context, it is possible to promote the theoretical and practical learning of Taekwondo, based on the access to information such as the values of the force applied in the strikes, the calculation of acceleration and speed of the movements performed. In this way, the creation of an appealing and objective interface is relevant, with the intention of reducing the athlete's analysis time and, simultaneously, contribute to the progressive performance of the athlete. The objective of the solution to be developed is that users, whether they are high competition athletes or beginners, can easily understand the structures and techniques of the sport.

This project is integrated in a work team whose focus is the development of the technological and design components. The elaboration of a system in which the basis is deep learning enables the access to information concerning the athlete's behavior. This technology analyzes the data in a similar way to what happens in the neural networks of the human brain. It is a method that drives autonomous learning on different devices by constantly processing data. Automating performance enables the ability to respond quickly to numerous adversities, such as perfecting positions characteristic of Taekwondo.

In short, with this study we pretend to develop an ergonomic solution, where all the components show their potential in contributing to the athlete's performance. With the help of methodologies focused on the optimization of the user's experience and in the objective analysis regarding the user's performance, we aim to consolidate the compatibility between new technologies and Taekwondo.

This paper is organized in 5 sections. Section 2 presents a description of the digital media in the Taekwondo; Sect. 3 presents the state of art of the main areas covered in this project; Sect. 4 details a benchmarking of available platforms dedicated to sports; and, Sect. 5 enunciates the main conclusions and suggestions of future development.

2 The Digital Media in Taekwondo

2.1 The Taekwondo Sport

Taekwondo is a combat sport originated in Korea. The word Taekwondo comes from the junction of three words: Tae, which means feet; Kwon, a term that symbolizes hands; and, finally, Do, which means path. The combination of these three words gives origin to the expression: the path of the feet and hands through the spirit. In summary, this sport is a combat technique where the objective is self-defense through the total use of the body and without the use of weapons. From the use of fists to foot movements its main differentiating factor from the others combat sports is the privileged use of the legs and the conjunction of kicking movements.

Taekwondo is a sport where the athletes' muscles are trained and exercised for long periods with a high level of intensity. Although Taekwondo has a vast number of practitioners in Portugal, the evaluation's methods of the athletes' activity and performance are essentially manual and rudimentary.

Therefore, the feedback process - a way to evaluate a certain action - from the coach to the athlete ends up not having the necessary speed and efficiency, which could be obtained with the support of technological means [2].

2.2 The Digital Influence in Sports

When feedback is presented and structured in the right way and at the right time, it plays a decisive role in the evolution of athletes. Several research led by authors such as Mike Hughes, have revealed that the more quantitative and pragmatic the feedback is, the greater the athlete's performance will be [3].

Currently, the adoption of technology in sports is increasingly recurring. Heart rate and running speed are just some of the values monitored by technological systems. The purpose is the acquisition of relevant data and statistics that later allow the coach or user to evaluate this information and based on it provide more accurate and consistent real-time feedback. This type of analysis covers a wide range of information: from strengths to weaknesses; assessment of unnecessary movements; speed; accuracy; and, strength levels. Through this type of knowledge it is possible to create individual and personalized workouts for each athlete considering their individual needs. In this perspective, one of the coaches' main objectives is to obtain as much information from the athletes as possible to make an effective evaluation. However, the vast amount of information, relative to the athletes' times and movements, requires technical support, so that it can later be consulted and analyzed. Thus, to meet this need, the concept of performance analysis, also known as performance notational analysis, was created for a better evaluation and more detailed observation of the various athletes. In other words, it is where a system, through advanced technologies such as artificial intelligence or deep learning, evaluates the numerous characteristics of athletes to produce specific and vital data about them [4]. In this way, according to a study conducted by Sports Tech Tokyo [5], which includes more than 30 countries (Fig. 1), we can observe that the "Training/Performance" category contains the highest overall percentage: 16.4%. The emergence of innovative strategies in sports with the use of technology has led to greater demand for athlete analysis platforms by coaches and athletes.

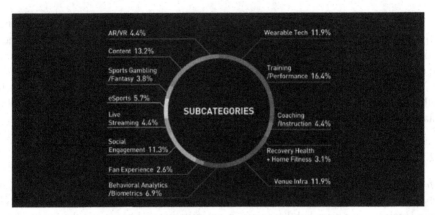

Fig. 1. Promising technologies in sports [5].

The determination to progress and display ever better performance results in a constant search for both current evaluation and analysis methods and new ways of training. Several systems of feedback between athletes and coaches are being studied with the premise that the adoption of these methodologies will contribute to a better performance be it of a team or of an individual athlete [6].

Briefly, the goal of the technologies is to record in detail the user's entire performance. New perspectives are portrayed, all information can be saved and consulted later. In this way, new knowledge is acquired, allowing a faster and more effective development of the athlete's performance.

3   State of the Art

3.1   Data Design and Structuring in Sports

The Importance of Data Visualization. Data and statistics assume a high importance in supporting the definition of strategies and exercises in martial arts [7]. In the case of Taekwondo, the relevant information focuses essentially on the speed, strength and acceleration of the athletes. However, to obtain this data, it is necessary to resort to a precise analysis of certain movements characteristic of this sport, such as the execution of a Miryio Tchagui: a kick used to push the opponent away.

For the athlete and the coach to understand the information about speed and strength, in the different phases of the movement for the execution of a Miryio Tchagui, it must be presented in a clear and objective way, for a correct and enlightening reading by the users. And this is a fundamental topic of Design, in guaranteeing the translation of the different data into a graphic solution that allows a simple and effective reading of the information. A data structuring is considered effective when it organizes all the information in a way that our brain can understand and our eyes can identify the different components. Stephen Few [8] has defined some effectiveness criteria to analyze to what extent the data presentation corresponds correctly to human perception. First, it is necessary to understand if it clearly indicates the type of content being presented. Then it is necessary to pay attention to whether it represents the elements and their values accurately. The next step is observing if the user can quickly evaluate the differences between the different elements. The structuring of the data should be segmented in a logical order. And finally, the criterion of showing how the information should be used [8]. Few [8] also argues that one should always judge the competence of data visualization considering some factors such as ease, efficiency, and accuracy of information since the change of balance between perception and cognition are the premises for acquiring good results.

The orientation and hierarchy of information is important because of the speed of perception: the action of seeing something. While this action is something almost immediate and often used to evaluate and perceive different data; on the other hand, cognition is much less efficient and slow. That is, using visual properties, such as colors, different typographic styles and different patterns, it becomes possible to perceive content and information faster and without the use of conscious thought [8, 9].

As far as the science of human perception is concerned, one of the first contributions made to this study was Max Wertheimer's "Experimentelle Studien über das Sehen von Bewegung" in 1912 [10]. The main goal was to understand what kind of patterns are created when humans observe something specific, later resulting in the well-known Gestalt Principles.

The Gestalt Principles. The way users view and interact with a digital solution should be a simple and intuitive procedure. The more elementary it is for the user to perform the various functionalities to achieve his or her goal the greater the motivation for further exploration of the product or service. Gestalt principles are not entirely concerned with people. The goal is to create dynamics that apply to all users involved in a given action [11].

Gestalt principles were developed by German psychologists Kurt Koffka, Wolfgang Kohler and Max Wertheimer in the 20th century during a study of cognitive psychology [10]. The word "Gestalt" derives from German and means "form." This theory essentially consists of a set of rules that express how the human being, more specifically the human mind, reacts in the face of data captured in the real world. These principles consider that when a visual stimulus appears in our brain it gets a set of different and varied signals, eventually grouping all those it considers similar. That is, at first, we perceive the object in its entirety and then we perceive its details [10]. In this sense, even if unconsciously, Gestalt principles are constantly present in various aspects of everyday life, from the way we interpret posters on the street to the way we combine different types of clothing in everyday life. This study, which analyzes the laws of perception based on the data that the human being acquires from the real world, proves to be relevant when it comes to UX (user experience) and UI (user interface) Design, since these are principles that influence the perception that users have when facing an interface.

Therefore, the Gestalt principles (Fig. 2) state that nearby objects appear to be more related than more distant objects - Proximity. However, when objects appear similar, the tendency is to deduce that they have the same function - Similarity. Therefore, it is scientifically proven that human beings not only tend to put symmetrical objects together - Symmetry -, but also group, as a rule, the first four points of a set (such as a row instead of a column) - Enclosure. Furthermore, elements that are arranged in a straight line or curve are easily perceived as correlated to each other - Continuity. Moreover, when we observe a set of complex elements, we tend to establish a recognizable pattern between them - Closure -, since humans can only focus on a single plane: the foreground or background - Figure & Ground. And finally, "Connectedness", the principle that argues that there is a tendency to see connected elements as being of the same category [10].

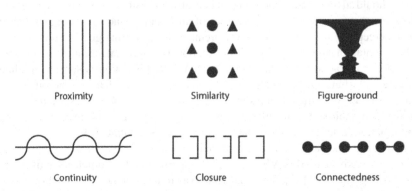

Fig. 2. The gestalt principles: proximity, similarity, figure-ground, continuity, closure and connectedness [12].

Thus, these principles show themselves relevant when it comes to Taekwondo and the perception of information and association of content. Several studies have already proven that a poor understanding of the exact position in which a technique should be executed can lead to a decrease in speed or performance of athletes [13].

However, this methodology also correlates with UX and UI Design. Nowadays, users evaluate a website in a short period of time which leads to the fact that the first impact of the user interface must be good and intuitive. This is because this first impact with the website supports the decision to continue browsing or close the browser window. In this way, a positive first moment can lead to the following impressions also being positive [14]. For example, the first principle - Proximity - is represented in filling the digital fields, where we regularly find the designation close to the space reserved for completing the information. The same happens with the second principle - Similarity - because in the case of forms, sometimes the fields and buttons are similar, but the fact that the button has a different color shows the user that it is a different component. However, not only design, but also gamification, an area focused on game development, often uses these principles. Since games are activities that make use of our mental capacity and quick thinking, we are constantly forced to assimilate sets of elements and extract visual or theoretical information from that interpretation.

3.2 Gamification

The premise of gamification is not only to understand what experience we want to pass to the user, but also to identify the type of content, elements and mechanisms that will be necessary to create this approach [15].

Currently, there is an attempt to understand and develop new ways to attract customers, with gamification emerging as a result. This area focuses on the use of elements and mechanisms divergent from games, whose main purpose is to contribute and encourage users to achieve one or more goals. The use of these methods aims to transform complex issues into more perceptible and easy-to-understand topics. They act as a stimulus to arouse interest and, at the same time, enhance creativity and imagination.

Gamification methodology, according to Yu Kai Chou [15], is subdivided into eight categories: Octalysis (Fig. 3). This structure is supported by 8 Core Drives and was developed with the purpose of identifying the basic psychology of human motivation and how it operates. Games are fun because they activate specific motivations within each individual, which make them want to repeat the experience. Although not all Core Drives need to be present in a single action, at least one of these categories should be evident. Each Drive has a different nature, from emotions, such as obsession and power, to feelings such as creativity and personal fulfillment [15].

Fig. 3. Octalisys [15]

In this way, the most relevant Core Drives for the present study were analyzed. Firstly, Accomplishment, whose focus is personal achievement, that is, the main motivation comes from the user himself to progress and develop his skills (the will to overcome the imposed challenges). This category is generally intertwined with rewards and rankings where the player can visualize his constant progress. Next, the core that includes all social components: Social Influence. In this Core Drive, content that recalls childhood memories, as an example, ends up encouraging and arousing interest to participate or compete in something. Nevertheless, the seventh Core Drive, Unpredictability, is driven by the unknown factor, the curiosity to find out what the next challenges are. The user is curious about something, which leads them to think about it several times throughout its day. And finally, the eighth, and last Core Drive, Avoidance, where the focus is on the motivation to avoid certain actions that could cause further damage in the future - as is the example of games that force the player to do daily missions to earn points.

Gamification is increasingly used in design, since by understanding and identifying the Core Drive in which the target audience fits, it is possible to solve numerous issues related to UX. Thus, it allows to analyze, in detail, not only the best mechanisms to use, but also the type of motivation that attracts users. In summary, both gamification and design have the same goal: to make the user experience as pleasant and engaging as possible.

3.3 UI/UX Design

UX and UI are two distinct but complementary areas. UX Design embraces the entire spectrum of user experience, also evaluating factors such as usability and utility. While UI Design is the way in which this same experience is achieved, being the junction of various types of elements and components, such as menus, search fields, videos, and images. Therefore, UX is the process that covers the entire user journey on a specific platform - from analysis of the various user behaviors to the elaboration of various scenarios and flows. This process is fundamental to ensure a user-friendly experience in the use of an online platform. UX Design consists, in essence, in identifying problems and difficulties of the user, to improve and optimize the operation, ensuring in the same way the quality of the interface. The primary objective is to meet the particularities and needs of the user, since each small interaction with the platform will have a different type of experience associated with it. This is an extremely important issue, since sometimes that experience and interaction are mostly fragments of our memory, which may or may not correspond to the total reality [16].

The first contact of the user with the platform is crucial, since in that very instant an initial perception is created, which evolves successively the greater the proximity or use of it. Thus, seven essential factors for creating a good user experience have been established, namely: valuable, useful, accessible, usable, desirable, credible, valuable, purposeful, and easy to identify. In other words, there must be a balance between these numerous areas to create the best possible experience [17].

The UI is the process that allows the user to control a device, software or application, and this management can be performed through menus, buttons or any other type of functionality that provides interaction between the user and the device in question. In other words, it is based on the improvement and optimization of interactive systems that allow fewer problems and errors affecting the user [18].

Accordingly, Dan Saffer [19] established five elements - motion, space, time, appearance, and sound - as the infrastructure of interaction design. Although it is not necessary to use all these elements together, at least one of these components must be present. This way, a connection will be created, even if unconsciously, between the designed interface and the user, developing in consequence an emotional connection that will benefit both, brand/product, and consumer.

UI Design is then responsible for developing a product, anticipating obstacles, and making sure that the interface has usable elements that allow the user to achieve his goal in the fastest and most effective way. This process requires continual refinement in terms of design, based on usability testing.

In the past only technology experts used computers. Thus, in the 1980s the term usability emerged to replace the term ease of use. Therefore, within the scope of evaluating the ease of interaction and understanding of a platform, this term emerged and was portrayed as a hemisphere represented by the human being and the system. That is, an area that analyzes whether the interface provides the user with a pleasant and easy way to interact without having to engage in complex processes that result in a negative experience [20].

3.4 Usability Heuristics

Jacob Nielsen [21] developed some general rules that became known as heuristic evaluation. Nielson's heuristics, a set of principles developed with the goal of optimizing various usability-related issues, act to promote an efficient experience. Usability heuristics are generally applicable to any type of device. Using these principles, it is possible to evaluate and develop an interface quickly, collecting large amounts of information regarding the needs of the interface [21]. Although they do not replace usability testing, these parameters make it possible to create a platform with a smaller number of errors and premature adversities. The application of these rules proves to be a fundamental procedure in the development of a digital solution allowing users to navigate the platform in an intuitive way. In this context, the following heuristics were relevant in this study and were later applied in the benchmarking analysis following the collection and comparison of data on competing platforms.

Based on the principle that all information and content should be arranged logically and cohesively to be easily understood by the user, the heuristic "Match between system and the real world" arises. In these situations, it is evaluated whether concepts are being used that are familiar to the user rather than complex and confusing terms. Thus, it will be simpler for users to learn how the interface works. On the other hand, the "User control and freedom" heuristic states that the user should be given control over the system they are using. Therefore, a user may select the button to delete some content in an unintended movement. This type of action should always coexist with a confirmation notification or the ability to reverse the action. However, it is necessary to understand which elements of the interface can have a negative character resulting in future inconvenience to the user: "Error Prevention". The designer must foresee which buttons or content may mislead the user. The interaction process between the user and the interface must be facilitated guided by the main aspects of the system: "Aesthetic and minimalist design". Interfaces, as a rule, should only contain information relevant to the user or give greater prominence to the main content [21].

Through these principles it is possible to develop more comprehensive interfaces focused on usability and the user. The goal is to prevent the user from feeling lost in the designed interface, since the user's path should be fluid and immediate with no gaps or deviations from the destination [22].

4 Benchmarking: Digital Platforms in the Sports Category

Benchmarking is a procedure where the main competitors are analyzed with the purpose of gathering information that describes the user experience in the time of use of the platform in question. By performing this analysis one can more easily establish benchmarks for future improvements. The purpose of this strategy is to compare the various platforms to outline which functionalities and features should be incorporated or developed to better meet the user's needs.

Nowadays, there are several platforms that work as a complement to the athletes' training, helping them to develop faster and more efficiently. Nonetheless, in Taekwondo, no similar platforms have been developed. Therefore, platforms from other sports were analyzed, such as Fitbit, HomeCourt and Strava (Fig. 4).

Fig. 4. Platforms: FitBit, HomeCourt and Strava [23–25]

These are applications used by brands and reference athletes, such as the NBA - National Basketball Association - one of the most important basketball leagues worldwide. Later and with the purpose of gathering information about digital methods developed for Taekwondo practitioners, the applications Mastering Taekwondo, Taekwondo Trainer, Dojanga and Taekwondo WTF (Fig. 5) were also considered, which despite not evaluating the athlete in real time, are platforms whose purpose is the learning and training of this martial art. Following this, a comparative analysis was prepared to analyze the functionalities of platforms for athletes.

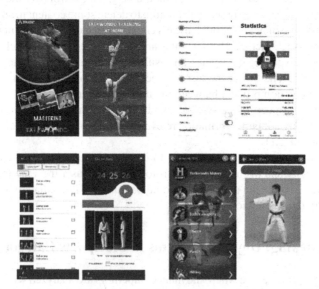

Fig. 5. Platforms: Mastering Taekwondo, Taekwondo Trainer, Dojanga and Taekwondo WTF [26–29]

In Table 1 and Table 2 are evaluated relevant issues such as the versatility of platform use in various devices, the way the training and exercises are presented to users and an analysis based on usability heuristics.

Table 1. Comparative analysis of functionality of platforms for athletes.

Platforms	Fitbit	Homecourt	Strava	Taekwondo trainer	Mastering taekwondo	Dojanga	Taekwondo WTF
Desktop	x	x	x				
Mobile	x	x	x	x	x	x	x
Login/Logout	x	x	x			x	
Different types of users					x		
Training	x	x	x	x	x	x	x
Training videos/Animations	x	x			x	x	x
Monitoring (Data and Statistics)	x	x	x	x			
Challenges/Events	x	x	x				
Extra Services	x						x
News Feed (from other users)	x	x	x			x	
Notifications	x	x	x	x	x	x	x
Camera's function utilization	x	x	x				

Table 2. Comparative analysis based on the heuristics studied

Platforms	Fitbit	Homecourt	Strava	Taekwondo Trainer	Mastering taekwondo	Dojanga	Taekwondo WTF
Match between system and the real world	x	x	x	x	x	x	x
User control and freedom	x	x	x	x	x	x	x
Error prevention	x	x	x		x		
Aesthetic and minimalist design	x	x	x			x	x

Regarding the platforms analyzed, it is noted that only three - Fitbit, HomeCourt and Strava - offer the athlete the versatility to be used in various types of devices, such as desktop, tablet, mobile and smartwatches. Although these platforms display a completer and more organized interface in terms of content, Mastering Taekwondo (the most indigent and devoid of content application of the interfaces present) ends up differentiating itself from the others, presenting a feature that the others do not have: the distinction between users. This interface was designed so that users can train and perform exercises according to their level of experience. This type of function provides users with continuous progress according to their current ability, distinguishing between beginners and seniors. Even without the profile feature, there is a wide range of pre-defined workouts according to the color of the user's belt (level of expertise).

The development of goals and challenges can be observed in the first three platforms, which demonstrates an active strategy of loyalty to its users, thus motivating them to use the interface regularly. One of the common points between all the platforms is the sending of notifications to remind users of training schedules or the occurrence of some momentary event. The clear backgrounds are a predominant factor in all platforms, highlighting the use of contrasting bright colors, such as oranges and blues, showing simultaneously the concern in the perception of information and clarity in reading. Following this and according to the effectiveness criteria defined by Stephen Few [8], regarding the presentation of data, it can be observed that the four platforms that monitor the athletes' data follow all the basic rules.

From the identification of the character of the information to the ease in identifying the order and classification of the values, all interfaces present a functional and direct data structuring. Thus, it becomes clear how essential it is for the athlete to have a quick perception of the various information relating to training. A small detail that makes it difficult to understand a specific value can complicate the whole exercise for the user, since a poor interpretation of the results will influence the athlete's future performance in the long term.

5   Conclusion

The inclusion of technology in sports is a fundamental procedure for the physical and mental development of athletes. The perception of the main adversities of Taekwondo was crucial in this phase of the project development, as well as the understanding of the relevance of design in the presentation and organization of relevant information. The correct digitalization and hierarchy of information allows athletes to explore new ways of improving their performance. Thereby it was necessary to explore interfaces allusive to other sports. With a perspective centered on user analysis and evaluation, examples like FitBit, HomeCourt, Strava, Taekwondo Trainer, Mastering Taekwondo, Dojanga and Taekwondo WTF were considered. Thus, through the study of complementary platforms to athletes' training (using technologies such as computer vision) the global panorama of the state of the art, benchmarking research and the main objectives of the interface were defined.

As a conclusion, the purpose of this first stage of the project was to explore the potential of technology in combination with design to optimize and develop the performance of Taekwondo athletes. Thus, the following needs were identified in relation to Taekwondo and its technological means:

- non-existence of evaluation systems for the athletes;
- absence of a database to store information related to the athletes' training;
- lack of organization regarding the learning content of the different techniques of the sport.

The next step will be to develop a solution that matches the needs of different users. To this end, personas focused on potential users will be developed, as well as the structuring of the information architecture to hierarchize the relevant information. Subsequently, usability tests will be developed to validate the prototype.

Acknowledgments. This work was funded through the FCT – *Fundação para a Ciência e Tecnologia* and FCT/MCTES in the scope of the project UIDB/05549/2020.

References

1. Federação Portugal Taekwondo (n.d.). http://portkd.com/inscricoes-na-nova-epoca-2020-21/. Accessed 10 Dec 2020. (in Portuguese)
2. Jia, Y.: Design of sports training system and motion monitoring and recognition under wireless sensor network. Mob. Inf. Syst. **2021**, 1–13 (2021). https://doi.org/10.1155/2021/3104772
3. Hughes, M., Franks, I.: Essentials of Performance Analysis in Sport. 2nd edn. Routledge, London (2015)
4. Hughes, M., Franks, I.: Notational Analysis of Sport. 2nd edn. Routledge, London (2004)
5. SPORTS TECH TOKYO - Connecting the World to Sports Innovation. (n.d.). https://sports tech.tokyo/achievements/. Accessed 23 June 2021
6. Liebermann, D., Katz, L., Hughes, M., Bartlett, R., McClements, J., Franks, I.: Advances in the application of information technology to sport performance. J. Sports Sci. **20**(10), 755–769 (2010). https://doi.org/10.1080/026404102320675611
7. Menescardi, C., Falco, C., Mendo, A., Sánchez, V.: Design, validation, and testing of an observational tool for technical and tatical analysis in the taekwondo competition at the 2016 Olympic games. Physiol. Behav. **224**(112980), 112980 (2020). https://doi.org/10.1016/j.phy sbeh.2020.112980
8. Few, S.: Information Dashboard Design: Displaying Data for at-a-Glance Monitoring. Analytics Press (2013)
9. Martins, N., Martins, S., Brandão, D.: Design principles in the development of dashboards for business management. In: Raposo, D., Neves, J., Silva, J. (eds.) Perspectives on Design II: Research, Education and Practice. Springer Series in Design and Innovation, vol. 16, 353–365. Springer, Cham (2022). https://doi.org/10.1007/978-3-030-79879-6_26
10. Gestalt psychology | Definition, Founder, Principles, & Examples | Britannica. (n.d.). https://www.britannica.com/science/Gestalt-psychology. Accessed 15 Apr 2021
11. Guberman, S.: Gestalt theory rearranged: back to Wertheimer. Front. Psychol. **8**, 1782 (2017). https://doi.org/10.3389/fpsyg.2017.01782

12. Burkhard, R.: Knowledge Visualization: The Use of Complementary Visual Representations for the Transfer of Knowledge: a Model, a Framework, and Four New Approaches (2005). http://www.researchgate.net/publication/36382932
13. Estevan, I., Jandacka, D., Falco, C.: Effect of stance position on kick performance in taekwondo. J. Sports Sci. **31**(16), 1815–1822 (2013). https://doi.org/10.1080/02640414.2013.803590
14. Möller, B., Brezing, C., Unz, D.: What should a corporate website look like? The influence of Gestalt principles and visualisation in website design on the degree of acceptance and recommendation. Behav. Inf. Technol. **31**(7), 739–751 (2012). https://doi.org/10.1080/0144929X.2011.642893
15. Chou, Y.: Actionable Gamification. Beyond Points, Badges, and Leaderboards. Octalysis Media (2015)
16. Norman, D., Nielsen, J.: The Definition of User Experience (UX) (2009). https://www.nngroup.com/articles/definition-user-experience/. Accessed 19 Apr 2021
17. Rosenbaum, S., Glenton, C., Cracknell, J.: User experiences of evidence-based online resources for health professionals: user testing of The Cochrane Library. BMC Med. Inform. Decis. Mak. **8**(1), 34 (2008). https://doi.org/10.1186/1472-6947-8-34
18. Charfi, S., Trabelsi, A., Ezzedine, H., Kolski, C.: Widgets dedicated to user interface evaluation. Int. J. Hum. Comput. Interact. **30**(5), 408–421 (2014). https://doi.org/10.1080/10447318.2013.873280
19. Saffer, D.: The Elements of Interaction Design: UXmatters (2006). https://www.uxmatters.com/mt/archives/2006/05/the-elements-of-interaction-design.php. Accessed 9 Jan 2021
20. Sauer, J., Sonderegger, A., Schmutz, S.: Usability, user experience and accessibility: towards an integrative model. Ergonomics **63**(10), 1207–1220 (2020). https://doi.org/10.1080/00140139.2020.1774080
21. Nielsen, J.: 10 usability heuristics for user interface design (2020). https://www.nngroup.com/articles/ten-usability-heuristics/. Accessed 16 May 2021
22. Pereira, L., Brandão, D., Martins, N.: Ageing related human factors to be addressed in the design of visual interfaces of digital applications developed for seniors: a literature review. In: Martins, N., Brandão, D., da Silva, F.M. (eds.) Perspectives on Design and Digital Communication II: Research, Innovations and Best Practices. Springer Series in Design and Innovation, vol. 14, pp. 65–80. Springer, Cham (2021). https://doi.org/10.1007/978-3-030-75867-7_5
23. Fitbit App & Dashboard (2020). https://www.fitbit.com/eu/app. Accessed 22 Dec 2020
24. HomeCourt (2020). https://www.homecourt.ai. Accessed 18 Dec 2020
25. Strava (2020). https://www.strava.com. Accessed 18 Dec 2020
26. Mastering Taekwondo (2021). https://mastering-taekwondo.pt.aptoide.com/app. Accessed 14 Sept 2021
27. Taekwondo Trainer (2020). https://apkpure.com/taekwondo-trainer/com.wtf.wtfapp. Accessed 14 Sept 2021
28. Dojanga (2018). https://play.google.com/store/apps/details?id=com.dojanga.dojangaios&hl=enUS&gl=US. Accessed 12 Nov 2021
29. Taekwondo WTF (2019). https://play.google.com/store/apps/details?id=com.mapbile.taekwondowtf&hl=pt_PT&gl=US. Accessed 12 Nov 2021

Multi-disciplinary Learning and Innovation for Professional Design of AI-Powered Services

Pontus Wärnestål[(✉)] [iD]

School of Information Technology, Halmstad University, Halmstad, Sweden
pontus.warnestal@hh.se

Abstract. Companies face several challenges when adopting Artificial Intelligence (AI) technologies in their service and product offerings. Adaptive behavior that changes over time, such as personalization, affects end-user experiences in sometimes unpredictable ways, making designing for AI-powered experiences difficult to prototype and evaluate. To fully make use of AI technologies, companies need new tools, methods, and knowledge that relate to their specific design context. This includes learning how to adapt design and development processes to fit AI-powered services, communication in cross-functional teams, and continuous competency development strategies. This paper reports on an innovation and learning program called AI.m that facilitates practical learning about how to use emerging AI technologies for human-centered design. The program has been executed for 15 companies and evaluated using interviews with researchers, design practitioners, and company representatives that have worked within the learning program. This study suggests and verifies a productive and efficient learning environment and process where companies, university research departments, and design agencies collaborate to produce AI-powered services and at the same time develop their competency in AI and human-centered design. The qualitative analysis provides a set of categories of learning implications organized as a framework of prompts to help organizations develop AI and design capabilities.

Keywords: AI · Design · Learning environments · Innovation · Digitalization

1 Introduction

The field of Artificial Intelligence (AI) has provided companies and organizations with new opportunities for creating personalized, adaptive, and autonomous service and product experiences. However, AI-powered services impact the end-user experience in complex and interconnected ways, rendering it difficult for organizations to keep a connected and holistic overview when designing service interactions [1]. The recent rise of data availability, access to powerful Machine Learning (ML) algorithms, and processing power have created new possibilities in assistive and agentive interfaces and automation of services [2]. AI is indeed claimed to be one of the most transformative technologies of our time [3]. Designers, developers, economists, researchers, and managers in all sectors

© ICST Institute for Computer Sciences, Social Informatics and Telecommunications Engineering 2022
Published by Springer Nature Switzerland AG 2022. All Rights Reserved
E. Brooks et al. (Eds.): DLI 2021, LNICST 435, pp. 21–36, 2022.
https://doi.org/10.1007/978-3-031-06675-7_2

need tools and practical know-how to support them in creating and evaluating designs that address the challenges and opportunities this new technology presents to society.

At the same time, AI is a heterogeneous collection of techniques and application areas and is therefore hard to define and learn to apply in practice. AI can make specific processes – such as searching, mining, and prediction based on big data – more efficient, and more advanced AI can be implemented to make services agentive – i.e., take the initiative and act on users' behalf. This affects how tasks and work are carried out and has substantial implications for how organizations orchestrate their workforce and what skillsets are prioritized [4].

There are multiple toolkits for *developing* and *applying* AI technologies from a technical point of view available. Google, Facebook, IBM, OpenAI, and other organizations have made ambitious AI-based development platforms available for developers to access algorithms and data sets. However, fewer support tools are available for helping designers and managers *understand* how designing services based on this technology affects business strategy, user experience, and ethical implications such as biased data and discrimination that may arise. Therefore, there is a strong need for designers and innovation leaders to be "AI literate" to make better use of AI technologies in human-centered services and products. This line of thought has led to the concept of "AI as a design material" [1, 5]. AI spans a large variety of aspects, ranging from different *approaches* (e.g., symbolic, sub-symbolic, or statistical AI), different *application types* (e.g., computer vision, expert systems, natural language processing), and different *service types* (e.g., assistive, agentive, or automated services). Designers and product managers need to navigate this space to make informed decisions on how AI can benefit their offering and value-creation and value-capture.

To this end, we have examined a practical learning and innovation program called AI.m[1] that aims to accelerate companies' ability to design human-centered AI-powered services. The model has been iterated in stages, and currently, 15 small and medium-sized companies from different sectors have completed the learning cycle. We present this learning environment and synthesize insights from interviews with participating designers, developers, innovation leaders, researchers, AI experts, and company leaders in the work reported on herein.

1.1 Aim and Research Question

The aim of this study is to provide a framework for how accelerated learning about human-centered AI as design practice can be facilitated in small and medium-sized companies. A second aim of the study is to evaluate the AI.m program experience from three perspectives: the company perspective, researchers' perspective, and the design agency perspective.

The rest of the paper is structured as follows. First, we describe the design and learning context for human-centered design when utilizing data-driven Machine Learning as a design material in Sect. 2. Then, in Sect. 3, the AI.m program process and surrounding ecosystem of actors are outlined. In Sect. 4, we report on the qualitative interview study

---

[1] www.aimhalland.se.

with representatives from the AI.m program and present the results of the analysis as a framework of design prompts. The paper is concluded in Sect. 5.

2 The Design and Learning Context for Human-Centered AI: State of the Art

As the complexity of digital services increases and becomes integrated into everyday life, organizations and firms face the daunting challenge of understanding how user experiences are affected through an ever-increasing number of touchpoints, channels, and media [6]. Within the field of Human-Computer Interaction (HCI), this has sparked a line of thought that the field is going through a paradigm shift, where interaction design and user experience (UX) design focus on situated and embedded complexities in a messy world [7, 8]. The multi-stakeholder view coupled with holistic experience design over digital and non-digital touchpoints is firmly grounded in Service Design practice [9]. The overlaps between interaction design, UX design, and Service Design have recently been re-framed and re-conceptualized [10].

The recent increase of AI technologies in digital services adds to this development. AI has been dominated by engineering and technology-centered disciplines for decades. Only recently have scholars started to re-conceptualize the *agency* of things in terms of AI and human-centered design (cf. [2, 8, 11–13]). At the same time, Harrisson et al. note that epistemologically, HCI has been moving away from the traditional engineering culture of the previous paradigm [7], rendering "the boundaries between technology and humans increasingly fuzzy" [8].

UX and Service Designers have a long history of crafting design tools that help them visualize, ideate, communicate, and validate their designs. Ever since the transition to the experience economy [14], the connection between the service platform complexity and user experience has required organizations to actively focus on a holistic view of their customers' complete service experience beyond interface design [15]. However, data-driven and AI-powered services are new territories for designers. The tools that make up the typical toolset of UX and Service Designers – such as Service Blueprints [16], Customer Journey Maps [17], Business Model Canvas [18], Personas and Scenarios [19–21], and Ecosystem Maps [9, 22] – are not explicitly tailored to describe user experience, impact, and value for services that rely on AI and algorithms. In particular, there is a lack of tools assisting in modeling how AI can augment human workers or operators and the resulting end-user (or customer) experience. The opportunities to apply AI technology – such as Machine Learning – in an HCI design context are multi-faceted. Generic challenges include designing for data collection and data maintenance, integrating ML functionality in user interface design, and augmenting human operators and change workflows with the help of AI technologies. Even though decades of work in the space of AI-powered design has produced several sets of HCI guidelines, it is clear that more knowledge and practical know-how are still needed [1, 13].

Just as AI and computation can be considered a specific design material that changes the context for designers [23, 24], the application of big data, algorithms, mobile technologies, and cloud computing also changes the design space for services. This development is sometimes referred to as "the platform economy" or "the third globalization."

Indeed, Kenney and Zysman [25] claim that: "We are in the midst of a reorganization of our economy in which the platform owners are seemingly developing power that may be even more formidable than was that of the factory owners in the early industrial revolution." (p. 62).

Digital platforms powered by emerging technologies allow firms to monetize human effort, assets, and data through various services that serve different user groups. The complexity of Business, Service, and User Experience design for AI-powered digital platforms is high, and service-providing organizations, therefore, need to understand (a) how key interactions and functionality are integrated to deliver value to the end-user (or customer), (b) how these components are interconnected to the organization and culture, and (c) how the organization generates and captures value through service interactions [26]. This includes orchestrating cooperation and co-learning between humans and AI agents, such as cognitive process automation, boosting human users' cognitive insight capabilities, and cognitive engagement opportunities [25]. It also includes competency development as well as facilitating multi-disciplinary communication within and between teams [1]. This adds complexity to the design context and requires designers and developers to consider such factors when designing AI-powered services. In effect, this shifts the focus from traditional human-centered design to interaction with *agentive* systems [2, 27] and explores what new workflows and skills are necessary for human operators [28, 29]. Indeed, designers often have a cliched understanding of AI and ML, such as viewing AI as a means for automating tasks [30].

Recent literature emphasizes that designers using AI-powered functionality in digital services could expand the design metaphor for enabling interactions to do more than rmerely react or respond as a "tool" [2, 31]. Rather, the metaphor for interacting collaboratively with humans could be seen as a "butler" or "valet" in "teaming" efforts between humans and AI-powered services [4] and focus on both *augmentation* and *automation* as they are interdependent [32]. Therefore, the design context is multi-disciplinary, and organizations need to take business impact, technology, and human behavior into account.

A significant challenge for enabling designers to embrace new technologies as design materials lies in orchestrating efficient learning and discovery of how such fast-changing emerging technologies such as AI can and should be used. Companies that design and develop digital services operate in fast-paced, time-critical contexts where formal, traditional learning opportunities might be scarce. Research indicates that such learning opportunities may exist only on paper, either because the execution of learning activities takes too long or because, once they get back to work, employees do not get opportunities to consolidate what they have learned in the regular work practice [33]. This provides an exciting opportunity for designing efficient and multi-disciplinary learning contexts for professionals that can be connected to everyday work practice.

In order to facilitate learning within and between groups of professionals in such a multi-disciplinary and complex design space, designers, developers, innovation leaders, and managers need to learn together and contextualize domain expertise in both AI and design in their work practice.

3   The AI.m Learning and Innovation Program

The context for the study presented here is an innovation program called AI.m – created by innovation arena and business incubator HighFive[2] and Halmstad University in a Swedish geographical region with a population of 330,000. The program aims to support small and medium-sized regional companies to fast-track their ability to utilize AI technologies in an impactful and sustainable way. A fundamental stepping stone for the program is the notion that the program is not only about AI technology per se but also incorporates business and user experience impact as a starting point. To this end, the program has identified that expert competency in both AI and human-centered design needs to be a part of a productive learning environment.

Following theories on design-based learning that is characterized by open-ended, hands-on, and multi-disciplinary craftsmanship on the one hand [34] and communication and interaction as "making meaning" in creative learning processes [35] on the other, the learning model is set up as a network of actors (see Fig. 1) and a formal process (see Table 1). The model aims to help identify business opportunities that create and capture value by implementing human-centered design and business modeling with AI technology. Tangible outcomes from the learning sequence in the program are one or more proof of concepts, or prototypes, that encapsulate concrete representations of how AI-powered services can enhance a specific company's service offering.

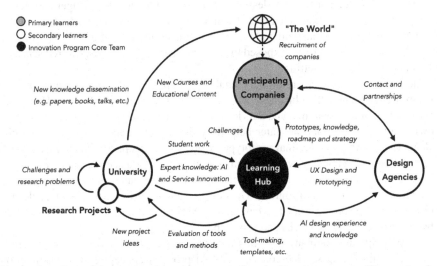

Fig. 1. Overview of the system of learners surrounding the learning program AI.m centered on the Learning Hub of HighFive. Participating companies get support from researchers and experts on AI and service innovation and practical UX design support from professional design agencies. New knowledge is captured in tools, templates, research papers, and other learning materials.

---

[2] https://h5halmstad.se/.

3.1 Learning Actors

The AI.m program consists of a learning hub hosted by innovation arena HighFive. The program is designed to coordinate learning and innovation processes between the actors of the system. The primary target group ("primary learners") are small and medium-sized regional companies from different sectors. Another actor in the network is the region's university (Halmstad University), which has strong research expertise in AI and Service Innovation. The third actor is a contracted group of design agencies consisting of professional UX and Service Designers that are tasked with prototyping work throughout the process. As the university and the design agencies serve by providing their expertise to the primary learners, they are considered secondary learners. However, as is evident from the evaluation of the learning program, both university researchers and design agencies boost their knowledge on how to design and develop AI-driven services as a result of the process (see Sect. 4).

Each company forms a team consisting of 3–5 key roles (including management, technical personnel, and domain experts). Depending on their data and digitalization maturity level, some companies provide several technical roles (CTO, data scientists, and developers), whereas others who might not have such roles defined within the companies typically bring senior management and product owners instead.

The core AI.m program team enlists one AI expert and one service innovation researcher from Halmstad University, one Business Designer from HighFive, a Service Designer, and one or two UX designers from the contracted design agencies. Later in the process, the team can be extended with design or engineering students from the university programs that can help build or evaluate the prototype being built. This allows the students to learn from being exposed to practical prototyping of AI-powered services in an authentic company setting.

The company brings a preliminary challenge hypothesis of how AI and service innovation could benefit their business or organization. The AI expert, Business Designer, Service Innovation Researcher, and Service Designer bring their perspectives and expert knowledge to the table and are later helped by the design agency team and possibly students for hashing out the final prototype or proof of concept. In return, researchers get insights and data about how innovation work using AI is carried out in practice. This also yields new tools and methods that can spawn new research project ideas for the university beyond the AI.m program. The design agencies provide high-quality design craftmanship to the project, and they benefit from rapid and efficient practical experience in building AI-powered services and prototypes.

The participating company gets tangible outcomes in the form of (a) one or more prototypes highlighting service concepts and AI proof of concepts, (b) a roadmap of possible next steps beyond the AI.m program, including financing and grant suggestions for future work, and (c) new contextualized knowledge about how to design and develop human-centered AI-powered services.

Another outcome of the ecosystem is the university's possibility of using case studies, developed tools and methods, research ideas for creating new educational content, and knowledge dissemination in the form of papers and ideas for research grant applications.

3.2 Process

The AI.m program process consists of five main stages. All the main actors from the ecosystem in Fig. 1 are involved in all stages to varying degrees. Table 1 summarizes the stages and sessions of the process. Typically, five companies run their sessions in parallel during a 6–8-week period, where about half of the calendar time is dedicated to prototyping an AI-powered proof of concept. Each batch of five companies is initiated with a kick-off where all the participating companies are gathered to get two inspiration talks; one about human-centered design opportunities and one introduction to AI from a technology perspective. In the same session, the companies spend two hours in a workshop where they outline challenges and opportunities together with AI and design experts from the core learning hub team.

Table 1. The program's learning process stages. Stage 1 is performed with a batch of 5 companies, stages 2–5 are performed with each company in parallel tracks.

Stage	Focus	Sessions and durations
1. Inspiration kick-off	Introducing AI Introducing design	1 two-hour session with inspiration talks and workshops (multiple companies)
2. Business design and innovation management	Aligning business goals with challenges and opportunities	2 two-hour workshops (1–2 weeks apart)
3. Service design	Definition of the desired impact Data inventory and maturity assessment Definition of key user journeys Ethics and risks Scope for prototype (including data requirements)	2 two-hour workshops (1–2 weeks apart)
4. UX design and prototyping	Iterative development of interactive prototypes and AI proof of concepts	3–4 weeks of design agency work and AI development, with continuous check-ins from the rest of the team
5. Dissemination and roadmap	Internal communication Defining next steps and new learning goals	1 two-hour session with a presentation of the concepts (multiple companies) Concluding individual discussion of learnings and roadmap for each company

After the common kick-off session, each company gets its individual schedule for stages 2–5 (see Table 1). In this first session of Stage 2, the company briefly presents its current business and possible steps it might already have taken in terms of AI or data-driven services. Based on this "ground truth," the Innovation Leader and Service Designer facilitate two workshops on possible routes for using AI to address the business challenges. An AI expert from the university is present to give insights on technical aspects of the business. In these workshop sessions, typical business development tools are used, such as business model canvas variants [18, 36] and ecosystem maps [22].

The outcome of the Business Design and Innovation Management stage is a shortlist of 5–10 possible service or project ideas where AI can make a positive impact for the company, as well as suggestions for business model developments based on available data and the company's challenges. At this stage, the company typically understands what kind of data they need to access – or even construct – to provide a business case and use case for the different ideas on the shortlist.

The shortlist of ideas is then reviewed independently by the core AI.m team and the company. During the first Service Design session (Stage 3), one direction is agreed upon, and a user journey mapping process commences. This decision is based on a discussion where the idea's communicative impact, the possibility of sustainable future developments, technical viability and availability of data, business feasibility, and positive user experience are reviewed. Due to the limited project time, the time factor for developing a prototype is also taken into consideration. The Service Designer facilitates two workshops where the user journey and interaction flows are mapped out. The AI expert, Service Designer, and company representatives shape a plausible and possible future state journey where AI technologies have in some way enhanced the service's impact on business and user experience outcome.

At the end of the second Service Design workshop, the UX designers increase their engagement and help set the prototype scope and detail form factor and target platform (e.g., tablet, smartphone, or digiphysical mock-up).

Stage 4 – UX Design and Prototyping – consists of 3–4 weeks of design sprint work, where the UX designers develop the prototype in an iterative fashion. Weekly check-ins on the progress being made so that the company and AI.m team can provide feedback and design critique. This stage is concluded with a presentation of the final prototype, where the AI-specific interactions and impact are in focus. In order to enhance cross-company learning, all five companies in a batch gather for the final presentation to see the other companies' solutions and progress. Stage 5 – Dissemination and Roadmap – also includes recommendations for future work for each individual company. Depending on the maturity level of both the prototype and the company itself, these recommendations typically center on how to bring the prototype into production, including plans for rigorous field tests and user studies. Staff at HighFive also provides recommendations for relevant grants, courses, third-party data sets, and other resources that the company can utilize in order to continue to develop its AI capabilities.

4 Evaluation

The AI.m program has been running in its current form between 2019 and 2021, with a total of 15 participating small- and medium-sized regional companies. The companies have a large spread, ranging from business-to-consumer smartphone app services and web-based online services to business-to-business IT platform solutions, IT security, medical technology, agricultural technology, and manufacturing plants. To evaluate the learning opportunities and effects of the AI.m program, a series of qualitative interviews were conducted.

4.1 Method

At the end of the three project batches of five companies each, respondents were recruited from (a) the participating companies, (b) HighFive, (c) the researchers at Halmstad University, and (d) the design agencies.

Semi-structured deep interviews were carried out individually. The interview themes focused on the learning and knowledge-building impact that the AI.m program experience had on the different actors. Respondents were asked to elaborate on their professional competency development during the project and reflect upon the various ways their understanding and knowledge of how human-centered design and business model innovation are affecting their business using AI technologies as enablers. The topics also included what worked well in the process, as well as problems and negative experiences of the project work. Towards the end of each interview, respondents were asked to talk about what they see as possible steps to continue to learn about AI and service innovation beyond the AI.m program.

In total, the data consist of 24 interviews (15 company interviews, 3 Business Design and Innovation Leader interviews from HighFive, 3 AI Researcher interviews from Halmstad university, and 3 UX designer interviews from three different design agencies). The interviews were analyzed qualitatively by service innovation researchers. Data also include written notes, whiteboard photographs, and digital collaboration areas that were created during the workshops. These auxilliary data were used to complement the interpretation of verbal anecdotes raised in the interviews in the analysis stage. In some cases, respondents used notes and images material in the interviews to explain their thoughts. These notes and sketches were also considered as a complement to the interview data.

4.2 Results

All 15 company representatives deemed the AI.m program to be a success and well worth the time invested. Even though the maturity level of the resulting prototypes varied, each company – except one – concluded the program with a demonstrator or proof-of-concept that captured an AI-powered service solution. The single company where a prototype was not completed had neither enough data nor the digital maturity level or culture to reach the prototype stage. However, they reported that their curiosity was sparked during the program and that the learning outcomes have strengthened their digital maturity and data analytics awareness in general. Several companies reported that the AI.m program enhanced their general data and digitalization awareness and that they are now more confident in further exploring emergent AI technologies as a result of their participation in the program.

The Business Designers and Innovation Leaders from HighFive reported an increased experience with, and understanding of, how data analytics and machine learning provide possibilities as well as challenges for business models and the organization.

Furthermore, a quality that the companies generally did not expect was that they ended up examining their business models in light of what AI and data analytics can provide. An example of this is a manufacturing company that previously considered internet-enabled machinery to be a premium offering with a higher price-point attached to it. This premium offer reduced the number of data-collecting sensors on the market compared to the cheaper machinery without an internet connection. However, during the business design and service design stages in the process, it became evident that the data such internet-enabled sensors could provide back to the company would be very valuable and enable new services such as predictive maintenance. In turn, this could reduce machine downtime for customers. Based on this, the company's approach to charge a higher price for internet-enabled machinery was questioned. This serves as an example of the importance of including business and management in the company's learning initiatives on AI and data analytics, and the impact this has on the way an organization thinks about value-creation in relation to AI- and data-specific features of service and business.

The agency designers reported that they previously had underestimated the characteristics with the design of AI-powered services when the first project started. They highlighted the importance of interdisciplinary communication and that they had acquired several new concepts, design patterns, and terminology from the AI and ML fields during the projects. This has made them better equipped to communicate with data scientists and AI programmers in future projects. The Service Designers, as well as the UX Designers, all expressed that the requirements on prototyping and innovation change when data-driven ML functionality becomes available. Examples of this include adaptivity, personalization, and ethical issues in terms of data collection and usage.

University researchers stressed the importance of seeing theory and data in practice. Practical application in authentic contexts-of-use presents problems that are typically not present in neat lab contexts. Examples include technical limitations in data formats, resolution, and processing speeds in already existing products that are out on the market in the hands of consumers and some companies' lack of resources and skills to handle business model changes internally. The project experience helped highlight such challenges for both researchers and companies alike. Both AI and service innovation researchers appreciated the opportunity to create and modify tools and methods during the process and reported that these had inspired new ideas in ongoing research projects outside the AI.m program (see Fig. 1).

Additional network effects occur in the learning system, as participating companies form bonds with design agencies. Several companies report that they had not considered UX Design as a possible service vendor before seeing what sort of value professional UX design could bring to their products and services. Even though companies are not required to disclose such information, several volunteered that they are renewing their business with the UX Design agencies beyond the AI.m program. From a regional perspective, this is a highly desirable outcome since it strengthens the business networking in the region.

Similarly, since there are five companies in each batch that meet each other at presentations, there are company-to-company partnerships forming as well. Even though some of the companies operate in different sectors and branches, there are examples of collaborations and other joint ventures that arise as a result of the AI.m program. Such experiences highlight boundary-spanning and continuous learning as a result of an orchestrated ecosystem of actors collaborating on common problems.

4.3 Analysis

The interview data were combed for meaning-bearing phrases related to learning experiences and design challenges. Phrases from the interviews were put on digital sticky notes and clustered into categories in a bottom-up fashion. The guiding principle for this categorization was in terms of experience design, learning effects, and business innovation implications for AI-powered services. As clusters emerged, they were named. For example: one company representative said, "we need to get a better sense of how AI makes the end-user experience different from non-AI services." This statement, and others related to functionality and interactions, were grouped in a category named "User Experience". In contrast, another respondent voiced concerns regarding potential negative effects and the ethical risks posed by biased data. Such statements were grouped in the category "Ethics and risks".

In total, 14 categories were generated and then discussed in a group format with the core stakeholders from HighFive, Halmstad University, and one of the design agencies. In the second analysis step, these categories were grouped into five over-arching themes, each corresponding to a different knowledge and skill learning implications for service innovation and design practice. The themes align with other mappings of AI and design-related challenges for service innovation, e.g. [1]. Table 2 summarizes these themes, categories, and learning implications.

Table 2. Summary of derived themes from interviews.

Theme	Categories	Learning implications
1. Knowledge	- Data and analytics - Culture and competencies	Theoretical and practical knowledge about different AI technologies and their impact on user experience design
2. Innovation	- Vision - Problem and consequences	The ability to create innovative solutions based on AI technologies
3. Impact	- Impact and values - Ethics and risks	Understanding long-term effects of AI-powered services on organization, skills, user experience, and value creation
4. Prototyping	- Algorithm effects - Augmentation - Service offering - User experience	The ability to rapidly prototype and evaluate specific use qualities due to AI-powered prediction, adaptivity, and agency
5. Communication	- External communication - Internal communication	The ability to communicate effectively in and between cross-functional teams, as well as with end-users and customers of AI-powered digital services

For each category, a set of *prompts* – formulated as questions – were derived from the interview categories and statements made in the interviews. These prompts provide an action-oriented framework for stakeholders in an extended design team to understand, discuss, and creatively support business model and service innovation using AI as a design material. As such, the themes, categories, and prompts can be seen as boundary objects that can facilitate discussions across professions and democratize the communication, coordination, and knowledge transfer between different roles in an organization [37].

1. Knowledge. ML affects both design and user experience and this relationship is seen as a knowledge gap to overcome by both designers and developers. This theme covers the technical knowledge of data science and analytics, as well as the human-centered design competencies related to data and digital technologies. This theme also includes cultural aspects and how the organization can become more AI- and design-ready.

Data and analytics questions include:

- What data sources do we have access to today? What quality do they have?
- Do we have access to useful information that we might not consider "proper data" today?
- What is our strategy for collecting and update our data?
- What kinds of patterns and relations do we see in our existing data set?
- What data attributes seem to be related?
- What new data attributes can we extract by aggregating existing attributes?
- How can new types of data grow our service offering?

Prompts in the *Culture and competencies* category include:

- What are our drivers, purpose, and attitudes?
- What defines us as an organization?
- What issues can be resolved with cultural drivers instead of more process and regulation?
- How do we track performance?
- How do we make design decisions?
- Do we have ownership issues regarding data within our organization?
- Do we have a "data-ready" culture?
- Are data science perspectives championed at the executive level at the company?
- Are design perspectives championed at the executive level at the company?
- What competencies are required? Which do we already have? Which are we lacking?
- What is our strategy to create a learning culture?

2. Innovation. The ability to use knowledge about AI and human-centered design to create innovative solutions for value-creation and value-capture is found in the positive vision on the one hand and the problems and consequences category on the other.

Vision prompts include:

- What is our vision and impact statement? (Why are we doing this at all?)
- What is unique?
- How is value created?
- How is value captured?

Problems and consequences focus on the negative aspects of the problem space, which can lead to innovative outcomes:

- What primary problem exists in our application space?
- What negative consequences of that problem are we eliminating or resolving?
- What will the consequences be if we do not do anything?

3. Impact. A particular aspect of user- and context-adaptive services is the continuous change and long-term impact enabled by data-driven ML and other AI technologies. To capture these aspects in the learning environment, the following prompts are used:
Impact and values:

- What values do we build for our different end-users?
- What metrics measure successful outcomes?
- What are our overall impact goals for our customers, our organization, and society?

Ethics and risks:

- What ideology is built into the design?
- How can the platform be misused?
- What may our services break or affect negatively (human conditions, other products, and resources)? Is it worth it?
- Whose perspectives have been heard and considered?
- To what extent are human safety, resources, and the organization's reputation at risk?

4. Prototyping is an essential part of human-centered design and consists of four different, but related, perspectives.
Algorithm effects include the ability to understand how ML algorithms affect the problem space:

- What are the possible outputs, outcomes, and impact of new attributes and other algorithmic effects?
- Does ML solve the problem better than other approaches?

Augmentation focuses on techniques for prototyping how AI-powered services affect work and skills:

- What becomes possible for workers?
- How will skills be augmented?
- What tasks will be replaced or augmented?
- Vulnerability: what is the likelihood that human operators working with the AI will distrust its decisions and override them and thereby making the functionality redundant?

The *Services* perspective is focused on prototyping how a complete service is orchestrated. It typically resonates with a Service Designer's lens of prototyping end-to-end holistic service experiences:

- What key service encounters occur, and in what order?
- How are different services on the platform related to each other?
- What does the customer/user experiential journey look like?

The *User Experience* perspective is highly related to the Services perspective but focuses more on the UX Designer's concrete design efforts for specific channels and platforms:

- In what ways does AI render the user experience "magical"?
- What are the UX effects of false positives and false negatives?
- What are the possible UX effects of biased data?
- Is the system's behavior understandable and explainable?

5. Communication. As highlighted by all respondents, developing skills to communicate both within a multi-disciplinary team and with external stakeholders is critical for success.

External communication is vital from a marketing and branding perspective and is essential for companies, but also for designers who aim to "prove" the service brand with their solutions:

- What is the relation between our brand mission and AI-powered services?
- How do we communicate AI-powered service functionality to customers and other stakeholders?

Internal communication prompts are in some ways highly related to Culture and competencies (see Knowledge, above) as they focus on continuous internal development:

- What tools and resources are we using to facilitate cross-functional communication about AI and service between teams?
- What educational initiatives do we need, and for whom, in the organization to build better communication between departments?

5 Conclusion

The AI.m learning ecosystem and process has successfully fast-tracked 15 small and medium-sized companies from a variety of sectors in their capability development of using emerging AI technologies in their business and service offerings.

The derived themes correspond to previous research on challenges with designing AI-powered services (e.g., as reported by Yang et al. [1]) and further develop these challenges into a framework of design and learning opportunities. The categories and associated learning prompts are derived from the input from AI experts, multi-disciplinary perspectives from company representatives, as well as Business, Service, and UX Designers. The themes, categories, and prompt questions presented herein can be used as a framework for addressing organizational and individual learning when designing human-centered services and products powered by AI technologies in a multi-stakeholder design context. As voiced by the participating companies, the AI.m program experience sparked their interest in using human-centered design and AI and increased their confidence in taking on new forms of digital service innovation initiatives. These are viewed as important factors for positive learning outcomes and helped companies view learning about design and AI through prototyping and support from academia as a value-creation activity. The learning ecosystem approach where multiple actors meet, and exchange knowledge and ideas has been fruitful in this case. As new connections between participating actors have formed and lasted several years in some cases, the AI.m program has demonstrated a sustainable way to stimulate regional development and at the same time strenghtened bonds between academia and companies.

References

1. Yang, Q., Steinfeld, A., Rosé, C., Zimmerman, J.: Re-examining whether, why, and how human-AI interaction is uniquely difficult to design. In: Proceedings of the 2020 CHI Conference on Human Factors in Computing Systems, pp. 1–13. Association for Computing Machinery. New York (2020)
2. Noessel, C.: Designing Agentive Technology: AI That Works for People. Rosenfeld Media (2017)
3. Brynjolfsson, E., McAfee, A.: The Second Machine Age: Work, Progress, and Prosperity in a Time of Brilliant Technologies. WW Norton & Company (2014)
4. Johnson, M., Vera, A.: No AI is an island: the case for teaming intelligence. AI Mag. **40**, 16–28 (2019)
5. Dove, G., Halskov, K., Forlizzi, J., Zimmerman, J.: UX design innovation: challenges for working with machine learning as a design material. In: Proceedings of the 2017 CHI Conference on Human Factors in Computing Systems, pp. 278–288. Association for Computing Machinery, New York (2017)
6. Forlizzi, J.: Moving beyond user-centered design. Interactions **25**, 22–23 (2018)
7. Harrison, S., Tatar, D., Sengers, P.: The Three Paradigms of HCI, pp. 1–18 (2007)
8. Frauenberger, C.: Entanglement HCI the next wave? ACM Trans. Comput. Hum. Interact. (TOCHI) **27**, 1–27 (2019)
9. Polaine, A., Løvlie, L., Reason, B.: Service Design: From Insight to Inspiration. Rosenfeld Media (2013)
10. Forlizzi, J., Zimmerman, J.: Promoting service design as a core practice in interaction design. In: Proceedings of IASDR 2013 (2013)
11. Verbeek, P.-P.: COVER STORY beyond interaction: a short introduction to mediation theory. Interactions **22**, 26–31 (2015)
12. Taylor, A.: After interaction. Interactions **22**, 48–53 (2015)
13. Amershi, S., et al.: Guidelines for human-AI interaction, pp. 1–13 (2019)
14. Pine, B.J., Gilmore, J.H.: Welcome to the experience economy. Harv. Bus. Rev. **76**, 97–105 (1998)
15. Lemon, K.N., Verhoef, P.C.: Understanding customer experience throughout the customer journey. J. Mark. **80**, 69–96 (2016)

16. Shostack, G.L.: Designing services that deliver. Harv. Bus. Rev. **62**, 133–139 (1984)
17. Nenonen, S., Rasila, H., Junnonen, J.-M., Kärnä, S.: Customer journey–a method to investigate user experience, pp. 54–63 (2008)
18. Osterwalder, A., Pigneur, Y.: Business Model Generation: a Handbook for Visionaries, Game Changers, and Challengers. Wiley, Hoboken (2010)
19. Pruitt, J., Grudin, J.: Personas: practice and theory, pp. 1–15. ACM (2003)
20. Cooper, A., Cronin, D., Noessel, C.: About Face: The Essentials of Interaction Design, 4th edn. Wiley, Indianapolis (2014)
21. Goodwin, K.: Designing for the Digital Age: How to Create Human-Centered Products and Services. Wiley, Indianapolis (2011)
22. Vink, J., Koskela-Huotari, K., Tronvoll, B., Edvardsson, B., Wetter-Edman, K.: Service ecosystem design: propositions, process model, and future research agenda. J. Serv. Res. **24**, 168–186 (2021)
23. Maeda, J.: How to Speak Machine: Laws of Design for a Digital Age. Penguin (2019)
24. Nelson, H.G., Stolterman, E.: The Design Way: Intentional Change in an Unpredictable World. MIT Press, Cambridge (2014)
25. Kenney, M., Zysman, J.: The rise of the platform economy. Issues Sci. Technol. **32**, 61 (2016)
26. Osterwalder, A.: The business model ontology: a proposition in a design science approach (2004)
27. Luciani, D.T., Löwgren, J., Lundberg, J.: Designing fine-grained interactions for automation in air traffic control. Cogn. Technol. Work **22**(4), 685–701 (2019). https://doi.org/10.1007/s10111-019-00598-9
28. Daugherty, P.R., Wilson, H.J.: Human+ Machine: Reimagining Work in the Age of AI. Harvard Business Press (2018)
29. Neary, B., Horák, J., Kovacova, M., Valaskova, K.: The future of work: disruptive business practices, technology-driven economic growth, and computer-induced job displacement. J. Self Gov. Manag. Econ. **6**, 19–24 (2018)
30. Yang, Q.: Machine learning as a UX design material: how can we imagine beyond automation, recommenders, and reminders? (2018)
31. Wärnestål, P.: Design av AI-drivna tjänster. Studentlitteratur, Lund (2021)
32. Raisch, S., Krakowski, S.: Artificial intelligence and management: the automation–augmentation paradox. Acad. Manag. Rev. **46**, 192–210 (2021)
33. Caporarello, L., Manzoni, B., Panariello, B.: Learning and development is the key. How well are companies doing to facilitate employees' learning? In: Gennari, R., et al. (eds.) MIS4TEL 2019. AISC, vol. 1007, pp. 80–88. Springer, Cham (2020). https://doi.org/10.1007/978-3-030-23990-9_10
34. Wärnestål, P.: Formal learning sequences and progression in the studio: a framework for digital design education. J. Inf. Technol. Educ. Innov. Pract. **15**, 35–52 (2016)
35. Selander, S.: Designs of learning and the formation and transformation of knowledge in an era of globalization. Stud. Philos. Educ. **27**, 267–281 (2008)
36. Joyce, A., Paquin, R.L.: The triple layered business model canvas: a tool to design more sustainable business models. J. Clean. Prod. **135**, 1474–1486 (2016)
37. Akkerman, S.F., Bakker, A.: Boundary crossing and boundary objects. Rev. Educ. Res. **81**, 132–169 (2011)

Evaluating Learning Analytics of Adaptive Learning Systems: A Work in Progress Systematic Review

Tobias Alexander Bang Tretow-Fish$^{(\boxtimes)}$ and Md. Saifuddin Khalid

Department of Applied Mathematics and Computer Science at the Technical University of Denmark, Kongens Lyngby, Denmark
compute@compute.dtu.dk
https://www.compute.dtu.dk/english

Abstract. There is currently no systematic overview of methods for evaluating Learning Analytics (LA) and Learning Analytics Dashboards (LAD) of Adaptive Learning Platforms (ALPs). 10 articles and 2 reviews are analyzed and synthesized. Focusing on the purposes of evaluation, methods used in the studies are grouped into five categories (C1-5): C1) evaluation of LA and LAD design and framework, C2) evaluation of performance with LA and LAD, C3) evaluation of adaptivity functions of the system, C4) evaluation of perceived value, and C5) Evaluation of pedagogical and didactic theory/context. While there is a relative high representation of evaluations in the C1-C4 categories of methods, which contribute to the design and development of the interaction and interface design features, the C5 category is not represented. The presence of pedagogical and didactical theory in the LA, LAD, and ALPs is lacking. Though traces of pedagogical theory is present none of the studies evaluates on its impact.

Keywords: Adaptive learning platforms · Learning analytics · Evaluation

1 Introduction

Adaptive Learning (AL) is not only a relatively new research area but also a multi-disciplinary field involving multiple synonymous and definitions. Adaptive learning, personalized learning, individualized learning, and customized learning are in some way interchangeable although adaptive learning is the most frequently used term of the four [13]. Various methods are applied for the design and evaluation of adaptive or personalized activities and contents of the digital learning platforms.

Existing reviews on Learning Analytic (LA), Learning Analytics Dashboards (LAD), and AL has not focused on the methods used to evaluate LA and LADs of Adaptive Learning Platforms (ALPs). For instance, the systematic literature

E. Brooks et al. (Eds.): DLI 2021, LNICST 435, pp. 37–52, 2022.
https://doi.org/10.1007/978-3-031-06675-7_3

review [7] presents six reviews on adaptive learning and seven reviews on learning analytics among others types of learning technologies but lacks focus on the methods for the evaluation of LA or LADs. The review [9] posed several questions on especially which methods have been employed for the evaluation of the systems. The review reports that the learners play an important role in the evaluation of intelligent tutoring systems, such as learners' experience when evaluating system usability. In the examined studies 5.66% of studies involving intelligent tutoring systems were evaluated only by learner experiences, while in combination with learner's performance, system's performance or both, learners' experiences have been used more frequently [9]. The review does not entail what methods were used for obtaining the learner experience or what types of usability tests were used.

The purpose of applying different methods of evaluation is therefore interesting to look into to get a better understanding of which perspectives are being evaluated from as well as how they are being evaluated.

This leads to the motivation for this systematic review. The motivation is to synthesize the evaluation methods applied in the design, development, and implementation of AL as they support pedagogical and learning related decisions for educators and students. Likewise, we want to examine how students' and educators' perceptions of LAD and LA are integrated in the evaluation methods. The study will contribute to the fields of usability engineering, user experience, and digital learning technology. The study on the methods of evaluating AL platforms is pivotal for improving the quality of learning experience and learning outcome, educators teaching experience and their adoption of the technology, and development process of companies and the implementation of the right evaluation methods.

The above-mentioned scope and motivation led us to devising the research question:

How to evaluate the Learning Analytics and Learning Analytics Dashboards of Adaptive Learning Platforms?

The desired outcomes is one set of methods for evaluating the functionalities and perceived experiences of the technological features, and the other set of methods on the evidence of improving learning outcomes, learning experience, and teaching quality. While the first contribute to the field of interaction design and the second contribute to the broader field of service design and innovation within the education and training domain.

2   Methods

Applying two different established methods, the protocol for the selection of papers and the protocol for the process of analysis and synthesis are conducted.

2.1 Selection of Papers: PRISMA

The selection of articles are conducted according to the Preferred Reporting Items for Systematic Reviews and Meta-Analyses (PRISMA) [11], which includes four phases: identification, screening, eligibility, and included (See Fig. 1). Since the aim is to review evaluation methods used for LA and LAD on ALPs, various combinations of the following keywords are used: evaluation, adaptive learning, learning analytics, learning analytics dashboards, assessment, etc. The searches were restricted to peer-reviewed papers, published in English, Danish, and Norwegian (considering authors' language skills), from 2011 to the search date September 1, 2021. In consultation with a librarian and after testing different combinations of keywords, four databases were selected, and different combinations of the keywords returned the following: Scopus [n = 75], ACM [n = 144], ScienceDirect [n = 106], and Taylor & Francis [n = 38]. We envision further inclusion of databases such as IEEE Xplore, JSTOR, Routledge, Springer, and ERIC in our continued work.

The exclusion criteria implemented in screening and eligibility stages are as follows: 1) A paper that does not mention LA or LAD in relation to ALP. 2) Papers with a focus on LA and LAD in other e-learning environments which do not meet the requirements of adaptivity for the learning platform. 3) Papers without empirical data examining LA or LAD on ALP. 4) For the conference proceedings, only included papers published as part of the main conference. Workshop papers and posters were excluded.

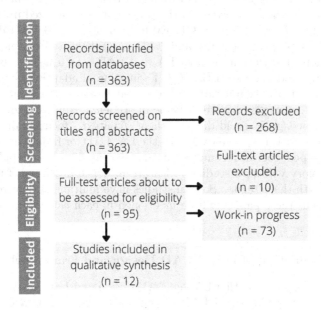

Fig. 1. PRISMA flow-chart

The two authors screened separate databases and only the papers selected by one author (n = 95) are included in this document. For this review, 10 articles and 2 reviews have been included for analysis and synthesis.

2.2 Constant Comparative Analysis Method

We applied the constant comparative analysis method for the analysis and synthesis [4]. The articles were encoded according to themes and then divided into categories. During this process, the coded sections were regularly compared to similar parts of texts containing the same codes. The intention was to create a connection between the texts and ensure the continuity of the codes' definitions [4].

Each included paper was read with the purpose of identifying methods, parameters, and purpose of evaluating LA and LAD. The data extracted from the papers are tabulated to synthesize: 1) The methods used when evaluating LA and LAD. 2) Parameters measured by the aforementioned methods to evaluate LA and LAD. 3) The purpose for the evaluation method applied. From the identified purposes a thematic analysis was initiated and categories were developed.

3 Analysis and Synthesis

In this section, we report the qualitative synthesis of the systematic review. The evaluation methods identified in the papers are summarized in the Table 1 are grouped into four categories. C1) Evaluation of LA and LAD design and framework - focusing on how LA and LAD is implemented on the platform. C2) Evaluation of performance with LA and LAD - focusing on user performance with LA and LAD statistics. C3) Evaluation of adaptivity - focusing on if and how the adaptivity functions of the system works. C4) Evaluation of perceived value - focusing on perceived value of students, educators, or users. C5) Evaluation of pedagogical and didactic theory/context - focusing on whether a pedagogical theory is the groundwork for the LA, LAD, or framework or if there are actionable pedagogical recommendations associated with the application.

Each category will have studies which are in depth described if their main focus aligns with the category. Several studies have multiple evaluations besides their main focus these papers will be mentioned in each category as evaluation features.

3.1 C1) Evaluation of la and LAD Design and Framework

Paper [1] focuses on evaluating LA and LAD design and framework whereas [8] only has evaluation of LA and LAD design and framework as a part of their study.

[1] propose EduAdapt, an architectural model for the adaptation of learning objects considering device characteristics, learning style and students' contextual

information. They develop an ontology (OntoAdapt) for recommending content to users. Particularly, for EduApadt the study wants to investigate if the use of ontology matches the learning objects adaptation scope.

The OntoAdapt [1] is an ontology which is evaluated in two phases. The first phase describes the development of the ontology and the second phase of applying it in a developed application. The first phase uses two strategies; scenarios and analyzing the quality and fidelity that OntoAdapt delivers against other ontologies. The scenarios identified different use cases from which they developed OntoAdapt. The analyzing of quality and fidelity of OntoAdapt compared to other ontologies was done with some evaluation metrics from full ontology evaluation (FOEval) (coverage, richness, and level of detail) and some provided by the software Protege (Annotations, Object property, Data property, Properties to the specific domain, Properties with specific range, Total number of classes, and Total number of subclass) to analyze the quality and the fidelity that OntoAdapt delivers in covering concepts on the associated subjects. These metrics were complemented with the tool Manchester-OWL Ontology Metric to validate and display statistics on OntoAdapts performance. These were used to calculate Attribute Richness (AR), Relation Richness (RR), Ontology Richness (OR), and Subclass Richness (SR).

The second phase, were the testing of the ontology. A mobile application prototype for Apple iOS mobile devices was developed and they used the prototype in an undergraduate course called Ubiquitous and Mobile Computing with 20 learners who used the Adapt application during 1 month. The study applied a survey using the Felder and Silverman index of learning styles with 44 items on a 5 point Likert scale on four dimensions (Active/Reflective, Sensing/Intuitive, Visual/Verbal, and Sequential/Global). Afterwards a pretest on the EduAdapt was preformed with 20 Learning Objectives (LOs). A post test was then offered after 1 month and to complete a survey on EduAdapt. The survey was based on the work of a two-tier test and a usability evaluation and was compounded of 10 statements, the students had to rate using a 5 point Likert scale to measure the level of user satisfaction. These results were evaluated on reliability with the Cronbach alpha approach and Wilcoxon-Mann-Whitney test to assess whether samples have the same distribution.

As one of the results in this expansive study "we can highlight as the main scientific contribution the proposal of a model for learning objects adaptation that employs inferences and rules in an ontology considering various contexts, including the student's learning style" [1, p. 83].

Besides this paper, an additional paper touch upon the evaluation of LA and LAD design and framework in their study. [8] presents a framework to frame user requirements of an adaptive system.

3.2   C2) Evaluation of Performance with la and LAD

Two papers focused mainly on evaluating user performance with LA and LAD and one additional paper mentioned the measurement of performance through LA and LAD but not as part of the main scope of its study.

Table 1. Review results

Author	Category	Evaluated unit	Methods	Parameters	Purpose
Di Mascio et al. (2013) [3]	C3, C4	Adaptive learning system TERENCE	Heuristic evaluation, expert reviewing, cognitive walk-through, observations, think-aloud and verbal protocols, controlled experiments, simulation and system performance indicators	Users' attitudes towards the system, users' performance and system performance	The qualitative methods (Heuristic, expert reviewing, cognitive walk-through evaluations etc.) are used to evaluate design choices for the system. Whereas, the simulations and system performance indicators are also used to evaluate the design choices but from a usability perspective on system performance
Bresó et al. (2016) [2]	C3, C4	Mechanism that adapts to stamina/mood	Surveys and simulations	Adaptability and variability	The simulation method was used to evaluated on the amount of possible outputs from the system. The surveys combined with a pilot case evaluated on the perceived levels of both variability and adaptability
Tlili et al. (2019) [14]	C3, C4	Method for modelling to learners personalities	Survey and LA student personality scores	Learner personality	LA was used to estimate learners' personalities and surveys were used to evaluate the validity of the personality models
Wei-Chih et al. (2015) [5]	C2, C3, C4	Adaptive learning algorithm	Surveys, pre- and post-tests, performance scores, and user satisfaction scores	Learner satisfaction scores and learning effectiveness	How does the algorithm performs (student performance) as well as what the learning satisfaction with the LAD were
Nye et al. (2021) [10]	C4	MentorPal, adaptive framework for virtual mentors	Formative user testing interviews, log data, pre- and post-surveys for career attitudes, and post-survey for usability	Feasibility for virtual mentoring	The LAD is evaluated on statistics which were used to check for the model quality, this was verified against users' subjective quality assurance testing

(continued)

Table 1. (*continued*)

Author	Category	Evaluated unit	Methods	Parameters	Purpose
Abech et al. (2016) [1]	C1, C4	Ontology model for LA and LAD	FOEval, user feedback, surveys, measurements of survey reliability, user scenarios, competence questions and usage patterns	Learners, learning objects, devices, context, context awareness, coverage, richness, and level of detail	The evaluations of the ontology goes through two phases. First phases evaluations are used for developing the ontology. Second phase evaluations are applied to compare it with other ontologies and to evaluate how the ontology performs in a learning context
Mavroudi et al. (2016) [8]	C1, C4	Teacher-led design on envisioned adaptive system	Evaluation questionnaire and Qualitative Comparative Analysis	Teacher perceptions and expectations	This paper proposes a methodology to frame requirements to a number of critical success factors in meeting the users' expectations of the system
Khawaja et al. (2014) [6]	C3, C4	Adaptive multitouch tabletop interaction application	Subjective ratings, Linguistic Inquiry and Word Count, and Advanced Text Analyzer	User's experienced cognitive load, Language Complexity Measures, and Linguistic Category Features	A method for a none-intrusive, non-manipulative adaptive learning design which adapts to users' cognitive load
Santos et al. (2015) [12]	C2, C3, C4	Ambient Intelligence Context-aware Affective Recommender Platform	Tutor Oriented Recommendations Modeling for Educational Systems methodology, user-centered design methods, data mining techniques, interviews, and SUS questionnaire	Learners' affective state, educators' tacit experiences, learner physiological signals	Exploration of ambient intelligence providing sensory-oriented feedback. How or if this improves personalized support through a recommender system
Zhang et al. (2021) [15]	C2, C4	Student-centered online one-to-one tutoring system	Pre- and post test of students' academic performance and system log files	Students' learning performance (academic), teachers' performance (attracting students)	Does such a system have a practical value

[5] developed a new algorithm, called the competency-based guided-learning algorithm (CBGLA). The study aimed to develop a CBGLA-based learning system that includes personalized learning paths which guide learners in achieving the learning objectives. The purposes of the guided-learning functions are to

accelerate and streamline the learning process. The system was tested on six third-year college students of electrical engineering before the experiment was conducted on 59 third-year college students of electrical engineering [Experimental group = 29, control group = 30]. To test the effectiveness of CGBLA a quasi-experimental research method was employed using a non-equivalent test design. The statistical mean, independent sample t-test, and one-way analysis of covariance (ANCOVA) was used to investigate the participants' learning effectiveness, satisfaction, and three dimensions of system validity through achievement of learning objectives, required learning time, and learning effectiveness. Learner satisfaction was investigated using a 16-item survey of five-point Likert scale covering three dimensions: interface design, design of adaptive guided-learning mechanism, and the perception of CBL. "The results of system validity experiments were significantly positive. This paper also conducted learning experiments to analyze learning effectiveness. Results showed that students learned more effectively under the guidance of the CBGL system than under the instruction of a teacher. [...] However, students expressed a lower degree of satisfaction when surveyed about their perception of CBL" [5, p. 124].

[15] presents the Student-Centered Online One-to-one Tutoring system (SCOOT), which deals with the cost of one-to-one tutoring. SCOOT is presented as a supplementary service where students can ask questions outside school to expand the flexibility of posing questions. The tutoring sessions with SCOOT is organized in four essential components: organization of teachers, student inquiry, and pair matching mechanism and the tutoring session. In SCOOT, teachers and students are able to communicate online through screen sharing, sending text and pictures, and speech. The teachers' interface of the application needs the teachers to log into the system and mark themselves as available for synchronous live conversations. The students' interface of the application require the students to log on and interact with the available teachers. These tutoring sessions are initiated by the students. The study seeks to evaluate the efficiency of SCOOT as well as examining how students' prior knowledge and the superficial patterns of tutoring sessions affected their learning. The evaluation include integrate students' learning performance and behavior log files instead of running between-subject experiments. The study ran for 50 days with a pre-test before and post-test afterwards. To get an in-depth understanding of how tutoring sessions affected students' learning, 40 tutoring sessions were randomly selected based on the criteria inferred and the sessions were manually labeled in detail with the coding schema developed from Chi's Interactive Constructive Active Passive (ICAP) framework. The participants consisted of 810 students in Grade 7 and 64 mathematics teachers and tutoring sessions which had a length of less than 1 min were omitted. Pretest performance combined with system usage factors was used to predict posttest performance by linear regression, this was done with Waikato Environment for Knowledge Analysis (WEKA). Common descriptive statistical analysis and Pearson correlation coefficient were computed. "The results suggested that system interventions are needed at both the student and teacher sides to facilitate good-quality tutoring interactions; otherwise, SCOOT

may further increase the difference between high- and low- achieving students" [15, p. 17].

Apart from the two above-mentioned papers [12] evaluates the effectiveness of supporting the learning process by e.g. giving affective and sensory input to help calm the user in a stressful learning context, and whether the input was helpful in the students' performance.

3.3   C3) Evaluation of Adaptivity

Four papers evaluated on the adaptivity of LA, LAD, or framework. Two additional papers mentioned adaptivity in their studies but did not present it as their main focus.

For defining personality in adaptive learning systems, [14] devised an evidence-based personality model by mapping students' participation in 15 functionalities of iMoodle learning management system against Big Five Inventory (BFI) dimensions (i.e. Extraversion, Agreeableness, Consciousness, Neuroticism, and Openness). The devised method is defined as an LA approach for defining the learners' personality. Based on 50 students data, Chi-square test is used as an assessment criterion to compare between the assessed personality levels from the results of LA approach and that assessed from the BFI results. Since the study is exploratory and little information is previously known, the obtained experimental data from their pilot experiment was validated using three methods namely, Chi-square, 10-fold cross-validation and Cohen's Kappa. The study concluded that the "LA approach with Bayesian network can model learners' personalities with an acceptable precision and a fair agreement compared to BFI for only three personality dimensions, namely, extraversion, openness and neuroticism" [14, p. 12].

To evaluate adaptability and variability of content from both simulations and user feedback, [2] presents the Personal Health System as a part of Help4Mood which supports users in not relapsing into depression, thereby learning to live with their condition. The Personal Health System is a developed tool that adapts its content to users stamina or mood. The design of the Personal Health System has been performed by adopting a user centred design methodology, which was done by involving a set of users, clinicians and caregivers. The evaluation is done through two methodologies one is producing simulated data and the second is collecting user feedback on the system. The simulation data was produced with two categories of scenarios in mind. The scenarios were designed on clinical requirements and were restrictive and flexible scenarios. Restrictive scenarios had a high number of constraints in the relative order and dependencies between tasks. They also had a high number of constraints in the periodicity and priority of the tasks. The flexible scenario in contrast had a minor number of constraints. The evaluation space corresponds to the multivariate combination of answers to all questions that might make sense given the context of the user. The simulations were done on 19 tasks and 31 subtasks and a task could be formed by one or more subtasks. There were 20.000 simulations of interactive sessions (restrictive n = 10.000 and flexible n = 10.000). In this study, adaptability was defined as how much the produced content of a session can change in relation to current and past information and inferred about the users' condition. Variability was defined as how the content order is offered depending both on user actions during the interactions and restrictions defined by clinicians. The second methodology encompassed two tests where users used the system and afterwards answered an 11-item survey with 3-point Likert scale on their perceived usefulness of different functionalities of the system. Two of these items referred to adaptability and variability. The paper concluded that "We can ensure that our framework provides a sufficient degree of adaptive and varied sessions, allowing the personalisation of the interactive sessions in order to improve the user experience" [2, p. 90].

In a study by [6], user's experienced cognitive load is examined to help improve performance in complex, time-critical situations by dynamically deploying more appropriate output strategies to reduce cognitive load. This is done through linguistic behavioral features as indices of user's cognitive load. A pilot study was conducted on a paper mock-up with two teams of four participants consisting of experts from fire management work roles. Their feedback improve the task design as the interaction design. The study examined a session where 44 participants (11 teams of four operators) participants strategically managed fire fighting tasks as a team. Participants interacted with a multi-touch tabletop screen that displays the fire management tasks and related information. All participants had general knowledge about firefighting, but none had ever participated in any actual firefighting, training fire fighting exercises, or used any fire management system before. Task design was set up with three different levels of task complexity or cognitive load. The levels were low, medium, and high (in the analysis combining low and medium to a single low category) Data consisted of participants voices which were recorded with wireless close-talk microphones recorded with the audio recording tool WaveSurfer and two video cameras which were used to record the operators' interactions. Further data consisted of logs of interactions with the touch table including operators' touch positions and dragging behavior as well as a survey on the self-rated perception of task difficulty as individuals and as a team on two separate 9-point Likert scales. The survey also contained an open question for general comments on task complexity, use of policy documents, and any communication issues. The analysis were done on observations, data transcription, feature extraction, and statistical analyses of the linguistic features with Linguistic Inquiry, Word Count, and Advanced Text Analyzer to investigate the variations in their behavior under different task load levels. In conclusion the paper states that: "An interaction system that is able to analyze users' speech and linguistic patterns to determine their current cognitive load could dynamically adapt its response to minimise the users' extraneous cognitive load and help them maintain task performance" [6, p. 362].

[12] presents an Ambient Intelligence Context-aware Affective Recommender Platform (AICARP) that applies Tutor Oriented Recommendations Modeling for Educational Systems (TORMES) elicitation methodology to sense changes in learners' affective state. AICARP delivers interactive context-aware affective

educational recommendations in an interactive way through complementary sensory communication channels. The recommendations are given to make users adjust breathing, stress etc. To evaluate the TORMES methodology, problem scenarios were used to identify the necessary requirements or user goals while taking into account the context of use elicited in the previous activity. Problem scenarios were used to develop solution scenarios that solved or avoided the problems posed by delivering interactive recommendations. To specify these solutions the recommendation modeling work with five dimensions; recommended action (what), recommendation rules (when and who), justification of the recommendation (why), recommendation format (how and where), and recommendation attributes (which). Evaluation of the scenarios were carried out by applying the user-centered design method Wizard of Oz. In this empirical study, a psycho-educational expert with experience in supporting learners face-to-face and online acted as the Wizard. Video of the participant and affective data (pulse, skin temperature, skin resistance, and skin conductance) was visualized to the wizard who in turn generated the associated recommend action (e.g. the green LED and the buzzer playing a pure tone). The study had six participants one of them being visually impaired. Before the study began participants completed the General Self-Efficacy Scale (GSE), the Big Five Inventory (BFI), and the Positive and Negative Affect Schedule (PANAS). As part of the study participants had to complete two tasks. Each of the task involved speaking for 5 min, while being recorded with the webcam. Before talking, participants had 1 min to think about what to say. Data consisted of AICARP system data (the previous mentioned physiological data), recordings from a webcam (facial expressions and voice), recordings from a video-camera (body movements), and time-stamped notes by an observer. The impact of the elicited interactive recommendation on the learner was evaluated at the end of the experiment by means of a questionnaire and an interview. The questionnaire was the System Usability Scale (SUS) 10-item 5 point Likert scale. The interview consisted of five open questions with the goal of understanding participants' opinions of their interaction with the system regarding perception, intrusiveness, and utility. Chi-square test was conducted to determine whether there were independence between the usability of the system and the effectiveness of the recommendations perceived by the participants. Answers given in the open questions were coded categorically. To verify these categories chi-square tests were again applied. The results cannot be applied as representative due to a very low sample size. The study concludes that "[...] this research opens a new avenue in related literature which focuses on managing the recommendation opportunities that an ambient intelligent scenario can provide to tackle affective issues during the language learning process when preparing for the oral examination of a second language learning course" [12, p. 50].

In addition to these papers, a number of papers mentions evaluation methods that evaluates on adaptivity. [3] presents usability associated with adaptivity and [5] effectiveness of adaptivity.

3.4   C4) Evaluation of Perceived Value

2 papers had their main focus on evaluating from users' perceived value or evaluation of users' perceived value. All of the rest 8 studies reviewed in this paper had in one way or the other included users' perceived value as a feature of their studies.

[3] describes the development of the TERENCE system's Graphical User Interface (GUI) prototypes through evidence based and user-centered design where they identified users' requirements and context of use by using users and domain experts. The first group were learners ($n \approx 170$), which here is described as 7–8 year old primary-school students who are poor comprehending and hard of hearing or deaf. The second group were educators ($n \approx 10$), who were primary school teachers, support teachers, and parents of learners. The last group were experts ($n \approx 10$) who were psychologists and linguists, who designed and developed the learning material. In evaluating the ALS TERENCE the GUI was assessed and it was assessed on two levels. The Learner GUI and the Expert/Educator GUI. Three evaluations were done and the two first ones were done with experts. The purpose for the expert evaluation were to assess whether the learning material were adequate for the learners and to evaluate the usability of prototypes, in particular whether the interfaces followed standard visual design guidelines, whether the interfaces supported the user's next step to achieve the task, and whether the interfaces provided appropriate feedback. The prototypes were evaluated using heuristic evaluation, expert review and cognitive walk through. More evaluations were conducted with end users. The purpose was to provide indications related to the pedagogical effectiveness of the prototypes and to evaluate their usability. The methods were: observational, think-aloud, verbal protocols, and controlled experiment. The paper informs about upcoming analyses of a large-scale evaluation with 900 end users. The initial findings and analysis is not included here. Their findings informs an expansion of usability testing to also include timing and focus of users' participation as well as system performance during the execution of users' tasks [3, p. 5-7].

[10] presents a virtual mentor system called MentorPal. In this empirical study the system gives career advice to high school students (n = 31) attending STEM internships who considering STEM careers. They participated in 3 sessions with MentorPal where they completed a pre-survey, interacted with MentorPal for 25–30 min, and then completed a post-survey. Researchers unobtrusively observed the students during usage and were available to help if needed. The STEM career advice were given with focus on STEM careers in the Navy. The system works as follows; the student asks one of four recorded virtually represented mentors by Free Text, Speech Input, or Topic Buttons about the mentor's career to get a better understanding of the career's alignment with the students interests and goals. MentorPal responds with the most suited answer. The primary pedagogical technique encouraged during recording of the mentors was the use of anecdotes and narrative. Development of MentorPal was done with three parameters in focus: Conversational Flow, Video-Chat Authenticity, and Low Cost. MentorPals performance was evaluated through pre- and post

surveys. Usability was evaluated with Unified Theory of Acceptance and Use of Technology constructs (UTAUT) survey on a 6 point Likert scale with 6 items. To evaluate change in attitude towards specific careers a survey was generate from variants of the CAPA Career Confidence Inventory and the CAPA Interest Inventory which resulted in respectively 50 items based on the approximately 400 CAPA items on a 5 point Likert scale. The results were tested and evaluated through traditional classifier statistics these were used to check for the direction of increases or decreases for model quality with 5-fold cross-validation accuracy scores, this was verified against subjective quality assurance testing. Their findings were limited on both sample size, sample diversity, and impact but one of the clear conclusions were that: "A panel of four mentors (even one hypothetically optimized through hindsight) is insufficient to cover either the main career interests or diversity representation of even 31 students. So, future research should investigate how students respond to self-reported or automatically personalized panels drawn from a larger set of mentors representing broader career choices and backgrounds" [10, p. 39].

In addition, several papers mentions the evaluation of perceived value. [1,2,12,14,15] present the evaluation of perceived value as a method for further informing performance of LA. [2,12] uses evaluation of perceived value to evaluate adaptability and variability and to assess the usability of the LA, [5] presents it to assess satisfaction levels of LA, [6] estimate perceived level of cognitive load, [15] assesses the practical value of the LA, and [1,8] developing the application.

3.5   C5) Evaluation of Pedagogical and Didactic Theory/Context

Three papers mentioned pedagogical theory as a contextual factor for their studies. None of the studies evaluated on how pedagogical or didactic theory was evaluated upon in either LA, LAD, or frameworks. The three papers that mentioned pedagogical were: [3] who had a second iteration of expert evaluation which consisted of 10 learning experts. As they applied the TERRENCE system to their prototype they included a pedagogical direction described as the pedagogical stimulation plan. The results from the user evaluation consisting of approx 170 users assessed whether the pedagogical effectiveness of the prototypes, the evaluation of its usability, and whether expectations to the pedagogical stimulation plan was met. This was done through observational, think-aloud, verbal protocols, and controlled experiment. [1] reviewed other works on ontology which had a pedagogical approach. This was compared to their own ontology's adaption to learning styles but their own ontology was not assessed on any pedagogical parameters. [5] used competency-based learning to develop their CBGLA algorithm but their study does not mention how CBGLA could or should be implemented in a pedagogical context neither how CBGLA resulted in the development of users' competencies.

4   Conclusion and Discussion

In this work in progress systematic literature review, we identified 12 relevant papers, synthesized 10 empirical papers, and covered two reviews as part of the introduction for establishing the scope of the paper. The methods that directly or indirectly contribute to the evaluation of LA or LAD of ALPs are grouped into five categories: C1) evaluation of LA and LAD design and framework, C2) evaluation of performance with LA and LAD, C3) evaluation of adaptivity functions of the system, C4) evaluation of perceived value, and C5) Evaluation of pedagogical and didactic theory/context. Figure 2 shows the number of papers covering the methods under the five categories as the central focus of their study.

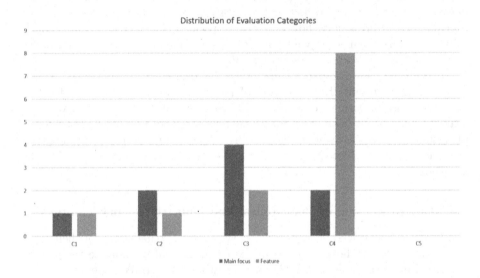

Fig. 2. Distribution of evaluation categories

Pedagogical and didactic theory/context (C5) as a theme occurred in multiple papers but none of the papers covered the evaluation of impact of an LA or LADs of ALP. LA and LAD are rarely examined in an educational context as a learning tool which informs either students and educators on making informed pedagogical or didactic choices framed by a pedagogical or didactic theory.

We experienced the lack of pedagogical theories and concepts such as motivation, engagement, gamification, and nudging to mention a few. For future studies, we raise the question, how do we improve learning and teaching quality with LA if there are no learning theory attached to the data collection and presentation? And how can LA and LAD lead to better learning or teaching if there are no actions associated with the data rather than just a presentation of learning objectives' difficulty, time spent on the platform or active users. Pedagogy and didactics needs to be connected with LA and LAD of ALPs to support teachers and students as they focus on cognitive and meta-cognitive impact, behavioral change, and social learning activities.

Broadly, we see assessments with ontologies, frameworks, methodologies, experimental designs, mathematical models, and LA statistics which are almost all the building blocks of a LA. Only evaluations of the visualization and the pedagogical elements are not present.

References

1. Abech, M., et al.: A model for learning objects adaptation in light of mobile and context-aware computing. Pers. Ubiquit. Comput. **20**(2), 167–184 (2016). ISSN: 1617–4909. https://doi.org/10.1007/s00779-016-0902-3. http://moodle.com. http://link.springer.com/10.1007/s00779-016-0902-3

2. Bresó, A., et al.: A novel approach to improve the planning of adaptive and interactive sessions for the treatment of major depression. Int. J. Hum. Comput. Stud. **87**, 80–91 (2016). ISSN: 10959300. https://doi.org/10.1016/j.ijhcs.2015.11.003

3. Di Mascio, T., et al.: Design choices: affected by user feedback? Affected by system performances? Lessons learned from the TERENCE project. In: ACM International Conference Proceeding Series, pp. 16–19, September 2013. https://doi.org/10.1145/2499149.2499171

4. Hewitt-Taylor, J.: Use of constant comparative analysis in qualitative research. Nurs. Stand. (Royal College of Nursing (Great Britain): 1987) **15**, 39–42 (2001). https://doi.org/10.7748/ns2001.07.15.42.39.c3052

5. Hsu, W.-C., et al.: A competency-based guided-learning algorithm applied on adaptively guiding e-learning. Interact. Learn. Environ. **23**(1), 106–125 (2015). ISSN: 1744–5191. https://doi.org/10.1080/10494820.2012.745432. https://www.tandfonline.com/action/journalInformation?journalCode=nile

6. Asif Khawaja, M., et al.: Measuring cognitive load using linguistic features: implications for usability evaluation and adaptive interaction design. Int. J. Hum. Comput. Interact. **30**(5), 343–368 (2014). ISSN: 1532–7590. https://doi.org/10.1080/10447318.2013.860579. https://www.tandfonline.com/action/journalInformation?journalCode=hihc

7. Martin, F., Dennen, V.P., Bonk, C.J.: A synthesis of systematic review research on emerging learning environments and technologies. Educ. Technol. Res. Dev. **68**(4), 1613–1633 (2020). ISSN: 1042–1629. https://doi.org/10.1007/s11423-020-09812-2. https://link.springer.com/10.1007/s11423-020-09812-2

8. Mavroudi, A., et al.: Teacher-led design of an adaptive learning environment. Interact. Learn. Environ. **24**(8), 1996–2010 (2016). ISSN: 1049–4820. https://doi.org/10.1080/10494820.2015.1073747. https://www.tandfonline.com/action/journalInformation?journalCode=nile. https://www.tandfonline.com/doi/full/10.1080/10494820.2015.1073747

9. Mousavinasab, E., et al.: Intelligent tutoring systems: a systematic review of characteristics, applications, and evaluation methods. Interact. Learn. Environ. **29**(1), 142–163 (2021). https://doi.org/10.1080/10494820.2018.1558257

10. Nye, B.D., et al.: Feasibility and usability of MentorPal, a framework for rapid development of virtual mentors. J. Res. Technol. Educ. **53**(1), 21–43 (2021). https://doi.org/10.1080/15391523.2020.1771640. https://www.tandfonline.com/action/journalInformation?journalCode=ujrt20

11. Page, M.J., et al.: The PRISMA 2020 statement: an updated guideline for reporting systematic reviews. BMJ **372**, n71 (2021). ISSN: 1756–1833. https://doi.org/10.1136/bmj.n71. https://www.bmj.com/lookup/doi/10.1136/bmj.n71

12. Santos, O.C., Boticario, J.G., Rodriguez-Sanchez, M.C.: New review of hypermedia and multimedia toward interactive context-aware affective educational recommendations in computer-assisted language learning toward interactive context-aware affective educational recommendations in computer-assisted language learning (2015). ISSN: 1361–4568. https://doi.org/10.1080/13614568.2015.1058428. https://www.tandfonline.com/action/journalInformation?journalCode=tham20

13. Shemshack, A., Spector, J.M.: A systematic literature review of personalized learning terms. Smart Learn. Environ. **7**(1), 1–20 (2020). https://doi.org/10.1186/s40561-020-00140-9

14. Tlili, A., et al.: Automatic modeling learner's personality using learning analytics approach in an intelligent Moodle learning platform. Interact. Learn. Environ. (2019). ISSN: 17445191. https://doi.org/10.1080/10494820.2019.1636084. https://www.tandfonline.com/action/journalInformation?journalCode=nile20

15. Zhang, L., et al.: Evaluation of a student-centered online one-to-one tutoring system. Interact. Learn. Environ. **0**(0), 1–19 (2021). https://doi.org/10.1080/10494820.2021.1958234. https://www.tandfonline.com/action/journalInformation?journalCode=nile

Personality in Personalisation: A User Study with an Interactive Narrative, a Personality Test and a Personalised Short Story

Waltteri Nybom[✉] and Mick Grierson

Creative Computing Institute, University of the Arts London, London, UK
w.nybom0620201@arts.ac.uk

Abstract. We present a user study developed to explore the use of psychological frameworks for the personalisation of narratives. Further, we explore using interactive narratives to understand the user's personality and narrative preferences. The study consists of three sections: an interactive narrative, a personality test, and a personalised short story. Whilst it would appear that at least this interactive narrative could not be used as a personality test per se, it was able to capture some traits. The personalisation appeared to work well, especially regarding relating with the protagonist. It was also found that extraverted people appear to prefer reading narratives with less formal language, and introverts prefer narratives with more formal language.

Keywords: Personalisation · Personality · Narrative

1 Introduction

What makes a good story? Any subjective answer to the question would, by definition, be down to the person answering the question. To present them a suitable story, we could find one matching their preferences, or, more intriguingly, make one fit them. Trying to understand the person using methods from psychology, the narrative could be made to have different variations for different personalities. But how do we get an understanding of the person's personality? Using their social media data would not always be possible or ethical. Using a personality test might not necessarily be much fun to the user. Then, why not use a method that should be fun for anyone interested in narratives: a narrative? That is what this study does: presents the users with an interactive narrative designed to capture their personality using the five-factor model (FFM) and the Need for Affect (NFA), and then personalises a narrative to match with their personality scores. This study seeks to consider various ways of personalisation at the same time, focusing on written, non-interactive narratives, and testing how this affects the reader experience.

© ICST Institute for Computer Sciences, Social Informatics and Telecommunications Engineering 2022
Published by Springer Nature Switzerland AG 2022. All Rights Reserved
E. Brooks et al. (Eds.): DLI 2021, LNICST 435, pp. 53–64, 2022.
https://doi.org/10.1007/978-3-031-06675-7_4

2   Background

2.1   The Five-Factor Model

The five-factor model (FFM) [16], often considered the gold standard of personality psychology, features five traits: extraversion, agreeableness, conscientiousness, emotional stability, and openness to experience. The factors have been found in many studies to influence preferences in narratives and media. [42] found that people with high scores in neuroticism, the reverse of emotional stability, had a strong preference for sad music and avoided light-hearted film genres, and psychoticism, an opposite of agreeableness, indicated a preference against comedy but one strongly for graphically violent horror movies. [47] found evidence that sensation seeking, represented by openness and extraversion, involved a preference for novel and arousing media across genres. Many such correlations have also been found in other studies [10,14,27,28,33,34,43,46]. Various other online activities, such as personal websites [39], Facebook profiles [4], emails [13] and even email addresses [3], can also reveal a person's personality to human observers. Computer-based personality judgments can indeed be more accurate than ones by humans, according to [44], who created an algorithm they found to accurately predict all FFM traits simply based on likes on Facebook.

Games have been used to research personality in several studies; [15], noting that games can have similar qualities to psychometric tests while being more engaging, propose a game for daily cognitive assessment. The Five Domains of Play theory [38] translates the FFM into five aspects of gaming motivation: people with a high score in openness to experience seek novelty; conscientiousness matches with challenge; extraversion with stimulation; agreeableness with harmony; and neuroticism with threat. [40] tested the model, finding that for participants younger than 60, four out of five personality traits correlated significantly but weakly with their corresponding game preference domains ($r = 0,13 - 0,30, p < 0,05$). [24] applied the FFM for adjusting difficulty in a first-person shooter game, with a linear regression model aiming to optimise enjoyment and gameplay duration. [37] found a correlation between gameplay metrics and all the five factors. [18] also created a method for generating a FFM profile during gameplay for the players, which is then used to define their quests.

2.2   Need for Affect

There have been various studies and versatile results on the topic of what sort of personal characteristics explain enjoyment of negative emotions in art. For example, [9] found that people with high empathy enjoyed tragic films more. [41] linked it to high openness to experience and empathy.

One promising approach could be the Need for Affect (NFA), which refers to how motivated people are to seek emotion-inducing situations and activities [21]. Media use or preference is not a part of its definition or operationalisation, but the study did have participants rate their willingness to see specific films after having read descriptions of how interesting, happy, and sad each of them was supposed to be. The willingness to see happy and sad films rather than less emotional films was higher for individuals with a strong NFA. [21] note that while sensation seeking is conceptually similar to the NFA, they found them empirically distinct.

High NFA scores appear to match with willingness to watch films with affectively negative content, but only in females [1]. [6] found that people with high NFA enjoyed horror films more. They found the NFA as the first personality trait found to be a consistent predictor of individuals' engagement with negative and ambivalent emotion experiences regardless of gender or genre. Therefore, using it in combination with the FFM could be helpful in determining possibly the most important issue in personalisation: whether the narrative should be ultimately happy or sad.

2.3 Narrative Personalisation

User modelling has been widely used to adapt computer games, but relatively little to determine storylines, often using factorial models of user types in interactive narratives, such as in PaSSAGE [5,35], Mirage [11], and [31]. Some assess the user's present emotional state, as in [32], or their comprehension of the narrative, as in [8]. It is also possible to focus on just narrative preferences, which can be treated as a collaborative filtering [17] problem, as in [45], whose drama manager learns a user's preferences from ratings on story fragments and then chooses successive plot points.

There is also some work on personalising language, typically with chatbots, such as in [30] who used the user's FFM personality type. The Personage system [22] produces utterances matching FFM profiles. It has also been used for making variations of stories slightly different stylistically, such as in the use of swear words, exclamation marks and stuttering [29] and, together with the Scheherazade story annotation tool [12], altering between first- and third-person narrators, and the shyness levels of their language [19,20].

3   Methodology

The study[1] had 59 participants (17 women, 36 men), volunteers of all ages above 18 who were found by posting about the study on internet discussion boards on interactive narratives and other relevant topics.

The first part is an interactive narrative specifically written for this study. It uses a 2nd person perspective where the user assumes the role of the protagonist and makes choices that determine what the protagonist does and how the plot advances. All but one of the 25 questions simulate a personality questionnaire on a five-point Likert scale, with the possible options ranging from one extreme to another, measuring either one of the factors in the Five-Factor Model (FFM) or the Need For Affect (NFA). The questions relating to FFM are about how the

---

[1] Available at https://cci.arts.ac.uk/~wnybom/zombies.

protagonist responds to the situation, for example in a very extraverted or a very introverted manner, and the questions measuring NFA are about deciding what happens next, ranging from something light-hearted to something very dark. Most choices do not affect the narrative trajectory, except for three questions, resulting in $2 \times 3 \times 5 = 30$ different ways the story could end up.

The participants then take a 10-item FFM questionnaire [26] and a 10-item NFA questionnaire [2]. Each question in both the narrative and the personality test is given a score from 0 to 4, and the total score for each trait is scaled in a normalised range from 0 to 1. Finally, the scores for the questions in the narrative are readjusted with ridit scores [7] to take into consideration how specific questions tend to get answered. Here too, a normalised range from 0 to 1 is used.

In the final part, the users are presented with a short story written for the experiment and personalised for them. Users are defined as being either high or low in a given trait and are given a version that matches with that. Group 1 have this done according to the results of the interactive narrative presented (henceforth referred to as IN), group 2 according to the personality test (PT), and one control group will get the opposite of what they'd get in group 1. The users are asked how much they liked the story and its language and how much they identified with the protagonist.

The narrative has two different versions: one with high, and one with low extraversion. This affects the use of language throughout every section. The story is then split into six different sections, and, apart from the section that is the same for everyone in the same extraversion pathway, there are two versions of each section under both extraversion pathways depending on whether the user has a high or low score in a given trait. The protagonist's personality depends on the user's FFM scores other than extraversion, and the ending on NFA: a high NFA indicates a preference for a more emotional, tragic ending; a low NFA a less emotional, somewhat happy ending. Therefore, there are $2^6 = 64$ different variations of the story.

FFM traits have been found to have various correlations with what sort of language people use, and here it is hypothesised that people would also like to read the sort of language they prefer to use. The most important FFM trait in this and many other respects has been found to be extraversion [23], and therefore, to avoid complicating things, it is the only trait used for personalising language in this study. Since it is used for this purpose, it is not used in other forms of personalisation; e.g. adjusting the protagonist's personality, to separate the effect of personalising language from that of personalising the character. Nevertheless, since extraversion is arguably the most important and the most widely understood FFM trait, it is the most likely one to affect identifying with the character, so if the other traits are helpful at all, extraversion would be highly likely to be so as well.

The way the use of language is personalised here is based on previous studies that have shown that people with high extraversion write using simple constructions; short sentences; few quantifiers; informal, affective language; the pronouns "we" and "which"; confident language featuring much words such as "want" and "need"; stylistic expressions such as "catch up" and "take care"; and a lot of semantic errors. Introverts, on the other hand, prefer the reverse: more long, formal and complex sentences; few errors; the pronoun "I"; negations; quantifiers; and less confident language such as "trying" and "going to" [23].

4 Results

4.1 Interactive Narrative

The personality scores given by the interactive narrative (IN) had varying correlations with the personality scores given by the personality test (PT), slightly improved by the ridit analysis (Table 1).

Table 1. Correlations of traits as judged by IN and PT, readjusted with ridit scores

Trait	Spearman correlation	p value
Extraversion	.425	.001
Emotional stability	.323	.012
Conscientiousness	.155	.241
Agreeableness	.128	.335
Need for affect	.035	.791
Openness to experience	.018	.89

It appears the IN was able to make an approximate assessment of the user's extraversion and emotional stability, but not the other traits. NFA(IN), or NFA according to the IN, did not have any significant correlations with anything, especially with NFA(PT), but got close to significant correlations with agreeableness(PT), $\rho = -.233$, $p = .076$, and with openness(PT), $\rho = -.211$, $p = .108$, both negative but not quite significant at $p < .05$.

The IN also appears good at judging openness in those identifying as women ($\rho = .469$, $p = .058$), but for men the correlation is actually negative ($\rho = -.273$, $p = .107$); neither are quite statistically significant. Particularly for women, statistical significance was hard to reach due to the small number of participants who identified as women (17).

4.2 Personalised Short Story

Some people took the experiment rather quickly and presumably carelessly, and one person confessed to just skim-reading the personalised narrative. Therefore, we exclude from the personalised short story analysis the 14 people who spent less than ten minutes on the test.

Table 2. Average scores by group, scale 1–5

Group	Liking story	Relating	Liking language
1 [n = 9] (IN)	3.56	2.78	3.55
2 [n = 19] (PT)	3.37	3.00	3.58
3 [n = 17] (Control, IN)	3.00	2.35	3.00
Kruskal-Wallis p value	.342	.197	.022

We can note that extraversion according to the PT had .387 correlation with relating with the protagonist in the high-extraversion version of the short story (n = 21), but −.24 in the low-extraversion version (n = 24), meaning that the more extraverted the user is, the more they relate with the protagonist if the language used is extraverted, but if the language is introverted, the reverse happens: the more introverted the user is, the more they relate! The p value for such a difference in correlations is .021. There were many such correlation differences, with only the statistically significant ones presented in Table 3.

Table 3. Significant correlation pairs, comparing groups presented with different version of the short story

Trait	Rating	IN			PT		
		Corr (high-trait group)	Corr (low-trait group)	p	Corr (high-trait group)	Corr (low-trait group)	p
Extraversion	Relating with protagonist				.387 [n = 21]	−.24 [n = 24]	.021
Extraversion	Liking the language	.136 [n = 24]	−.41 [n = 21]	.037	.389 [n = 21]	−.638 [n = 24]	< .001
Conscientious-ness	Relating with protagonist	.381 [n = 29]	−.176 [n = 16]	.044	.109 [n = 29]	−.426 [n = 16]	.048
Stability	Relating with protagonist	.104 [n = 26]	−.422 [n = 19]	.044			
Openness	Liking sad ending				−.364 [n = 25]	.333 [n = 20]	.012
NFA	Relating with protagonist more in sad ending	.169 [n = 25]	−.382 [n = 20]	.038			

Gender was also a major factor with the ending. For men, the ending made little to no difference, as versions with the happy ending were found just marginally better (3.27 [n = 15] vs. 3.07 [n = 15], Mann Whitney U p = .24). However, for women, the sad ending was greatly preferred (3.71 [n = 7] vs. 2.6 [n = 5], Mann Whitney U p = .014) (Table 4).

Table 4. Ratings by gender

	Men			Women		
	Happy ending [n = 15]	Sad ending [n = 15]	Mann Whitney U p	Happy ending [n = 7]	Sad ending [n = 5]	Mann Whitney U p
Liking	3.27	3.07	.24	2.6	3.71	.014
Relating	3.0	2.4	.071	2.4	3.0	.11
Language	3.4	3.33	.41	3.0	3.57	.043

5   Discussion

5.1   Interactive Narrative

As noted above, the IN was able to make an approximate assessment of the user's extraversion and emotional stability, but not the other traits. It should be noted that its way of measuring NFA did not match with the way NFA is tested, but with the way the authors of NFA describe the preferences for art that people with high NFA are expected to have: the more emotional and intense, the better. This study would give some indication that this is not necessarily the case.

The scores given by the IN followed a more standard distribution than those from the PT, particularly with ridit scores. According to the PT, the participants had a particularly low average score in extraversion (.32) whilst being high in openness to experience (.77), for example, which makes sense given the way they were recruited, but this could skew the results given by the IN, which had all of the average scores between .43 and .54 before ridit, and .45 and .50 after ridit. Some choices in the IN were far more popular than others, typically with bias in favour of the middle options. When the bias was away from the middle options, however, the ridit scores pulled the scoring closer to the middle.

In question 23, the user is asked whether to slip a housemate's medications into his drink. The choice is presented only to add to the user experience and the user's sense of control, and has no influence on personality scores. Interestingly, almost half of the users (26/59) decided to do so, and of those who did, few (8/26) wanted to see him unwell afterwards, though this was very common (28/33) in the group that chose not to! This was the only question where previous choices could have such influence on answers, being avoided specifically for issues like this. This gives some clue that while people often want to see suffering in interactive narratives, they don't want to feel like it's their fault.

5.2   Personalised Short Story

According to Kruskal-Wallis tests, the only statistically significant inter-group difference for the ratings for the story (Table 2) was with the language, $p = .022$. However, the scores between the groups are not directly comparable; for example, group 2 got the sad ending much more than others, which could skew the results slightly in their favour, since that ending was more liked on average. This is because users tended to get high NFA scores in the PT (average .61), which defined the personalisation of group 2, but the results were more balanced in the IN (average .45), which was used in groups 1 and 3. Nevertheless, it is easy to note that the control group performed the worst in every aspect, suggesting the personalisation did improve the experience.

Looking at Table 3, we can note that adjusting the language depending on level of extraversion worked well regarding liking the language, and, in the case of the PT, also with respect to relating with the protagonist (who was also the narrator). Personalisation based on conscientiousness and emotional stability(IN) also worked particularly well in making the protagonist relatable. Openness(PT) indicated liking the happier, less emotional ending, and therefore would apparently have been better for personalising the ending than NFA was, though NFA(IN) appeared to work too, but did not quite reach significance $(-.028$ vs. $-.45$, $p = .079$). NFA(PT) seemed to have the opposite effect, which would have reached significance without removing the fast experiment takers. However, NFA(IN) did work in making the protagonist relatable. Generally, the IN worked in many ways much better than the PT, though many correlations weren't found quite significant and therefore weren't mentioned here.

6   Conclusions

It was found that extraverted people appear to prefer reading narratives with less formal language, and introverts prefer narratives with more formal language, or specifically, the types of language extraverts and introverts have been found to write; this does not appear to have been tested before. Whilst it would appear that at least this interactive narrative could not be used as a personality test per se, it was able to capture some traits, specifically extraversion and emotional stability. It is possible that with agreeableness, conscientiousness and openness to experience, people might indeed have a preference to act within fiction differently from how they would in reality; for example, someone who is agreeable in reality might want to get a safe experience of what it is like to be rude. Whether they would then want to see protagonists behaving like this as well, or preferably like they would in reality, is an open question.

We should also consider the possibility that the personality tests did not measure traits ideally. Short versions were used to not bother the participants too much, but longer versions might have been more accurate. On the other hand, some people could have been rather uninterested in the personality test section and clicked through it rather carelessly, and making it longer could have exacerbated such a problem. It is therefore possible that interactive narratives could capture at least some aspects of personality even better than personality tests, and in fact the IN was at least as good as the PT for personalisation. Questions in personality tests can to be rather abstract and open to interpretation, even ambiguous, but in an interactive narrative, the user is put into a specific situation in a rather concrete manner. NFA, however, did not appear to work as intended, except with the way the IN interpreted it. Therefore, perhaps NFA(IN) could be re-defined simply as a preference for tragic rather than lighthearted themes in narratives – perhaps this could be called Preference for Tragedy, or PFT.

The personalisation with individual FFM traits also appeared to work well for relating with the protagonist. However, the effect could have been limited by the fact that the sections displaying the protagonist's personality were rather brief. Therefore, that a type of personalisation did not appear to work with this story does not mean that it could not work when done better, in a longer narrative, or with more participants, and that it did appear to work here could in some cases be down to just chance. Similarly, at least some of the questions in the interactive narrative could have been just poorly made. Therefore, more similar studies would be helpful. Other ways of personalisation could also be done based on FFM, such as more novelty for people with high openness for experience. Next, we plan to try NLP for altering the writing style, which could vastly ease the process.

In the future, it should be studied how interactive narratives could better capture personality. More such narratives should be written, and the kinds of choices that best correlate with personality scores should be chosen for further usage. Such choices would not necessarily have to be on a Likert scale. Collaborative filtering could also be used, and with enough participants and questions, surprising links could be found, which in turn could help personality research as well. Finally, the user profile thus created could also later be used for a recommender system, particularly with narratives, but possibly with other domains, as well; it has indeed been found that FFM can be useful in recommenders, particularly when there is little data available on the user [36], as well as for increasing the diversity of recommendations [25]. Ultimately, the approach could be used to personalise just about every aspect of narratives, as well as to recommend and perhaps generate more.

References

1. Appel, M.: Manche mögen's heiß. Diagnostica **54**(1), 2–15 (2008)
2. Appel, M., Gnambs, T., Maio, G.R.: A short measure of the need for affect. J. Pers. Assess. **94**(4), 418–426 (2012)
3. Back, M.D., Schmukle, S.C., Egloff, B.: How extraverted is honey. bunny77@ hotmail.de? Inferring personality from e-mail addresses. J. Res. Pers. **42**(4), 1116–1122 (2008)
4. Back, M.D., et al.: Facebook profiles reflect actual personality, not self-idealization. Psychol. Sci. **21**(3), 372–374 (2010)

5. Barber, H., Kudenko, D.: A user model for the generation of dilemma-based interactive narratives. In: Workshop on Optimizing Player Satisfaction at AIIDE, vol. 7 (2007)
6. Bartsch, A., Appel, M., Storch, D.: Predicting emotions and meta-emotions at the movies: the role of the need for affect in audiences' experience of horror and drama. Commun. Res. **37**(2), 167–190 (2010)
7. Bross, I.: How to use Ridit analysis. Biometrics Mag. **14**, 18–38 (1958)
8. Cardona-Rivera, R.E.: A model of interactive narrative affordances. Ph.D. thesis, North Carolina State University (2019)
9. De Wied, M., Zillmann, D., Ordman, V.: The role of empathic distress in the enjoyment of cinematic tragedy. Poetics **23**(1–2), 91–106 (1995)
10. Denden, M., Tlili, A., Essalmi, F., Jemni, M.: Educational gamification based on personality. In: 2017 IEEE/ACS 14th International Conference on Computer Systems and Applications (AICCSA), pp. 1399–1405. IEEE (2017)
11. El-Nasr, M.S.: Interaction, narrative, and drama: creating an adaptive interactive narrative using performance arts theories. Interact. Stud. **8**(2), 209–240 (2007)
12. Elson, D.K., McKeown, K.R.: A tool for deep semantic encoding of narrative texts. In: Proceedings of the ACL-IJCNLP 2009 Software Demonstrations, pp. 9–12 (2009)
13. Gladis, S.D.: WriteType: Personality types and writing styles. Human Resource Development (1993)
14. Gunter, B.: Dimensions of television violence. New York: St (1985)
15. Holmgård, C., Togelius, J., Henriksen, L.: Computational intelligence and cognitive performance assessment games. In: 2016 IEEE Conference on Computational Intelligence and Games (CIG), pp. 1–8. IEEE (2016)
16. John, O.P., Donahue, E.M., Kentle, R.L.: Big five inventory. J. Pers. Soc. Psychol. (1991)
17. Koren, Y., Bell, R.: Advances in Collaborative Filtering. In: Ricci, F., Rokach, L., Shapira, B. (eds.) Recommender Systems Handbook, pp. 77–118. Springer, Boston, MA (2015). https://doi.org/10.1007/978-1-4899-7637-6_3
18. de Lima, E.S., Feijó, B., Furtado, A.L.: Player behavior and personality modeling for interactive storytelling in games. Entertainment Comput. **28**, 32–48 (2018)
19. Lukin, S.M., Reed, L.I., Walker, M.A.: Generating sentence planning variations for story telling. arXiv preprint arXiv:1708.08580 (2017)
20. Lukin, S.M., Walker, M.A.: Narrative variations in a virtual storyteller. In: Brinkman, W.-P., Broekens, J., Heylen, D. (eds.) IVA 2015. LNCS (LNAI), vol. 9238, pp. 320–331. Springer, Cham (2015). https://doi.org/10.1007/978-3-319-21996-7_34
21. Maio, G.R., Esses, V.M.: The need for affect: individual differences in the motivation to approach or avoid emotions. J. Pers. **69**(4), 583–614 (2001)
22. Mairesse, F., Walker, M.A.: Towards personality-based user adaptation: psychologically informed stylistic language generation. User Model. User Adap. Inter. **20**(3), 227–278 (2010)
23. Mairesse, F., Walker, M.A., Mehl, M.R., Moore, R.K.: Using linguistic cues for the automatic recognition of personality in conversation and text. J. Artif. Intell. Res. **30**, 457–500 (2007)
24. Nagle, A., Wolf, P., Riener, R.: Towards a system of customized video game mechanics based on player personality: relating the big five personality traits with difficulty adaptation in a first-person shooter game. Entertainment Comput. **13**, 10–24 (2016)

25. Onori, M., Micarelli, A., Sansonetti, G.: A comparative analysis of personality-based music recommender systems. In: Empire@ RecSys, pp. 55–59 (2016)

26. Rammstedt, B., John, O.P.: Measuring personality in one minute or less: a 10-item short version of the big five inventory in English and German. J. Res. Pers. **41**(1), 203–212 (2007)

27. Rawlings, D., Ciancarelli, V.: Music preference and the five-factor model of the neo personality inventory. Psychol. Music **25**(2), 120–132 (1997)

28. Rentfrow, P.J., Goldberg, L.R., Zilca, R.: Listening, watching, and reading: the structure and correlates of entertainment preferences. J. Pers. **79**(2), 223–258 (2011)

29. Rishes, E., Lukin, S.M., Elson, D.K., Walker, M.A.: Generating different story tellings from semantic representations of narrative. In: Koenitz, H., Sezen, T.I., Ferri, G., Haahr, M., Sezen, D., Ç atak, G. (eds.) ICIDS 2013. LNCS, vol. 8230, pp. 192–204. Springer, Cham (2013). https://doi.org/10.1007/978-3-319-02756-2_24

30. Ritschel, H., Baur, T., André, E.: Adapting a robot's linguistic style based on socially-aware reinforcement learning. In: 2017 26th IEEE International Symposium on Robot and Human Interactive Communication (RO-MAN), pp. 378–384. IEEE (2017)

31. Sharma, M., Ontañón, S., Mehta, M., Ram, A.: Drama management and player modeling for interactive fiction games. Comput. Intell. **26**(2), 183–211 (2010)

32. Tanenbaum, J., Tomizu, A.: Narrative meaning creation in interactive storytelling. Int. J. Comput. Sci. **2**(1), 3–20 (2008)

33. Tekofsky, S., Van Den Herik, J., Spronck, P., Plaat, A.: Psyops: personality assessment through gaming behavior. In: Proceedings of the International Conference on the Foundations of Digital Games. Citeseer (2013)

34. Teng, C.I.: Online game player personality and real-life need fulfillment. Int. J. Cyber Soc. Educ. **2**(2), 39–50 (2009)

35. Thue, D., Bulitko, V., Spetch, M., Wasylishen, E.: Interactive storytelling: a player modelling approach. In: AIIDE, pp. 43–48 (2007)

36. Tkalcic, M., Kunaver, M., Košir, A., Tasic, J.: Addressing the new user problem with a personality based user similarity measure. In: First International Workshop on Decision Making and Recommendation Acceptance Issues in Recommender Systems (DEMRA 2011), vol. 106 (2011)

37. Van Lankveld, G., Spronck, P., Van den Herik, J., Arntz, A.: Games as personality profiling tools. In: 2011 IEEE Conference on Computational Intelligence and Games (CIG 2011), pp. 197–202. IEEE (2011)

38. VandenBerghe, J.: The 5 domains of play: applying psychology's big 5 motivation domains to games. In: Game Developers Conference, GDC Vault (2012)

39. Vazire, S., Gosling, S.D.: e-perceptions: personality impressions based on personal websites. J. Pers. Soc. Psychol. **87**(1), 123 (2004)

40. de Vette, A.F.A., Tabak, M., Dekker-van Weering, M., Vollenbroek-Hutten, M.M.: Exploring personality and game preferences in the younger and older population: a pilot study. In: ICT4AgeingWell, pp. 99–106 (2016)

41. Vuoskoski, J.K., Thompson, W.F., McIlwain, D., Eerola, T.: Who enjoys listening to sad music and why? Music. Percept. **29**(3), 311–317 (2011)

42. Weaver, J.B., III.: Exploring the links between personality and media preferences. Pers. Individ. Differ. **12**(12), 1293–1299 (1991)

43. Yee, N., Ducheneaut, N., Nelson, L., Likarish, P.: Introverted elves & conscientious gnomes: the expression of personality in world of warcraft. In: Proceedings of the SIGCHI Conference on Human Factors in Computing Systems, pp. 753–762 (2011)

44. Youyou, W., Kosinski, M., Stillwell, D.: Computer-based personality judgments are more accurate than those made by humans. Proc. Natl. Acad. Sci. **112**(4), 1036–1040 (2015)
45. Yu, H., Riedl, M.O.: Personalized interactive narratives via sequential recommendation of plot points. IEEE Trans. Comput. Intell. AI Games **6**(2), 174–187 (2013)
46. Zammitto, V.L.: Gamers' personality and their gaming preferences. Ph.D. thesis, Communication, Art & Technology, School of Interactive Arts and Technology (2010)
47. Zuckerman, M., Litle, P.: Personality and curiosity about morbid and sexual events. Pers. Individ. Differ. **7**(1), 49–56 (1986)

Tools and Models

Tools and Models

Jeanette Sjöberg[1] ⓘ and Eva Brooks[2] ⓘ

[1] Halmstad University, Kristian IVs väg 3, 30118 Halmstad, Sweden
jeanette.sjoberg@hh.se
[2] Aalborg University, Kroghstræde 3, 9220 Aalborg, Denmark
eb@hum.aau.dk

Abstract. In this section of the volume, contributions from EAI DLI 2021 explores different aspects of digital technologies being used as tools for various reasons, such as for interactions and experience design, to enrich existing and novel design practices and to affect the interaction process and engagement. In addition, it focuses on how models can be developed as useful assets for innovative approaches while using digital tools. Overall, the section shows examples of different ways to investigate and ensure that learning can be enhanced through the use of digital tools.

Keywords: Computational thinking · E-Learning · Evaluation model · Game design · Mediating artefacts · Multisensory interaction · Pedagogical tool · Production-oriented approach · Spatial interaction · Teaching model · User interface design

1 Introduction

1.1 Scope

The second section of this volume is themed "Tools and Models", and it focuses on different aspects of digital technologies being used as tools for learning and how they in turn can be evaluated and validated in relation to learning. Digital tools for learning are widely debated as a concept since it challenges institutional traditions of learning; the technologies do not merely support learning; they transform how we learn and how we come to interpret learning [1]. Thus, there is a need to study and evaluate digital tools used for pedagogical support in various learning settings as well as to develop models that can be used for innovative approaches in educational contexts. An example of this is games and gamification, which has increased rapidly in recent years. Game-based reforms of transforming entire schools from start to finish designed by the means of key mechanisms and participation strategies from the world of digital games to create an ideal school, are being discussed [2]. As a consequence of this and other examples, researchers involved in innovative processes of learning development by the aid of digital technologies must therefore consider not only what a person can do with the technology but also what the technology can do with the person. An important aspect here is to distinguish when digital tools add value to a learning situation and when they don't. This part of the EAI DLI 2021 proceedings exemplifies different existing and novel practices where digital tools for learning are being assessed in various ways according to organisational, pedagogical and design challenges. Using problem solving as a basis for learning, the contributions here are characterised by experimental design and creativity.

The first contribution in this second section discusses an evaluation model proposed in this study, based on the Production-oriented Approach of Teacher-Student Collaborative Assessment, which focuses on how to effectively carry out course evaluation in the online and offline blended learning in the information age. The second contribution includes an overview of the concept of computational thinking in relation to mathematics, in which the background that relates to how students can develop their mathematical understanding through computational thinking is also considered when establishing an analysis model. The third contribution examines organisational and pedagogical challenges in an ongoing pedagogical development project in which game design is used to let students both learn and reflect upon different perspectives of ethics during the length of an entire master program. Finally, the last contribution in this second section addresses the question of how to use sonic interaction design as a tool for interactions and experience design, to enrich existing and novel design practices and affect the interaction process and engagement.

The following text snippets elaborate from each contribution to further assist readership.

2   Research on Evaluation Model of College English Online and Offline mixed Learning under Digital Environment

The paper is authored by Yongqin Wang and titled Research on Evaluation Model of College English Online and Offline Mixed Learning under Digital Environment. Here, the author discusses an evaluation model based on the Production-oriented Approach (POA) of Teacher-Student Collaborative Assessment (TSCA). TSCA highlights the leading role of teachers and enhances students' learning participation. In traditional college English classroom teaching, there is no lack of evaluation links, but it is often a formality. Teachers simply leave comments or record student test results. TSCA requires teachers to select typical evaluation samples in advance, and then guide students to conduct individual, group, and team evaluations, with all members working together to evaluate. In addition, TSCA also promotes the achievement of language goals and communication goals. Furthermore, TSCA has realised the promotion of learning by evaluation and the promotion of teaching by evaluation. The author claims that the construction of online and offline college English courses is now the general trend in reforming college English courses, and that classroom evaluation is an important part of judging whether the reform of college English online and offline curriculum can effectively achieve the teaching goals. The model proposed in this study focuses on how to effectively carry out course evaluation in the online and offline blended learning in the information age. The study concludes that, based on TSCA, the proposed college English online and offline classroom teaching evaluation model has a positive impact on students' learning motivation, learning methods, and learning behaviours, and at the same time enhances students' evaluation abilities, and promotes the development of speculative and cooperative abilities.

3   Orchestration Between Computational Thinking and Mathematics

The paper Orchestration Between Computational Thinking and Mathematics, authored by Camilla Finsterbach Kaup, includes an overview of the concept of computational thinking (CT) in relation to mathematics, in which the background that relates to how students can develop their mathematical understanding through CT is also considered. The aim of the study, on which the paper is based, is to use computational thinking and mathematics to establish an analysis model and recognize CT's utilisation in maths teaching. Additionally, meaning of signs that occur as part of students' development of mathematics concerning CT are also emphasised. The study draws on a socio-cultural viewpoint on learning to examine the relationship between CT and mathematics, which was significant for the development of the proposed model, and by applying a socio-cultural perspective, the mediation theory provides new opportunities for understanding the mediation process involved in the introduction of digital artefacts, such as robots in mathematic teaching. The model - "Orchestration between CT and mathematics" - consists of two dimensions: where one of them concerns which perspective that is applied (either teacher- or student-centred), and the other dimension concerns the synergy between CT and mathematical concepts. These two dimensions produce different representations and are initiated in various ways. The interplay between CT and maths emerges through theoretical perspectives, which are essential to how teachers mediate and construct teaching activities to support their students' development of mathematical, scientific concepts. The concept of "orchestration" relates to teachers' function in facilitating various activities that mediate the creation of student symbols and the relationship between signs and scientific concepts. If teachers can use CT to convey mathematics content to promote and coordinate various teaching activities, then it is appropriate to include CT in mathematics teaching. The author concludes that the study has relevance for mathematics teachers as well as researchers and that it can help them determine how teachers can incorporate digital artefacts to support CT concerning mathematics teaching.

4   Game Design as a Pedagogical Tool for Learning and Reflection: The Case of the Ethics Experience

The paper titled Game Design as a Pedagogical Tool for Learning and Reflection: The Case of the Ethics Experience is authored by Lena Hylving, Andrea Resmini, Bertil Lindenfalk and Oliver Weberg and reports on an ongoing pedagogical development project in which game design is used to let students both learn and reflect upon different perspectives of ethics relevant to the master program they are enrolled in; the DSI program - a two-year master's program on Digital Service Innovation – at Halmstad University. In the paper, the authors address organisational and pedagogical challenges with the application of game approaches across the length of an entire master program. The course plans in the program all include ethical considerations to some degree, and it was decided by the program manager that ethics and the role it plays in digital service innovation should be emphasised even more by implementing a "core theme" of ethics and ethics in design running throughout the entirety of the program, and also in relation to game and game design. The authors use an action design approach where the problem is grounded in the challenge of engaging students in learning opportunities that have no curriculum credits assigned to them and where the students will follow an applied design methodology in their own design process. The authors argue that in terms of design education, games offer a safe, controllable, and observable space for simulating experiences, hence it could have an enhancing effect for learning. Using an experiential learning approach to closely follow that provided by games and formalised in game design, the authors explain the underlying logic behind the pedagogical process where students develop their own game and at the same time learn about different perspectives of ethics in relation to courses that they are currently taking. Even though the project is ongoing, the team has gained some preliminary insights: the requirement of careful planning for the pedagogical process, the necessity to keep students involved and engaged and reflections of how to handle the entire process in terms of treating ethics as culturally bounded. Furthermore, this approach to game design as a pedagogical tool to engage and democratise the learning experience is new and increasingly relevant for both students that play games on an everyday basis, but also students that are new to games.

5   Designing User Experience with the Sonic Metaphors

Predrag K. Nikolić authored this paper titled Designing User Experience with the Sonic Metaphors, which is addressing the question of how to use sonic interaction design (SID) as a tool for interactions and experience design. SID is a multisensory design approach where sound has a primary role in developing users' interactions with electronic devices or digital systems and giving meaning to user engagement. As part of performing user research, the study includes several informal interview sessions and personal observations during the public art-work exhibitions and controlled lab environment with participants in the Sonic Metaphors' interactive installation "Before & Beyond", exhibited at the Maison Shanghai Finally Fantasy exhibition in 2016. In the installation, this activity relates to given sound control, which helps users enrich their experience through given metaphors. The activity is mediated by the contextual pattern built into the artwork's concept. The installation is conceptualised as a responsive, playful environment where visitors have physical interactions that stimulate their internal processes, such as motivating them to collaborate, bodily interact and communicate. The installation space responded to visitors' body movements, the direction of walking and the distance between participants. After entering the installation, visitors were attached to the visual String of Energy projected on the screen in front of them, with characteristic colour and sound as an abstract metaphor of their existence in a virtual world they stepped in. Animated strings with a specific tone, user movements and social interactions were elements of the aesthetic experience. Theoretically, the authors are using activity theory as a foundation in design evaluation and human-device problem analysis, where it serves as a helpful framework for understanding presented works in the broader sound interaction design context. The main contribution of the study is that it offers new creative vocabulary based on sound meanings and utilises acoustic information patterns as a novel way of enabling access to the digital environment. The authors propose that sonic metaphors can be used as a creative vocabulary to enrich exiting and novel design practices, significantly when sensory limitations can vastly affect the interaction process and engagement.

6   Epilogue and Acknowledgements

This second section, Tools and Models, introduced four contributions to promote readership of each full paper that are presented in the following chapters. In doing so, the authors of this chapter acknowledge the contributions from each author whose original work was presented in the EAI DLI 2021 online conference events on December 2nd, 2021.

References

1. Säljö, R.: Digital tools and challenges to institutional traditions of learning: technologies, social memory and the performative nature of learning. J. Comput. Assist. Learn. **26**(1), 53–64 (2010)
2. Prensky, M.: Teaching Digital Natives: Partnering for Real Learning. Corwin Press (2010)

Research on Evaluation Model of College English Online and Offline Mixed Learning Under Digital Environment

Wang Yongqin[✉]

Harbin University of Science and Technology,
No. 52 Xuefu Road, Nangang District, Harbin, China
wangyongqin0926@163.com

Abstract. Based on the Production-oriented Approach (POA) of Teacher-Student Collaborative Assessment (TSCA), an online and offline college English teaching evaluation model is proposed and combined with teaching examples to analyze the impact of the evaluation model on students' learning motivation, learning methods, and learning behaviors, so that the purposeful and efficient English learning of the students' is carried out in the digital age, so as to improve students' thinking ability and cooperative evaluation ability.

Keywords: Production-oriented approach · Teacher-Student Collaborative Assessment · Teaching model · e-learning

1 Introduction

With the issuance of the "Notice of the General Office of the Ministry of Education on the Implementation of the 'Double Ten Thousand Plan' for the Construction of First-class Undergraduate Majors", various colleges and universities are carrying out characteristic development and classified development. Many colleges and universities have carried out college English teaching reforms, such as classified teaching according to student level, general English, academic English, etc., but no matter what kind of teaching transformation, the construction of online and offline college English courses is the general trend. Classroom evaluation is an important part of judging whether the reform of college English online and offline curriculum can effectively achieve the teaching goals. Therefore, in language learning, based on the Teacher-Student Collaborative Assessment (TSCA) link proposed by Wen Qiufang, the impact of "assessment" on students' learning motivation, learning methods and learning behaviors is analyzed, so as to promote teaching by assessment and promote teaching by assessment. The effect of learning, enhance students' thinking ability and cooperative evaluation ability.

This paper is granted by Heilongjiang Province Educational Science Planning Project GJB1421070 "Research and Practice of College English Teacher-Student Collaborative Assessment Based on SAMR Model". Heilongjiang Province Educational Science Planning Project GJB1421065. Heilongjiang Province Economic and Social Development Key Research Project (foreign language discipline special project) WY2021041-C.

E. Brooks et al. (Eds.): DLI 2021, LNICST 435, pp. 71–76, 2022.
https://doi.org/10.1007/978-3-031-06675-7_5

2   Teacher-Student Collaborative Assessment (TSCA)

2.1   The Theoretical Basis of TSCA

The Production-oriented Approach (POA) proposed by Wen Qiufang's team is a teaching theory with Chinese characteristics aimed at the practical problems of foreign language education in China. The theory takes "learning-centered theory, integrated learning-use theory, and whole-person education theory" as its core concepts, covering the hypothesis of output drive, input facilitating, and selective learning. The theory emphasizes the intermediary role of teachers and must be effectively realized in the teaching process, driving, facilitating and assessing [1].

The Teacher-Student Collaborative Assessment (TSCA) used in this article is the last part of the POA teaching process. The evaluation objects of the teaching examples are the output tasks related to the unit topics in the college English textbooks. The evaluation subjects include teachers, students, Machine automatic scoring, etc. The specific implementation of the evaluation link is mainly embodied in TSCA pre-class preparation, in-class implementation and after-class activities.

2.2   The Role of TSCA

First of all, TSCA highlights the leading role of teachers and enhances students' learning participation. In traditional college English classroom teaching, there is no lack of evaluation links, but it is often a formality. Teachers simply leave comments or record student test results. TSCA requires teachers to select typical evaluation samples in advance, and then guide students to conduct individual, group, and team evaluations, with all members working together to evaluate.

Secondly, TSCA promotes the achievement of language goals and communication goals. TSCA's evaluation points focus on these two goals, testing language acquisition before, during and after class, such as testing vocabulary, sentences, paragraphs, text and grammar, etc.; at the same time, it will also evaluate the effectiveness of actual communication, such as whether the speaker correctly expresses its conversational meaning, attitude, ideas, and emotions to the listener. Through the development of TSCA activities, students clarify the key points of evaluation and promote the achievement of learning goals.

Thirdly, TSCA has realized the promotion of learning by evaluation and the promotion of teaching by evaluation. Through self-analysis, evaluation of others, and acceptance of others' evaluation opinions, students have made it possible to promote learning through evaluation and take advantage of others to make up for their shortcomings. Teachers combine students' language expressions of evaluation points and students' communication with each other to keep abreast of student dynamics and mastery of knowledge points in a timely manner, and then adjust teaching content and promote the realization of teaching goals.

3　TSCA-Based Online and Offline Classroom Teaching Evaluation Model for College English

TSCA has been implemented in many college English classes. The model proposed in this article, taking our university as an example, focuses on how to effectively carry out course evaluation in the online and offline blended learning in the information age.

3.1　Online Evaluation Before Class

In view of the reduction of college English teaching hours in our school, students have online platform tasks to complete before each class, such as written expressions, oral expressions, micro-class learning, pre-class quizzes, pre-class questionnaires.

For students, online evaluation combines personal evaluation and peer evaluation. Taking online composition as an example, the topic is to write opinions on the foreign translation of Chinese film culture. Firstly, personal evaluation is carried out. Students submit essays online, and students conduct self-evaluation and peer evaluation based on the feedback from the automatic evaluation system. For peer evaluation before class, it includes two aspects. One is that each student should mark his peer's composition according to the system's designation, point out mistakes and score according to the scoring standard, expand their thinking, and think about the similarities and differences between their own writing and others' writing; The second is to evaluate the peer's pre-class learning effectiveness based on the peer's self-evaluation, consultation and discussion, and make a record and give feedback to the teacher.

For teachers, in pre-class online evaluation, teachers obtain many values from big data as reference, such as machine scores, the number of students' self-evaluation corrections, the number of students' mutual evaluations, and the distribution of errors, etc., and then conduct micro-evaluation; at the same time, learn from students' mutual evaluations. Commentary notes, grasp the students' learning attitude, learning behavior, and learning weaknesses in time, and give a macro evaluation. According to the TSCA philosophy, teachers' pre-class preparation is an important part of giving full play to the guiding role, accurately selecting typical samples and designing exercises that can effectively achieve the teaching goals, without asking for all-round comments, but focusing on the emphasis and difficulty, and promoting the achievement of the teaching goals.

3.2　Offline Evaluation

Under the guidance of TSCA, when conducting comprehensive offline classroom evaluations, teachers can use online mobile Apps to analyze teaching effects faster and more conveniently, adjust teaching progress in a timely manner, enrich teaching content, and carry out teaching evaluations.

In offline classrooms, there are rich evaluation forms, and teacher-student cooperative assessment that integrate individual evaluation, peer evaluation, group evaluation and teacher evaluation are conducted around typical samples. In-class links are the key and difficult points for teachers to implement evaluation (Sun Shuguang 2019) [2]. Taking the written expression composition in the above pre-class session as an example, the teacher sends typical samples and evaluation criteria to the students in class. For example, the evaluation criteria checklist: whether the prescribed writing tasks are completed, whether the required writing content is included, whether the structure is complete, whether the sentences are fluent, etc.

Students self-evaluate and mutually evaluate typical samples, and then communicate and exchange in the group to propose rectification plans. Each team sends a member to report within 3 min, and other members of the team can make supplements within 30 s. At the same time, well-prepared teachers integrate the difficulties of pre-class preparation and the results of on-site student evaluations, use mobile apps to initiate voting and keyword discussions, and ask students to select the group with the best evaluation display (not to select their own group). The reference data in the mobile app helps teachers use their time to evaluate efficiently, so as to evaluate and promote teaching.

After the teacher's evaluation, use the mobile app to randomly select people, and let one or several student analysts collaborate to evaluate the results, for example, whether to agree to the rectification plan, and what are the reasons. In order to clarify whether the students really mastered the important and difficult points, and sample the achievement of the language goal. The offline evaluation of a typical sample of teacher-student cooperation has actually experienced five processes of individual, peer, group, teacher, and teacher-student cooperation of the sample. Then let the students complete the exercise tasks prepared by the teacher before the class in the mobile app, so that the students once again clarify the key points of the course and strengthen the use of the knowledge they have learned. The data feedback on the online platform is helpful for teachers and students to check for deficiencies, complete offline evaluations in the classroom, and promote learning.

3.3 Online and Offline Evaluation After Class

Based on the above evaluation of typical samples, each student revised his personal composition again and completed the online output task. In this link, online peer evaluation and offline group evaluation are the main ones, and teacher evaluation is a supplementary one. The implementation principles of TSCA are: goal-oriented before class, focus on key points, problem-driven in class, gradual support, process monitoring after class, promotion and demonstration (Sun Shuguang 2020) [3]. Under the guidance of the TSCA, students have already analyzed typical samples under the guidance of teachers in class, and the evaluation process can also draw inferences about the samples that have been used for reference in the final output tasks of the individual. Peer mutual evaluation should compare the similarities and differences of peer output tasks before and after class, and record the evaluation experience. Each group organizes their own offline discussions, and makes transcripts and photographs. If conditions permit, they can make video recordings. Each group selects one excellent work, and attaches recommended comments to share with the whole class. After the online and offline evaluation of the students is completed, the teacher will give comments, and at the same time turn on the voting, questionnaire, discussion and feedback functions of the mobile app to provide reference for future output tasks and evaluation activities.

4 The Influence of College English Online and Offline Classroom Teaching Evaluation Model

According to interviews with students and questionnaire surveys, we know that the TSCA-based college English online and offline classroom teaching evaluation model we adopted has a certain impact on students' learning motivation, learning methods and learning behaviors.

4.1 Impact on Learning Motivation

Foreign language learning requires the cooperation of students' internal psychological processes, that is, based on specific goals, the interest in learning is generated from the heart. The college English online and offline classroom teaching evaluation model creates an immersive English learning environment for students, maintaining personal, peer and group communication before, during and after class, allowing students to truly use and acquire language from the external environment Start to strengthen learning motivation. With the exertion of students' subjective initiative, students' pursuit of foreign language learning no longer simply stays at the stage of language learning, but pays more attention to the learning of culture and thinking. In this way, internal pursuits counteract external communication, and external causes act through internal causes. Students will strive to achieve language goals and communication goals.

4.2 Impact on Learning Method

Online and offline blended learning in the information age can greatly improve learning efficiency. The big data evaluation results of the online platform can help students find the lack of vocabulary, grammar, sentence patterns, etc., achieve effective input, accumulate necessary language knowledge, and achieve language learning goals. In terms of learning methods, in addition to traditional recitation, silent reading, speed, notes, etc., driven by the information age, students use online and offline evaluations to actively accumulate knowledge for effective language expression, and explore the world, expand their horizons, and enrich Personal imagination. Teachers can make timely adjustments to teaching resources and students can learn about the learning condition of their peers, which will stimulate students' selfreflection [4]. Through teaching practice, it is found that the promotion of reading by evaluation is better, and students actively think and discuss through reading. However, with the popularization of the Internet and the abundance of resources, the factors that cause distraction of students have also increased. Teachers and students should pay attention to self-monitoring and external monitoring when using online resources to ensure learning efficiency and cultivate a correct learning outlook.

4.3 Impact on Learning Behavior

The college English online and offline classroom teaching evaluation model plans the learning process before, during and after class for students, which is conducive to the development of good study habits. Moreover, in the evaluation process, students also gradually shifted from the initial micro-evaluation of language to the aspects of responsibility, love, courage, respect and belief, so that students can not forget their original intentions, convey their ideas correctly, and shape a sound personality. The evaluation of teacher-student cooperation strengthens the communication and discussion between students and between teachers and students, and realizes the improvement of students' dominant status (Zhang Pengjiu 2020) [5]. In the implementation of specific behaviors, students are also willing to discover humorous, vivid, beautiful, rich or accurate language from classic stories, drama and poems, celebrity speeches, and current affairs news, so as to enrich themselves and complete output tasks.

5   Conclusion

Based on TSCA, the proposed college English online and offline classroom teaching evaluation model has a positive impact on students' learning motivation, learning methods and learning behaviors, and at the same time enhances students' evaluation abilities, and promotes the development of speculative and cooperative abilities. Students will lay a solid foundation for communication in life and work in the future.

References

1. Wen, Q.F.: The production-oriented approach: a pedagogical innovation in university English teaching in China. In: Wong, L., Hyland, K. (eds.) Faces of English: Students, Teachers, and Pedagogy, pp. 91–106. Routledge, London, New York (2017)
2. Sun, S.G.: Dialectical research on "teacher-student cooperation evaluation". J. Mod. Foreign Lang., 419–430 (2019)
3. Sun, S.G.: An example analysis of the principles of teacher-student cooperation evaluation in the "output-oriented method". J. Front. Foreign Lang. Educ. Res., 20–27 (2020)
4. Yongqin, W., Mingming, H., Fei, L.: Teaching effect of college english based on cloud class platform. In: Liu, S., Glowatz, M., Zappatore, M., Gao, H., Jia, B., Bucciero, A. (eds.) eLEOT 2018. LNICSSITE, vol. 243, pp. 27–32. Springer, Cham (2018). https://doi.org/10.1007/978-3-319-93719-9_4
5. Zhang, P.J.: Probe into several problems in the teaching of college English writing. J. Educ. Theory Pract., 54–56 (2020)

Orchestration Between Computational Thinking and Mathematics

Camilla Finsterbach Kaup$^{(\boxtimes)}$ (iD)

Aalborg University, Kroghstræde 3, 9220 Aalborg East, Denmark
cfk@ikl.aau.dk

Abstract. The use of computational thinking (CT) in educational settings has increased in popularity in the last twenty years. The aim of the paper is there-by to unfold both CT and mathematics to develop an analytical model for analyzing mediating processes in teaching mathematics including CT. By applying a socio-cultural perspective, the mediation theory provides new opportunities for understanding the mediation process involved in the introduction of digital artifacts, such as robots in mathematic teaching. The research has a specific focus on the construction of knowledge through signs. The suggested model is intended as a tool to analyze the mediating processes that occur when using CT in mathematics and mathematics education. The proposed model includes two dimensions, where one of them concerns which perspective that is applied (either teacher- or student-centered), and the other dimension concerns the synergy between CT and mathematical concepts. These two dimensions produce different representations and are initiated in various ways.

Keywords: Computational thinking · Mathematics · Primary level · Mediating artifacts

1 Introduction

1.1 Computational Thinking in Mathematics

Over the last few years, researchers and educators have recognized computational thinking (CT) as a strong educational approach [1]. Wing (2006) introduced the prevailing discussion about CT. However, the concept of CT can be tracked back to Papert's work in the 1980s [2]. According to Wing, CT can be seen as "a way to solve problems, design systems, and understand human behavior by using the basic concepts of computer science" [3:33]. According to Wing's [3] definition, CT is a problem-solving method that can be used to explain a problem so both humans and computers can recognize the solution. Due to logical structure and mathematical modeling problems [4], a natural and historical connection links CT and mathematics. According to Pérez [5], CT can help students understand mathematical problems through programming, algorithmic thinking, and creating computational abstractions. According to Li et al. [6], CT is "a model of thinking that is more about thinking than computing" [6:4], and CT should be a part

© ICST Institute for Computer Sciences, Social Informatics and Telecommunications Engineering 2022
Published by Springer Nature Switzerland AG 2022. All Rights Reserved
E. Brooks et al. (Eds.): DLI 2021, LNICST 435, pp. 77–85, 2022.
https://doi.org/10.1007/978-3-031-06675-7_6

of students' abilities in the 21st century. Similarly, Chongo et al. [7] defined CT as "…a process of thinking and a tool for solving problems using computer concepts either with a computer (plugged in) or without one (unplugged)" [7:160]. These two definitions are similar because they relate to a cognitive and systematic process and clarify that CT can be used with or without a computer. Indeed, CT can be a thought process that is independent of technology [1]. Several researchers have concluded that students can learn and acquire knowledge from CT early in their learning careers. However, researchers must first focus on problem-solving and how students can express themselves using mobile learning, coding apps, and digital artifacts [19]. This paper considers the background that relates to how students can develop their mathematical understanding through CT. The paper draws on a socio-cultural perspective to focus on the thinking process and peer collaboration [7]. However, there is still a gap within the proposed theory about CT in mathematics and its practical utilization in practice, especially in low-level mathematics education. This article aims to use computational thinking and mathematics to establish an analysis model and recognize CT's utilization in math teaching. This article also emphases the meaning of signs that occur as part of students' development of mathematics concerning CT. This type of study is relevant for mathematics teachers and researchers because it can help them determine how teachers can incorporate digital artifacts to support CT concerning mathematics teaching.

This paper uses a socio-cultural viewpoint on learning to examine the relationship between CT and mathematics. These perspectives are presented in a model that combines both of them. To illustrate the analytical model, an empirical example is provided at the end of the theoretical framework.

1.2 A Sociocultural Perspective

In this paper, a socio-cultural perspective frames the model development process. Knowledge creation is entrenched in different contexts and is mediated by signs and artifacts that involve students and teachers in social activities. Cultural meanings regulate the relationships between humans and their surrounding environments through signs and artifacts developed by humans over time. Every function in children's cultural development will appear twice; first, at a social level between people and then on the individual level inside the child [8].

Language plays a vital role in this intermediary, which transfers from the outside to the inside through internalization. Internalization describes how humans reconstruct external influences as internal understanding. Mediation connects humans' perceptions of the world [8]. According to the socio-cultural point of view, humans are connected to the social and physical by signs and artifacts. This can be related to the higher mental processes that humans use to mediate understanding and definitions of being in the world [9]. Students often work to accomplish abstract ideas in mathematics education; here, cultural artifacts can make learning visible through signs and symbols [10]. In this context, looking further into semiotic mediation can be useful. How students or teachers mediate information, meaning, thoughts, and ideas through artifacts and symbols is central to semiotic mediation [11]. It is essential to recognize what a sign represents and its interpretation to understand the semiotic mediation process [12].

In the developed model, mediations play a vital part in the use of tools and signs in mathematics and CT. Therefore, it is essential to reflect on the background of each sign. The semiotic perspective is helpful because it examines the relationships between signs that are included in the learning context of introductory CT in mathematics.

1.3 Knowledge Creation

According to Brandsford et al. [13], every student brings a viewpoint to the learning process. Learning can be understood as a process that allows students to construct new knowledge based on already known knowledge. Therefore, teachers must pay attention to the understanding that students already have. Otherwise, students' knowledge and experiences in the classroom may be different from their teacher's intentions. It is difficult for students to learn new concepts without considering their existing knowledge [8, 13].

In the process of knowledge creation, a student's learning must be visible to the teacher so that the teacher can help each student with misunderstandings. Brandsford [13] believes that by participating in discussions, asking questions, and using artifacts, students can thoroughly discover content that motivates learning and gain a deep understanding of mathematical concepts. With this in mind, students who study mathematical concepts by themselves will recognize the process of integrating CT into mathematics, CT-related symbols, and mathematical concepts [14, 15]. During growth, students develop spontaneous concepts, as well as scientific concepts with the support of adults or knowledgeable peers [8].

1.4 Connections Between Computational Thinking and Mathematics

Researchers have found that some inherent characteristics of CT can help students contextualize certain mathematical content by both working with and without digital artifacts [16]. During an investigation of the course guide and CT definition, Barcelos et al. [17] highlighted high-level skills related to CT:

- *Alternating between different semiotic representations*, which involves translating a model that is expressed as one symbolic representation into another symbolic representation. These representations can take many forms, including charts, tables, verbal expressions, algorithmic representations, or drawings.
- *Establishing relationships and identifying patterns* in situations that require students to identify patterns, use decomposition, or establish a formation rule. In mathematics, this skill is often applied to numerical regularities and abstraction used in problem-solving.
- *Building descriptive and representative models* by means of math or algorithmic language that describes and exposes students' considerations of a problem.

Determining the skills that are connected to CT and mathematics provides an opening for analyzing and understanding the relationship between CT and mathematics.

Recently, researchers have found that it is important for students to develop their own opinions and understandings regarding engagement in computation [6, 18]. By dealing with the connection between spontaneity and scientific concepts, students can start to recognize mathematical concepts in depth. CT highlights the meaning of students' thinking about the fundamentals of mathematics [6]. Mediation offers a connection to social and cultural processes and personal higher mental developments. From this point of view, students can internalize the intermediary process provided by teachers who are grounded in cultural, social, and institutional strengths.

2 Orchestration Between CT and Mathematics

Developing the theoretical basis for this paper led to the development of the following model: "Orchestration between CT and mathematics" (Fig. 1). This model consists of two dimensions, one of which is based on the interplay between CT and mathematics. The second dimension is established on the interplay concerning teacher- and student-centered perspectives. The interplay between CT and math emerges through theoretical perspectives, which are essential to how teachers mediate and construct teaching activities to support their students' development of mathematical, scientific concepts. "Orchestration" relates to teachers' function in facilitating various activities that mediate the creation of student symbols and the relationship between signs and scientific concepts [15]. If teachers can use CT to convey mathematics content to promote and coordinate various teaching activities, then it is appropriate to include CT in mathematics teaching [15].

The future of applying CT in math is based on the perspective concerning teacher-centered and student-centered activities that provide various content in traditional math lessons or more problem-based methods. Signs that are associated with CT and mathematical concepts appear in multiple forms. Teachers can understand the relationship that connects CT and math and examine students' learning conditions [15]. The cross-tabulation of these dimensions indicates the four-domain model of CT methods in mathematics teaching. When adopting this model, a teacher should examine the meaning of combining CT and math teaching. The model illustrates areas of relationships between CT and math learning. The model may be utilized as an analytic instrument for understanding the connection among CT and math and can also be used as a tool for using digital artifacts and CT to mediate activities in mathematics. Additionally, teachers can use the model to construct activities that focus on various aspects and symbolic representations of mathematical learning.

Computational Thinking

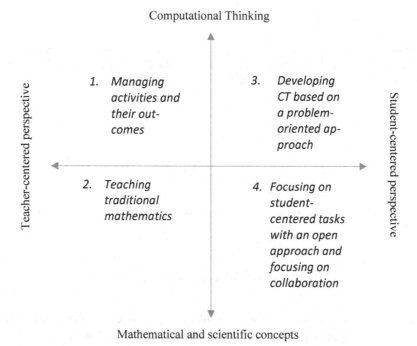

Mathematical and scientific concepts

Fig. 1. Orchestration between computational thinking and mathematics

The model presents 4 squares, every referring to diverse teaching activities that can take place during a teaching sequence. Square 1 illustrates the focus on managing activities and student outcomes; here, the teacher controls the activities. Square 2 portrays the more traditional approach to mathematics, which incorporates a textbook-driven approach. The teacher also manages these activities. Square 3 presents the focus on developing CT based on a problem-oriented approach in which tasks are student-centered [6]. Square 4 presents the focus on student-centered tasks in which tasks incorporate an open approach and focus on student collaboration [13, 18].

2.1 A Case with Beebot

This case utilizes data from a second-grade class. The class used Beebots as a digital artifact. The tasks explained in this case are the first and third tasks of a teaching sequence. The students worked in groups of two with one Beebot for each pair; there were ten teams in the class. This example involves tasks and activities that encouraged the students to classify geometric figures and use appropriate words.

An iterative process of didactic cycles followed the teaching sequences.

The first didactic cycle involved the robots. The students had to become familiar with the robots and understand how they worked.

The second didactic cycle required the students to have their robots make a square, and then they had to investigate how small or large the robots could make the square.

According to CT, the students were asked to create an algorithm for constructing the square.

During *the third didactic cycle*, the students were asked to work with the geometric properties of polygons. The task (Fig. 2) was to make the robots land on, for example, all squares, triangles, etc. and describe the characteristics of the individual polygon.

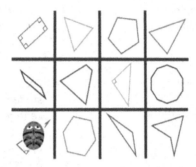

Fig. 2. The task involving geometric properties

The fourth didactic cycle involved a problem-solving approach; the students had to figure out which type of polygon the robots could make. The students were required to investigate the type – from one-sided to ten-sided polygon – that each robot could make and see if they could make any generalizations from it [21].

The next section covers the first and third didactic cycles to unfold the use of the developed model.

2.2   Familiarity with the Robot

Based on the model in Fig. 1, the first part is characterized by Square 1 and 3.

The students worked together in pairs, and each team had one robot. During the first task, the students were required to familiarize themselves with the robots. The teacher provided a short overview of the different buttons on the robots, and after that, the students were asked to figure out what the different buttons were used for, which aligned with Square 1. Subsequently, the teacher followed up on this activity during the class discussion. The following excerpt illustrates what some of the groups were struggling with:

Student 1: We clicked a whole lot, but it did not do what we wanted it to.
Student 2: It was because we forgot to press "delete." Then we clicked two forwards and two to the side, two backward and two to the side.
Teacher: What did you think it was doing? A square?
Student 1: Yes, but it did not. It just started driving around and going backward [the student moves his body to reveal what the robot had done] because we forgot to press "delete."
Teacher: If you had clicked on "delete," would it then have made a square? Did you try it?

Student 3: You must press two forward, one left, two forward, one left, two forward, one left, two forward, and one left.

This is an excellent example of what the students were struggling with during the first task. Many had trouble remembering to clear the robot after ending the activity and had problems creating a new activity. Student 1 also used his gesture to show the movement of the robot, which helped him make the movement more understandable [21]. During the first task, the students worked in Square 3 to investigate how the Beebots worked. During the class discussion, the teacher became aware of the students' misunderstandings. Giving the students time to explore the Beebots and following up in conversation with help from teachers and other students helped the struggling students focus more on the mathematics in the later exercises. The switch between Square 1 and 3 helped the students investigate the robots' features and still be aware of some of their misconceptions.

2.3 Mediating Artifact

In the third teaching cycle, students performed two activities. For the first task, they were asked to deal with the geometric properties of the polygons (see Fig. 2). Students must let the robot land on all squares, triangles, etc., and describe the characteristics of each polygon. When students sort the polygons, it helps them focus on the features of each polygon. This allows them to increase their knowledge of individual polygons. Students must establish a connection with the robot through CT to create an overview of the polygons on the worksheet and create an algorithm to move the robot from one triangle to another [21]. The students use the robots as a mediating artifact to describe the characteristics of the polygons. Some of the students used gestures to convey the directions in which the robots should turn. The task can be related to Square 4 since the students investigated how to characterize the different polygons from a student-centered perspective.

Students must also classify different polygons according to criteria related to right angles, acute angles, etc. This helps to support students' research on various attributes such as "right angle" and "equal length side." The classification of the polygons in Fig. 2 according to the new standard helps support students' reasoning at a higher level of abstraction [20, 21]. This also enables students to distinguish polygons and understand the standard features of polygons that do not seem to have the same characteristics. By classifying polygons, students learned that different polygons could have the same characteristics. When students use the robot as an intermediate workpiece, they work with CT to program the robot. Through CT, students try to make the robot move in a different order; for example, make the robot move to all triangles (Fig. 2). If the robot does not land on the required polygon, the students will constantly debug and correct their code during the task. In this way, students receive CT training when they introduce their work to the classroom and solve reward tasks [21].

The students used various signs to construct the meaning of the activity. The mediation process enhanced the students' understanding of the signs that appeared in various activities, which transformed into the psychological development of thinking and memory [9]. This activity embodies the transition from the teacher- to the student-centered perspective. In this case, the students used CT to develop their understanding of mathematical science concepts in relation to geometry.

3 Concluding Remarks

Using BeeBots, the students worked on new forms of geometric representation, and the learning content was presented in a new way that helped develop the students' mathematical and scientific understanding. The teacher worked to create an interaction between spontaneous and mathematical scientific concepts at the beginning of the lesson. The students understood the task through this interaction, so they were later able to perform it by mediating the task's computational and mathematical intentions. The mediation thus became essential for the teacher to help the students in their acquisition of mathematical and scientific concepts. The teacher was given a central role in the mediation process since it was significant. Therefore, CT that is implemented in composing an intermediary process can help students understand their math and CT better.

The teacher's conversation with the students during the class discussion also became necessary for the mediation process to support the students' development of scientific and mathematical concepts. However, little knowledge is available about how teachers can include CT in mathematics teaching and how CT can support students' mathematical and scientific understanding and problem-solving processes. The developed model can help teachers who implement CT in math. The model can also be expended to analyze the mediating processes that appear when CT interacts with math. The model-based consideration reveals the common sense of applying CT in mathematics teaching; however, more research is needed to study the model further.

References

1. Bocconi, S., Chioccariello, A., Dett ori, G., Ferrari, A., Engelhardt, K.: Developing computational thinking in compulsory education – implications for policy and practice. EUR 28295 EN. Rapport. Publications Office of the European Union, Luxembourg (2016). https://doi.org/10.2791/792158
2. Papert, S.: Mindstorms. Children, Computers and Powerful Ideas. Basic Books, New York (1980)
3. Wing, J.M.: Computational thinking. Commun. ACM **49**(3), 33–35 (2006)
4. Gadanidis, G., Cendros, R., Floyd, L., Namukasa, I.: Computational thinking in mathematics teacher education. Contemp. Issues Technol. Teach. Educ. (CITE J.) **17**(4), 458–477 (2017)
5. Pérez, A.: A framework for computational thinking dispositions in mathematics education. J. Res. Math. Educ. **49**(4), 424–461 (2018). https://doi.org/10.5951/jre-sematheduc.49.4.0424
6. Li, Y., et al.: Computational thinking is more about thinking than computing. J. STEM Educ. Res. 3(1), 1–18 (2020). https://doi.org/10.1007/s41979-020-00030-2
7. Chongo, S., Osman, K., Nayan, N.A.: Level of Computational Thinking Skills among Secondary Science Student: Variation Across Gender (2020)
8. Vygotsky, L.S.: Mind in Society: The Development of Higher Mental Processes. Harvard University Press, Cambridge (1978). https://doi.org/10.2307/j.ctvjf9vz4

9. Wertsch, J.V.: Mediation. In: Daniels, H., Cole, M., Wertsch, J.V. (eds.) The Cambridge Companion to Vygotsky, pp. 178–192. Cambridge University Press, New York. (2007). https://doi.org/10.1017/CCOL0521831040.008

10. Steinbring, H.: What makes a sign a mathematical sign? – An epistemological perspective on mathematical interaction. Educ. Stud. Math. **61**(1–2), 133–162 (2006). https://doi.org/10.1007/s10649-006-5892-z

11. Hasan, R.: Semiotic mediation and mental development in pluralistic societies: some implications for tomorrow's schooling. In: Wells, G., Claxton, G. (eds.) Learning for Life in the 21st Century: Sociocultural Perspectives on the Future of Education (2002)

12. Ma, J.: The synergy of Peirce and Vygotsky as an analytical approach to the multimodality of semiotic mediation. Mind Cult. Act. **21**(4), 274–389 (2014)

13. Brandsford, J.D., Brown, A., Cocking, R.R.: How People Learn, Brain, Mind, Experience, and School. National Academic Press, Washington D.C. (2000)

14. Lockwood, E., DeJarnette, A.F., Asay, A., Thomas, M.: Algorithmic thinking: an initial characterization of computational thinking in mathematics. In: North American Chapter of the International Group for the Psychology of Mathematics Education (2016)

15. Bartolini Bussi, M.G., Mariotti, M.A.: Semiotic mediation in the mathematics classroom: artifacts and signs after a Vygotskian perspective. In: English, L., Bartolini Bussi, M., Jones, G., Lesh, R., Tirosh, D. (eds.) Handbook of International Research in Mathematics Education, 2nd edn., pp. 746–783 (2008). https://doi.org/10.4324/9780203930236

16. Barcelos, T.S., Silveira, I.F.: Teaching computational thinking in initial series: an analysis of the confluence among mathematics and computer sciences in elementary education and its implications for higher education. In: XXXVIII Conferencia Latinoamericana En Informatica (CLEI) (2012). https://doi.org/10.1109/CLEI.2012.6427135

17. Barcelos, T., Muñoz-Soto, R., Villarroel, R., Merino, E., Silveira, I.: Mathematics learning through computational thinking activities: a systematic literature review. J. Univers. Comput. Sci. **24**, 815–845 (2018)

18. Li, Y., Schoenfeld, A.H.: Problematizing teaching and learning mathematics as "given" in STEM education. Int. J. STEM Educ. **6**(1), 1–13 (2019). https://doi.org/10.1186/s40594-019-0197-9

19. Stamatis, P.: The impact of coding apps to support young children in computational thinking and computational fluency. A literature review. Frontiers Educ. **6**, 1–12 (2021). https://doi.org/10.3389/feduc.2021.657895

20. Goldenberg, P., Dougherty, B., Zbiek, R.M., Clements, D.: Developing Essential Understanding of Geometry and Measurement for Teaching Mathematics in Pre-K-Grade 2, National Council of Teachers (2014)

21. Kaup, C.F.: Examining educational staff's expansive learning process, to understand the use of digital manipulative artefacts to support the students' computational thinking and mathematical understanding. In: Donevska-Todorova, A., et al. (eds.) Proceedings of the 10th ERME Topic Conference: Mathematics Education in the Digital Age (MEDA), pp. 53–60. Johannes Kepler University Linz (2021)

Game Design as a Pedagogical Tool for Learning and Reflection: The Case of the Ethics Experience

Lena Hylving[1]([⊠]) [iD], Andrea Resmini[1] [iD], Bertil Lindenfalk[2] [iD], and Oliver Weberg[1]

[1] Halmstad University, 301 18 Halmstad, Sweden
lena.hylving@hh.se
[2] Jönköping University, 553 18, Jönköping, Germany

Abstract. This paper sets out to present an ongoing pedagogical project where game design is used to let students both learn and reflect upon different perspectives of ethics relevant to the master program they are enrolled in. The paper explains the underlying logic behind the pedagogical process where students develop their own game and at the same time learn about different perspectives of ethics in relation to courses that they are currently taking. With an open and iterative method, we let the students explore, discuss and design a game that can be used by future students. By letting the students decide and lead the development we democratize the learning-process and engage them in a learning experience. More so, this approach to game design as a pedagogical tool to engage and democratize the learning experience is new and increasingly relevant for both students that play games on an everyday basis, but also students that are new to games. Also, it is a constant and dynamic process for both students and teachers.

Keywords: Experiential learning · Game design · Gamification · Pedagogical tool · Experience design

1 Introduction

In 2013, the highly anticipated sandbox video game "Grand Theft Auto V" by American publisher Rockstar Games/Take-Two Interactive sold copies for 800 million USD on its first day [1]. Stores opened up at midnight to long lines of prospective buyers, the likes of which we have come to associate with Apple. "Grand Theft Auto V" is far from being an isolated exception: in a remarkably short period of time, the video game industry, a behemoth worth 147 billion USD in 2019, has become the most lucrative entertainment industry, eclipsing the film industry, grossing 42 billions USD, and the music industry, worth 20 billions USD [2].

If, in 2007, a survey conducted by the NPD Group revealed that 72% of the US population aged 6–44 had played video games in the course of the year [3], statistics for 2021 place the number of video game players at 2.8 billion worldwide, forecasting that the 3 billion threshold will be crossed in 2023 [4]. The games market is maturing and

E. Brooks et al. (Eds.): DLI 2021, LNICST 435, pp. 86–96, 2022.
https://doi.org/10.1007/978-3-031-06675-7_7

diversifying under these generational and gender changes that see more older players and more women players make up a substantial part of its customer base, with video games acquiring a position of cultural influence and of increasing "artistic sophistication" [5, p. 7]. Convergence phenomena (Jenkins 2008) are also extending this influence through the dissemination of game content, game logic, and game culture in a variety of media, for example through live streaming of gameplay or esport competitions on Twitch or YouTube reviews, walkthroughs, and reactions. Additionally, the 2020–2021 COVID-19 pandemic has pushed many towards mediated forms of remote interaction, including online games. Established success stories such as Epic Games online multiplayer game "Fortnite" have seen their numbers surge [6], and forgotten games such as "Among Us" have become overnight successes [7, 8].

What is true of video games is true of games in general: while smaller, the global board games market has been growing steadily in the past twenty years and has been projected to keep growing at a 13% rate in the next five years, for a total of 30 billion USD worth in 2026 [9]. Games and gaming, that is the activity of playing games, also have a consolidated history of proven efficiency as educational tools [10], and they have been variously used in educational contexts [11] to *"enliven teaching topics"*, to *"appeal to different learning styles"*, to *"encourage collaborative problem solving"* and *"peer support"*, and have proven *"especially effective for dealing with problem solving and key concepts"* [12, p. 3]. Recent developments have education innovators such as Prensky [13] discuss game-based reforms that do not just see schools using games to teach students, but thoroughly recast the ideal school as *"a game, from start to finish: every course, every activity, every assignment, every moment of instruction and assessment would be designed by borrowing key mechanics and participation strategies from the most engaging multi player games"* [14, p. 128].

During the coming two years, a cohort of students from the Master's in Digital Service Innovation (DSI) at Halmstad University will engage in a design exercise that will see them working in groups and moving through a number of clearly specified stages to conceptualize, design and prototype a game that centers on specific ethical or sustainability problems, such as intersectionality, the common good, norm-critical design, judicious development, the tragedy of the commons, and human flourishing. The plan is to This design exercise is meant to help develop a pedagogical path for design education structured around the design of a game that deals with a yearly chosen core theme, ethics and ethics in design in this case, to be thoroughly explored throughout the two year study period.

A common way to use games in education is to play them and reflect after play so that extrinsic perspectives may be brought into the game's own context. For example, investigating the problematic relationship between ludic gameplay and narrative fiction in the video game "Grand Theft Auto" as a way to discuss in-game actions and behavior from a civic ethics standpoint [15]. In research, games have been developed to both allow students to *"practice real life clinical settings"*, for example in the context of healthcare [16], or to develop critical thinking skills by *"try(ing) out various choice paths and while doing it gain knowledge about how to make more appropriate choices"* [17, p. 69].

While it is not uncommon for educational institutions to apply game logic or game approaches to individual courses, as it is the case for example for the undergraduate course on Interactive Prototyping at Halmstad University, it is fairly less common to introduce such an approach across the length of an entire program, and further intertwine its primary design task throughout all of its courses in order to infuse the program with a specific core topic, in this case ethics, and a specific pedagogical approach, that of game design. This unusual and organizationally demanding situation has its own challenges, besides those that traditionally accompany the development of such initiatives: organizational ones, such as how to engage students in a learning process that runs as a parallel addition to mandatory program courses; and pedagogical ones, such as how to make sure such a process is consistent, coherent, relevant, and meaningful for the students, and how its outcomes should be evaluated, reused, and improved upon.

1.1 Organizational and Pedagogical Challenge

"Nothing ever becomes real 'til it is experienced" John Keates (1795–1821).

The authors used an experiential learning approach to closely follow that provided by games and formalized in game design. Experiential learning is based on a learning cycle that includes experiencing, reflecting, thinking and acting (Miettinen 2000). Students developing their own learning materials have a more concrete and direct experience of the subject of interest. At the same time, students gain new practical and theoretical insights as they act their way throughout the preparations, development and implementation [18]. In this sense, experiential learning is learning as a *"holistic process of adaptation of the world"* [19, p. 5] and has been used in several areas such as tema development [20], entrepreneurship [21], and engineering education [22].

Using problems as a foundation for learning assists in developing life-long knowledge and skills. Being tasked with solving a concrete, situated problem, one learns not only how to factually apply knowledge in a given context, but is also forced to reflect on what knowledge is missing. The problem itself is then an incentive to learn [23], meaning that instead of having to understand theories, concepts, and methods because a course plan says so, students learn in order to solve a problem they face and that they find relevant and interesting. Games, and especially video games, play an important gateway role here, as they are an extremely influential cultural artifact for current convergence culture [24] and especially for the Millennial and Gen Z generations, comparable to film and TV for previous generations [25]. Methods and styles from old media are retained and reinterpreted, for example narrative from film, and new *"forms of engagement, or media consumption, that are distinct to games and media properties, such as interactivity"* become more central [26, p. 4].

In collaborative settings, the process of solving a problem is not only a way to gain new knowledge but also training for important soft skills such as the capacity to listen, critical thinking, empathy, and rhetoric [27]. Collaborative problem-based learning helps in the process of constructive linking [28] as students *"enter"* a problem with certain knowledge assets, which throughout the process they develop and refine as they interact with teachers, peers, and the learning environment.

1.2 Game-Based Approach

Games can be described as *"a closed formal system that subjectively represents a subset of reality"* [29, p. 7] in a way that it can be experienced safely by players, since *"the results of a game are always less harsh than the situations the game models"* [29, p. 14]. More generally, *"(r)educed to its formal essence, a game is an activity among two or more independent decision-makers seeking to achieve their objectives in some limiting context"* [30, p. 6] Fullerton, echoing Crawford [29], describes a game as *"a closed formal system that engages players in structured conflict and resolves its uncertainties in unequal outcomes"*.

A number of important characteristics of games that matter in the context of design education are introduced by these definitions: the idea that games can be used to model real or fictional events or activities, what Crawford calls *"representation"*, the fact that players experience these by actively engaging in conflicts that are nonetheless safe, since the *"game is an artifice"* [29, p. 14] that excludes the physical realization of any situation of play, and their being structured, subject to rules, what Abt calls the *"limiting context"*. Rules constitute a framework that players use to understand and enact play situations and for structuring relationships within the game.

Games are also extremely valuable learning tools [14, 30] as they are adaptable, flexible, and *"can be moulded to suit a variety of learning settings and environments"* to support peer learning, collaborative knowledge creation, and divergent thinking amongst students [12]. Additionally, they have been found to facilitate distance learning students [12], which was also an important factor when conversations started in the spring of 2021.

In terms of design education, they offer a safe, controllable, and observable space for simulating experiences. Playing a game means to directly experience the interplay of information flows, human agency and desires, within the settings of hard environmental constraints that maintain focus on a specific "goal" and avoid "spillovers" [29–31]. Remixing existing games, that is altering their design and behavior to obtain a somewhat different game, is a significant hands-on way to learn how to creatively repurpose parts of a service or product to provide a different or improved experience, a common activity in the design professions. Analyzing a game and then modifying it in ways that allow it to fit *"an enhanced purpose, a new audience, a new level of complexity, or a new learning outcome"* [32], as much as designing a game anew to explore a specific problem, teaches students to manage complexity while considering coherent, clearly defined boundaries in relation to a manageable problem space. In this sense, game design theory offers a consolidated body of knowledge dealing with both formal (rules, players, resources, mechanics) and dramatic (premises, themes, characters, story, settings) elements that can be used for (re-)designing any type of experiences [31, 33].

Fullerton [33] highlights that games share characteristics with complex systems: for example, the fact that their outcomes cannot be predicted from their initial setup. In game terms, these *"unequal outcomes"* mean that while it is known that there will be one or more winners and one or more losers by the end of the game, it is impossible to determine at the beginning who will be what and through which precise steps that outcome will be achieved. This has two important consequences. As *"closed formal systems"*, games offer the possibility to model a complex system and to provide rules of engagement for players to experience it first-person, for any number of times during which they can decide to follow varying strategies. For example, place players in the role of commanders whose army needs to defeat their opponent's, in a game of chess.

As systems of formalized relationships between *"formal elements"* such as rules or resources, games can be *"dressed up"* through the use of what Fullerton calls, in opposition, *"dramatic elements"* [33]. Fullerton stipulates that games can be better understood by structurally addressing their formal and dramatic elements as separated but interdependent systems. The formal elements set includes players, rules, resources, or objectives. Dramatic elements include premise, story, characters, and settings. For example, *"Monopoly"* is a game of multilateral competition between two to eight players whose objective is to bankrupt opponents to win. Player relationships, in-game currency, and title deeds are resources. Story-wise, in the original game players take the role of early 20th century US landowners who attempt to buy land and build a real estate empire in a rapidly growing metropolis.

The interplay of formal and dramatic elements is what allows players to experience the strife for the emancipation from slavery in 19th century North America (in Freedom: The Underground Railway), group survival on a deserted island after an airplane crash (in Ravine), or the fragility of democratic processes (in Secret Hitler) through, in accordance with Crawford, representation (games as self-sufficient subsets of reality); interaction (games as exploratory systems); conflict (games as the pursuit of competing goals); and safety (games as artifices that simulate but do not concretize danger).

Building on Fullerton [33], Crawford [29], and Schell [34], two of the authors of this paper have consolidated an extended framework for approaching the analysis and design of games that has also been applied to the analysis and design of services and experiences. Retaining the distinction between formal and dramatic elements formalized by Fullerton, the extended framework introduces a third set, that of spatial elements, to account for *"the most fundamental human experience of apprehending oneself as a body located in space"* [35, 36] and to acknowledge the reinforcing role played by material anchors [37] in stabilizing conceptual blends [38] such as those happening in design activities. These spatial elements bridge between game-centered heuristics, and spatial and architectural primitives such as proximity, separation, sequence, and nesting [39].

The idea of a space as an important element of games harkens back to the seminal work of Huizinga [40], who characterized ludic activities as *"standing quite consciously outside 'ordinary' life"* and having their *"own proper boundaries of time and space according to fixed rules and in an orderly manner"* (p. 13). The commingling of digital and physical in our daily lives is also increasingly *"tak(ing) players away from the 'gaze' cultures of film and the 'glance regime' of TV and into the space of the haptic (touch) dimension of gameplay"* [26, p. 5] and digital games have been designed that directly interact with a person's embodied self in physical space [41].

Fullerton's framework does not conceptually identify spatial components as different: they are generically grouped under the label of *"boundaries"* and considered part of the formal elements set [33, p. 78]. Schell, while stating that *"every game takes place in some kind of space"* and investigating a number of structural spatial patterns [34, p. 130–134], considers space a game mechanic, and thus just an individual element part of his foundational structure of games built on an *"elemental tetrad"* comprising mechanics, story, aesthetics, and technology [34, p. 41].

The introduction of a set of spatial elements provides a more granular way to analyze and discuss games, and gives the design process a way to influence how embodiment comes into play in the context of the game. For example, how the experience of a game of chess changes greatly if we play with a regular board, on a mobile phone, or as part of a live chess extravaganza. Size, positioning, textures, haptic feedback, one's proprioception in respect to the game, aural and visual cues or commands are all significantly different and produce different effects, even if the architecture of chess, its rules, is the same.

1.3 The "Gamify Ethics" Design Experience

The DSI program is a two-year master's program: the initial three semesters consist of eight courses focusing on different aspects of Digital Service Innovation, such as Intelligent services and Design Research Methods, Academic communication and Emergent Themes in Digital Service Innovation Research; the final fourth semester has the students working on their master's theses. While the course plans all include ethical considerations to some degree, the program manager decided that ethics and the role it plays in digital service innovation should be emphasized even more by implementing a *"core theme"* running throughout the entirety of the program.

The implementation of this core theme consists in a number of activities that can be structurally divided in four stages. The first stage includes an introduction to different games and gameplay. Board games and card games as well as digital games are played, analyzed, and discussed, in order for the students to be acquainted with the idea of playful reflectivity that will carry through all of the four stages. This introductive part is also meant to inspire, illustrate the possibilities of addressing problems by means of a game, and have fun. The second stage focuses on the extended game design framework discussed above: students are introduced to the *Formal, Dramatic,* and *Spatial* elements in detail and apply these to analyze and then remix existing games. In the third stage, the students plan, design, and prototype a game focusing on an ethical issue they have encountered in the program courses. The goal is to learn as much as possible about such issues through game-design-centered experiential learning, and to create a tool, the game prototype, that allows others to safely and playfully experience that same problematic situation. Teaching staff provides continuous support in the form of lectures, supervision, collaborative work, and game workshops. In the fourth and final stage, the various game prototypes are brought in to be played by the upcoming student cohort to provide a tangible demonstration of what their two-year involvement in the core theme initiative intends to achieve. It will be a good introduction to different ethical issues connected to the program (Fig. 1).

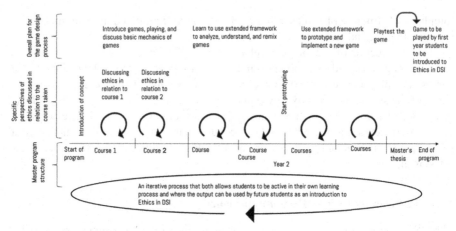

Fig. 1. A diagrammatic view of the core theme process across the two years of the master's program

Students and teaching staff meet regularly every other week to keep the process going. Since the meet-ups are not compulsory, practical activities and theoretical moments have to be finely balanced so that students remain interested and engaged. Game playing and post-game reflections play an important role in this respect, as does allowing the students to bring in their favorite, or least favorite, games for analysis and debate.

It is important to note that while the extended framework used can be applied to the analysis and design of video games as well as board and card games, the current core theme implementation strongly encourages students to primarily consider the design of board and card games. This is a consequence of both pedagogical and design process-related reasons. The pedagogical reasons include the need to embody and directly manipulate abstract concepts through material anchors that facilitate the learning process [37]. For example, manipulate the idea of "contingency", a game mechanic that requires players to complete their goals before a future event occurring in-game after an unpredictable amount of time [42], through movable or eliminable tokens; and a lowering of the barriers to entry for students, since no specific programming skills are necessary. The design-related reasons include the need to focus on the structural and experiential aspects of the process and how they allow one to untangle ethical questions, rather than on the coding, hand-eye coordination issues, game engine expertise, or visual design expertise that would be necessary to implement a digital game. Card and board games can be easily prototyped with pens and paper and no graphics.

A number of intrinsic and extrinsic organizational constraints have also influenced the process, including the current impossibility to assign credits to core theme activities, the diverse background expertise of students in terms of their undergraduate studies, and the restrictions imposed by the ongoing pandemic.

2   Methodology and Empirical Process

This research uses an action design approach [43] where the problem is grounded in the challenge of engaging students in learning opportunities that have no curriculum credits assigned to them. Students will follow an applied design methodology in their own design process. The setting is a master's program where a core theme is being implemented. The core theme runs throughout the two-year program and connects with each and every course included in the program. The core theme of the program is ethics and ethics in design.

This process started with a brainstorming session during which author #1 of this paper was tasked with implementing a *"core theme"* for the DSI program at Halmstad University. The intention of the core theme was to infuse ethics in all the different courses throughout the program to continuously enable opportunities for students to learn about, and engage with, ethics. A list of all the different courses was created and ethical questions that could be linked to each course were added. For example, the course on Academic Communication was connected to issues of plagiarism, and the course on Intelligent Systems to the handling, storing, and use of personal data.

As the core theme project would have no curricular credits connected to its completion, innovative ways of getting the students to get engaged were to be considered. Author #1 then contacted the other authors of this paper at different stages to collaborate on the development of the concept.

A second list was created containing a number of board and card games that could be used to illustrate the relationships between game choices and goals and the ethical questions from the previous list. This proved to be an ill-fitting process, with a very uneven distribution of games across the different questions and at times a rather thin relationship between the games themselves and the actual questions. The authors entertained the idea of creating an entirely new narrative game that could include the different relevant perspectives of ethics and ethics in design that the students should come in contact with. A narrative skeleton was created by means of a commercial card-based *story engine* built around "agents", "anchors", "conflicts" and "aspects" so that a basic storyline could be outlined to work with. A number of alternatives were generated. For example, *"A bossy designer wants to solve the problem of a device. But they will have to act against the community they belong to and protect a hated rival"* or *"An organisation is harming their local community with bad working conditions but protects the rest of the world"*. A prototype was also quickly produced using Twine (twinery.org), an open source tool for creating online interactive, non-linear narratives. The idea was discarded in the end since it either took away the students' design agency entirely, if they were simply given a complete narrative to explore, or introduced a rather steep programming learning curve, if they were to be directly involved in the design of the game.

A decision was taken to have the students design, prototype, and playtest their own game as part of their learning process. Such a set up would satisfy a number of pedagogical goals the team wanted to achieve: in accordance with experience learning principles, having to set their own goals would improve the learning outcomes for students [44]; it would engage students in a way that simply playing through a game presenting them with ethical choices would not; the game design process itself would place them in a position where discussions on ethics as they relate to the content of the game would become a constant occurrence. Additionally, the finished games at the end of the two-year cycle could be used to introduce future students to the core theme and to the design process, and could be listed in the students' portfolios when applying for jobs.

Consequently, the core theme project will see students design and prototype a game artefact addressing ethical challenges in the context of design and digital service innovation. During the design process, teaching staff will meet students regularly to offer help with the framing of ethical questions and for game design supervision. The various scheduled meet-ups, one every other week, will include game workshops, playing sessions, storyline development, workshops focusing on game design theory, and critique sessions. Meeting every second week will allow for continuous contact between students and teaching staff and a regular progression in their investigation of the core theme through the game design process. It will also allow students to discuss questions and concerns that might arise with specific points of the process as they emerge. Given the current pandemic situation, some of these meet-ups will take place on campus while others will be remote.

3 Conclusions and Further Work

This paper presents an ongoing project using games and game design as a way to guide the students through a two-year experiential learning process. This process runs in parallel to their master's studies and focuses on infusing a core theme, ethics in this case, all throughout the curriculum. Students are immersed in a social and cultural environment in which games occupy a relevant role, and research shows that games are a successful learning tool for tangling with complex problems as they provide immersion and agency while preserving safety [29]. This makes them an interesting conceptual tool to introduce the students to the analysis and simulation of design solutions that respond to ethical problems, an important concern for all processes concerned with the digital transformation process [45].

During the course we have adopted a modified and extended version of Fullerton's [33] framework where dramatic, formal and spatial elements are connected to ethical explorations. These three sets allow game designers, and in this case students, to precisely identify which elements of a game are embodying ethical aspects connected to the specific problem space. For example, how dramatic elements such as "premise" or "character" can make an entire game offensive to play through simple linguistic substitutions, say by changing "werewolves" to "immigrants" in a game of *"Werewolf"*. Reflective moments to discuss and add perspectives on ethical decisions that arise as they conceptualize, design, prototype, and playtest their games are part of the design process.

Although the project is ongoing, the team has gained a number of preliminary insights. First, much planning is required to simply be able to start the pedagogical process. For the students to benefit from the parallel core theme process, both content (literature, examples) related to the core theme itself, ethics in this case, as well as the necessary theoretical and practical notions related to designing games, have to be in place. Yet, as the process adapts constantly to the opportunities and constraints offered by what the students are doing and the way they are advancing, planning happens primarily ad hoc via what are agile-like maneuvers of constant adjustments to keep the pedagogical method of experiential learning via game design and the core theme in focus. A secondary element is the necessity to keep students involved and engaged. Finally, as DSI expresses a students' cohort of different social, cultural, religious, and political backgrounds, an additional dimension was added to the way the entire process is handled to treat ethics as culturally bounded. Possibilities for open and interesting discussions in safe and comfortable settings were enabled through this process, something the teaching staff also profits from.

Although this specific project focused on how to infuse ethics and ethics in design throughout a master's program, the authors believe that the pedagogical method, once stabilized, could be generalizable and used in different organizational settings, not necessarily connected to formal education, and for different core themes.

Reflections on the different parts of the core theme process, for example whether and how the setup described in this paper solved, and to what degree, the initial problem of engaging students and infusing ethical themes throughout the length of a master's program, are expected as the project progresses. Evaluation of the whole experience from a student's perspective is also planned at the end of the initial run, together with an assessment of the learning outcomes of the process.

References

1. Goldfarb, A.: 'GTA 5' Sells $800 Million in One Day (2013)
2. Richter, F.: Gaming: the most lucrative entertainment industry by far. https://www.statista.com/chart/22392/global-revenue-of-selected-entertainment-industry-sectors/
3. Faylor, C.: NPD: 72% of U.S. population played games in 2007; PC named 'driving force in online gaming'. https://www.shacknews.com/article/52025/npd-72-of-us-population
4. Clement, J.: Number of active video gamers worldwide from 2015 to 2023. https://www.statista.com/statistics/748044/number-video-gamers-world/
5. Tavino, G.: The Art of Videogames. Wiley-Blackwell, Chichester (2009)
6. Clement, J.: Daily active users of the Fortnite app after the coronavirus outbreak in Sweden (2020). https://www.statista.com/statistics/1116089/daily-active-users-of-the-fortnite-app-after-the-coronavirus-outbreak-in-sweden/
7. Stuart, K.: Among Us: the ultimate party game of the paranoid Covid era. https://www.theguardian.com/games/2020/sep/29/among-us-the-ultimate-party-game-of-the-covid-era
8. Rodriguez, S.: How Among Us, a social deduction game, became this fall's mega hit (2020)
9. Arizton: Board Games Market: Global Outlook and Forecast 2021–2026. https://www.arizton.com/market-reports/global-board-games-market-industry-analysis-2024
10. Oblinger, D.G.: Games and learning. Educ. Q. **29**, 5–7 (2006)
11. Squire, K., Jenkins, H.: Harnessing the power of games in education. InSight **3**, 5–33 (2003)
12. Boyle, S.: Teaching toolkit (2011)
13. Prensky, M.: Teaching digital natives: partnering for real learning (2010)
14. McGonigal, J.: Reality is Broken: Why Games Make Us Better and How They Can Change the World. The Penguin Press, New York (2011)
15. Kampmann Walther, B.: Using ludo-narrative dissonance in grand theft auto IV as pedagogical tool for ethical analysis. In: Liapis, A., Yannakakis, G.N., Gentile, M., Ninaus, M. (eds.) GALA 2019. LNCS, vol. 11899, pp. 3–12. Springer, Cham (2019). https://doi.org/10.1007/978-3-030-34350-7_1
16. Kim, T.W., Werbach, K.: More than just a game: ethical issues in gamification (2016)

17. Sader, J., Audetat, M., Nendaz, M., Hurst, S., Clavien, C.: Design bioethics, not only as a research tool but also a pedagogical tool. Am. J. Bioeth. **21**, 69–71 (2021)
18. Kolb, A.Y., Kolb, D.A.: The Kolb Learning Style Inventory. Hay Resources Direct, Boston (2007)
19. Kolb, A.Y., Kolb, D.A.: Learning styles and learning spaces: enhancing experiential learning in higher education (1999)
20. Kayes, A.B., Kayes, D.C., Kolb, D.A.: Experiential learning in teams. Simul. Gaming. **36**, 330–354 (2005). https://doi.org/10.1177/1046878105279012
21. Mason, C., Arshed, N.: Teaching entrepreneurship to university students through experiential learning: a case study. Ind. High. Educ. **27**, 449–463 (2013)
22. Gadola, M., Chindamo, D.: Experiential learning in engineering education: the role of student design competitions and a case study. Int. J. Mech. Eng. Educ. **47**, 3–22 (2019)
23. Wood, D.F.: Problem based learning **326** (2003)
24. enkins, H.: Convergence Culture. New York University Press, New York (2008)
25. Rose, F.: The Art of Immersion. Norton, London (2012)
26. Hjorth, L.: Games and Gaming. Berg, New York (2011)
27. Hmelo-Silver, C.: Problem-based learning: what and how do students learn? Educ. Psychol. Rev. **16**, 235–266 (2004)
28. Elmgren, M., Henriksson, A.-S.: Universitetspedagogik. Norstedts (2010)
29. Crawford, C.: The Art of Computer Game Design: Reflections of a Master Game Designer. McGraw Hill, New York (1984)
30. Abt, C.: Serious Games. The Viking Press, New York (1970)
31. Atkins, B.: More than a Game: The Computer Game as Fictional Form. Manchester University Press, Manchester (2003)
32. Baker, B.: Gaming as a Teaching Tool. https://penntoday.upenn.edu/news/gaming-teaching-tool
33. Fullerton, T.: Game Design Workshop. Morgan Kaufmann, Burlington (2008)
34. Schell, J.: The Art of Game Design. Morgan Kaufmann, Burlington (2008)
35. Ryan, M.-L., Foote, K., Azaryhau, M.: Narrating Architecture/Spatializing Narrative. Ohio State Press, Columbus (2016)
36. Tversky, B.: Mind in Motion: How Action Shapes Thought. Basic Books, New York (2019)
37. Hutchins, E.: Material anchors for conceptual blends. J. Pragmat. **37**, 1555–1577 (2005)
38. Fauconnier, G., Turner, M.: The Way We Think. Basic Books, New York (2002)
39. Norberg-Schulz, C.: Existence, Space, and Architecture. Littlehampton Book Services (1971)
40. Huizinga, J.: Homo Ludens: A Study of the Play-Element in Culture. Routledge, Abingdon (1949)
41. Resmini, A., Lindenfalk, B.: Mapping experience ecosystems as emergent actor-created spaces. In: Hameurlain, A., Tjoa, A.M., Chbeir, R. (eds.) Transactions on Large-Scale Data- and Knowledge-Centered Systems XLVII. LNCS, vol. 12630, pp. 1–28. Springer, Heidelberg (2021). https://doi.org/10.1007/978-3-662-62919-2_1
42. Hopson, J.: Behavioral Game Design. Game Developer. https://www.gamedeveloper.com/design/behavioral-game-design
43. Sein, M.K., Henfridsson, O., Purao, S., Rossi, M., Lindgren, R.: Action design research. MIS Q. Manag. Inf. Syst. **35**, 37–56 (2011). https://doi.org/10.2307/23043488
44. Miettinen, R.: The concept of experiential learning and John Dewey's theory of reflective thought and action. Con. Int. J. Lifelong Educ. **19**, 54–72 (2000). https://doi.org/10.1080/026013700293458
45. Govers, M., van Amelsvoort, P.: A socio-technical perspective on the digital era: the lowlands view. Eur. J. Work. Innov. **4**, 142–159 (2019)

Designing User Experience with the Sonic Metaphors

Predrag K. Nikolić(✉) 🔘

Faculty of Liberal and Fine Arts, University of The Bahamas, University Drive, Nassau 4192, New Providence, Bahamas
predrag.nikolic@ub.edu.bs

Abstract. In this paper, we present project three experimental installations under the conceptual topic of Sonic Metaphors. We use sound as the main tools to establish interaction between users' interface, physical and virtual space. We are trying to elicit memories and meanings, which plays a crucial role in designing desirable user engagement. We aim to use sonic metaphors as a tool for interactions and experience design. Furthermore, it offers new creative vocabulary based on sound meanings and utilizes acoustic information patterns as a novel way of enabling access to the digital environment.

Keywords: Sonic interaction design · User experience · User interface design · Multisensory interaction · Metaphors · Spatial interaction

1 Introduction

Sonic Interaction Design (SID) is a multisensory design approach where sound has a primary role in developing users' interactions with electronic devices or digital systems and giving meaning to user engagement [1]. SID research falls within a diverse range of emerging disciplines and research approaches toward a better understanding of sonic experience's various aspects [2]. All those approaches aim to explore everyday human perceptual experience to design more fluid and intuitive encounters with digital technologies [3]. One of the central sonic interaction design questions are; How actions can be guided with sound? How is perception affecting the process of embodiment? Who or what performs the interaction when using sound as a tool for interaction? Sound has spatial and environmental characteristics due to acoustic principles such as resonance, reverberation, diffraction, and refraction. It also has a temporal nature and depends on how we modulate it throughout time, distinguishing it from other sensory modalities. Related to interaction design is also the materiality of a sound and how interaction changes, shapes, or transforms sonic material and how interaction with sound helps form further embodied action [2].

Sonic interactions experience is designed upon the relationship between objects, environments, actions, and sounds, and as such, should be considered an essential element in interactive media art creative vocabulary. Previous works in this field show that

© ICST Institute for Computer Sciences, Social Informatics and Telecommunications Engineering 2022
Published by Springer Nature Switzerland AG 2022. All Rights Reserved
E. Brooks et al. (Eds.): DLI 2021, LNICST 435, pp. 97–112, 2022.
https://doi.org/10.1007/978-3-031-06675-7_8

sonic feedback coupled to action can change human performance and social and aesthetic experience. However, the conceptualization of new experimental interactive installations based on continuous sound and tactile feedback could have benefited from metaphors inspired by real-world manipulations. It can also deepen our knowledge about the utilization of acoustic patterns in tactile information, put them in proper interactive context and perform a wide range of perceptual and motor tasks. This could lead us toward the conception of novel ways of enabling digital information access via movement and sound [4]. In this paper, we will present three experimental interactive installations, "Before and Beyond", "Vroom", and "Sensynesthetic Sculptures", conceptualized to engage users and design their experience through the usage of sound metaphors as sensory stimuli.

We are using Activity Theory, Pragmatist Aesthetics [5] and Merleau-Ponty's integrated view of action and perception for the theoretical framework for our experiments with sonic interaction design. Activity Theory has been used as a theoretical foundation in design evaluation and human-device problem analysis. It serves as a helpful framework for understanding presented works in the broader sound interaction design context. In Activity Theory, the unit of analysis is motivated activity directed toward a goal [6]. In the Sonic Metaphors' interactive installations, this activity relates to given sound control, which helps users enrich their experience through given metaphors. The activity is mediated by the contextual pattern built into the artwork's concept. With an application of Merleau-Ponty's philosophy [7] to human-computer interaction, we got a new understanding of interaction as perception. By seeing interaction as a perceptual process involving both "Body" and "Mind", we overcome the Tool/Media dichotomy. When perception is understood as an active process involving our body's totality, it no longer makes sense to see it as a passive reception of information through a medium.

Similarly, when action is an expression of our being-in-the-world, it no longer has meaning to see as a purely "bodily" activity. For Pragmatist Aesthetics, the aesthetic experience is of the highest importance. It is central to understand an object socio-cultural context as an object's meaning and value change with the constantly altering context of experience, between cultures, between persons and even within persons [8]. Petersen et al. agree that aesthetics has an instrumental dimension 'related to actual human needs, values and fears'. In their view, aesthetic interaction promotes curiosity, engagement, and imagination in exploring an interactive system [9].

Key novelties in the Sonic Metaphors Projects are using sonic metaphors as the new tool for interactions, the development of new creative vocabulary based on sound meanings, and utilizing acoustic information patterns as a novel way of enabling access to the digital environment.

This paper will first describe three interactive installations that belong to the Sonic Metaphors research project. Furthermore, we will explain the conceptual and cognitive approach used in the design process. As part of performed user research, we did several informal interview sessions and personal observations during the public artwork exhibitions and controlled lab environment. The results will be presented within the installations descriptions chapter. To conclude, we will validate the interactive concept applied in the design of three experimental installations, "Before and Beyond", "Vroom", and "Sensynesthetic Sculptures", and experiential dimensions possible to achieve in human-machine sound interaction and stimulation.

2 Background

Arjen Mulder – biologist and media theorist, defines the concept of interaction as follow: "interaction is a mode of bringing something into being – whether a form, structure, a body, an institute or a work of art and on the other hand, dealing with it" [10]. An interaction can have different aspects such as visual, sonic, smell, taste and tactile. Moreover, each or a combination of them can be either input or output of an interaction system.

SonicTexting is a system that takes tactile as input and presents it in the form of audio to provide control over the texting process to reduce visual load. Texting in the dark, texting capability for visually impaired people or texting while driving is examples of this project [11]. The Sound of Touch is a system for filling the gap between electronic and acoustic audio by adding acoustic spontaneity to electronic music instruments via sensing the pressure on the instrument's body, bending, and changes in tilt or temperature. This project aims to explore the sound produced by a verity of textures [12]. PebbleBox, CrumbleBag, and Scrubber is another project in musical instruments that tried to extend available perceptual outcomes by maintaining the existing relationship between tactile actions and audio response [13]. Exploring the interaction with a couch based on tactile connection and audio feedback is the aim of ZIZI. In this work, researchers made a couch that is responsive to the actions of users. The couch can express different feelings via sounds related to each action, such as yipping as a sign of excitement, whining when it is boring or growling when the user touches it softly. Authors claim that making couch satisfied can provide user's satisfaction [14]. A combination of new interfaces for musical expression and approaches from human-centred design is presented in the A20 to explore personal music experiences to identify new themes from the listener's daily life interaction with music and propose an advanced interaction approach with these themes [15].

In conceptualizing and designing our experimental interactive installations, we followed some of the ideas related to the usage of sound and sonic interactions presented in the mentioned works. The common ground for all this example is sound as an emotional and cognitive trigger rather than just meaningless audio warning for the system mail function or urgent action required from the user. Multisensory interaction where audio experience has a crucial role in arousing users' meanings and motivation to engage has ultimate value in our user experience designing approach.

3 Interactive Installation Before and Beyond

Interactive Installation Before (our existence) & Beyond (our perception) (https://goo.gl/FhJF5G) is a multisensory interactive metaphorical voyage inspired by String Theory and body distance-related socio-emotional relationships development. As stated in Quanta Magazine, "Among the attempts to unify quantum theory and gravity, string theory has attracted the most attention. Its premise is simple: Everything is made of tiny strings." [16]. According to the California Department of Education, socio-emotional relationships development starts in early infancy as explained: "social interactions with peers increase in complexity from engaging in repetitive or routine back-and-forth interactions with peers to engaging in cooperative activities. Social interactions with peers also allow older infants to experiment with different roles in small groups and in different situations such as relating to familiar versus unfamiliar children." [17]. Interactive Installation Before & Beyond is conceptualized as a responsive, playful environment where visitors have physical interactions that stimulate their internal processes, such as motivate them to collaborate, bodily interact and communicate. Furthermore, through audio-visual elements to communicate ideas related to the origins of the Universe and human existence and to provoke social interactions between visitors. The installation was exposed at the Maison Shanghai 2016 event as part of the Final Fantasy exhibition. The installation space responds to visitors' body movements, the direction of walking and the distance between participants. The introductory animation represents the author's visual metaphor of the Universe creation, followed by the background sound composed of five of the most mysterious melodies found there. After entering the installation, visitors are attached to the visual String of Energy projected on the screen in front of them, with characteristic colour and sound as an abstract metaphor of their existence in a virtual world they step in. Animated strings with a specific tone, user movements and social interactions are elements of the aesthetical experience. To increase tracking accuracy and the intimate relationship between participants and the projected strings, we are using sensory-based technologies, Kinect movement detection placed on the wall, and Beacons integrated into the medallion around the neck of the participants (Fig. 1).

Fig. 1. After entering the installation space, every participant gets his String of Energy projected on the screen (© Predrag K. Nikolic. Photo: Predrag K. Nikolic)

Personal Strings (animated two-dimensional circles, enriched with a specific violoncello's tone and colour) projected on the screen are following the visitor's movements and reacting on distances between them. When participants are close enough to each other, their Strings join in one and vice-versa when they separate the joint String splits back to personal strings (Fig. 2).

Fig. 2. Depending on the distance and established relationships between visitors visual and audio appearance of the Strings changes (© Predrag K. Nikolic. Photo: Predrag K. Nikolic)

Furthermore, the experience articulates sensory stimuli such as dynamic and colourful behaviour of the strings, background sound and strings' tones. Conceptually they are the perceptive connection between visitors and the artwork's inspiration rooted in string theory and socio-emotional ability to establish positive and rewarding relationships with others [18].

Interactive installation Before & Beyond tends to intrigue visitors to explore their virtual existence and correlate it with others in the artwork's space. During that process, they acquire new personal properties such as colour, shape and sound attached to their String. For example, the given tone is becoming a metaphor for them. By playing and interacting with others in the installation, they make a musical composition based on relationships developed. Sonic and visual personification is giving them opportunities to express themselves and communicate with others in an alternative way. Likewise, to trigger a visitor's social behaviour change and engage them in collaboration, which will result in new relationships development within a given context. The physical and virtual space of the artwork is becoming a place for body and social interactions.

Interactive installation Before & Beyond tends to provoke social situations that affect the installation appearance by using human interactions, multisensory stimuli, scientific context, and playful surroundings. For example, the degree of intimacy and how people will move and behave reflects aesthetic and interaction concepts that will work well [19]. In the installation Before & Beyond users are moving around in the responsive space in front of the display. The interaction space between the users and the display is an agent that connects visitors' efforts and physical space actions with visual and sonic metaphorical outputs. By moving around and interacting with each other, participants shape social space the same way they are doing with their everyday living surroundings.

New types of sonic, visual, and socio-bodily interactions within the artwork can unify participants into groups where all individual efforts are dedicated to shared goals and generate new interpersonal and emotional relationships.

3.1 Observations and Informal Interviews

The installation was seven days exhibited at the Maison Shanghai Finally Fantasy exhibition in 2016. During that period, the author and one research assistant gave instructions to the visitors and observed how they interacted with the installation. Also, the detailed explanation of the installation concept, the author's inspiration, instructions, and the way to interact were printed and presented to the participants before entering the artwork's interactive space (Table 1).

Table 1. User profiles

Gendre	Age	Education	Profession	Experience
Male	28	High School	Carpenter	No
Male	43	High School	Driver	No
Female	37	University	Designer	Moderate
Female	37	University	Designer	Moderate
Female	52	University	Teacher	Yes
Male	21	University	Student	Moderate
Male	23	University	Student	Yes
Male	20	University	Student	Yes
Male	46	High School	Entrepreneurs	No
Female	24	University	Student	Yes
Male	32	University	Administration	Moderate

Observations

We observed the way and time needed for the participants to understand how to use the system. In severe failure or confusion, the research assistant was trained to assist the visitors and give necessary explanations. Also, the author was recording personal video and photo journal.

Interview

We conducted an informal interview with the participants we interviewed just after they finished their interactive session in the installation. Our questions were focused on the following aspects:

- What is your interpretation of the sound in the installation?
- Did you focus on sound during the session? Why?
- How did you correlate your actions with the audio response?
- Do you think the installation would provoke the same reaction and impression without the sound?

3.2 Findings

The sound had an important role in attracting visitors to interact with the installation. They believed that sound was involved to avoid an unwanted collision as they needed to control proximity between other participants. Every personal String had its authentic sound, but they personalized more with their video then audio representation. They did not care much once they lost their sonic identity after merging their strings with others.

The participants who read the introductory text at the installation entrance had a much better conceptual understanding of the sonic experience and the reasons for being part of the installation. Nevertheless, after some time, all the visitors used the sound as the navigation tool to prevent unwanted collisions in physical space and the merging of the strings in the projected virtual space. The users with the previous experience of playing in the interactive installations did focus on the sound despite those without experience who even found it annoying at a certain point. Nevertheless, both groups agreed that sound played an important role, and the installation experience would not be so profound without using it (Table 2).

Table 2. User experience research interview results

Gendre	Age	Interpretation	Correlation	Focus/Need
Male	28	Navigation	Direction/Collision	No/Yes
Male	43	Navigation	Direction/Collision	No/Yes
Female	37	Conceptual/Navigation	Direction/Collision	Yes/Yes
Female	37	Conceptual/Navigation	Direction/Collision	Yes/Yes
Female	52	Navigation	Direction/Collision	Yes
Male	21	Conceptual/Navigation	Direction/Collision	Moderate
Male	23	Navigation	Direction/Collision	Yes
Male	20	Conceptual/Navigation	Direction/Collision	Yes
Male	46	Navigation	Direction/Collision	No
Female	24	Conceptual/Navigation	Direction/Collision	Yes
Male	32	Conceptual/Navigation	Direction/Collision	Moderate

4   Interactive Installation Vroom

The installation is inspired with the children mimicking car engine sound once they want to imitate them driving a vehicle: For example, kids are using every opportunity to jump into father's car, take the wheel and by imitating the sound of a car engine to go on an imagined trip, enter fictional situations, make a story based on sonic narrative. Experience related to mimicking sounds of various vehicles to simulate movement is deeply emotionally attached to our childhood memories. For us, it is a metaphor we are addressing to specific situations and attaching meanings upon which we can develop our sonic stories and even synesthetic experience. In the interactive installation Vroom (https://goo.gl/bW4LKv), visitors were invited to shout the sound of a car engine in the microphone, which had a consequence illusion of moving forward on the road projected on the screen. Depending on sound intensity, they could regulate their speed along the road (Fig. 3).

Fig. 3. Interacting with the road in a virtual environment and controlling movement by making the car engine sound and modulating its intensity. (© Predrag K. Nikolic. Photo: Predrag K. Nikolic)

Additionally, we used road signs and arrows as metaphors related to decisions and choices in our lives and transformed them into visual narrative language. As such, visitors are not exposed only to virtual road trip experience controlled by the intensity of the imitated car engine sound, but they could also have followed and influenced the visual story that goes on the road surface (Fig. 4).

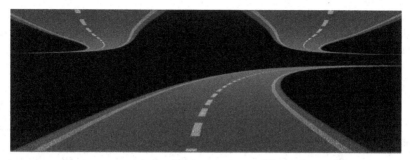

Fig. 4. A dreamful surrealistic story narrated with road symbols (© Predrag K. Nikolic. Photo: Predrag K. Nikolic)

The installation interface was purposely made of dumped car parts and then re-assemble into a new aesthetical form, as an intuitive and narrative metaphor clear enough to trigger desirable interaction between users and the sound installation (Fig. 5).

Fig. 5. The intuitive, meaningful interface made of dump car parts (© Predrag K. Nikolic. Photo: Predrag K. Nikolic)

We followed readymade creative practice and used meanings people are already attaching to particular objects. Hence, we created genuine aesthetical artefact people could interact passively or actively by taking a virtual ride controlled by the specific metaphorical sound required to trigger animated visual respond.

4.1 Observations and Informal Interviews

Like the experimental installation "Beyond & Before", The Vroom was also seven days exhibited at the Maison Shanghai The Final Fantasy exhibition in 2016. We applied the same procedure using observation and interview methods in our user experience research.

In the Vroom installation case, we decided not to go with the detailed instructions and test the intuitive aspects of the interface. This time we selected nine visitors who agreed to answer the interview questions (Table 3).

Table 3. User profiles

Gendre	Age	Education	Profession	Experience
Female	21	University	Student	No
Male	12	School	Student	No
Male	14	School	Student	Moderate
Male	20	University	Student	Moderate
Female	34	High School	Self-Employed	No
Male	35	High School	Self-Employed	No
Male	19	University	Student	Yes
Female	20	University	Student	Yes
Male	22	University	Student	Moderate

Observations

Like in the previous case with the installation "Before & Beyond", we observed how and time needed for the participants to understand how to use the system. In case of confusion, the research assistant was trained to assist the participants. The author was recording personal video and photo journal for later analysis.

Interview

We conducted an informal interview with the participants with interest in:

- What sounds meant to them in this installation?
- Did they find the interface intuitive enough?
- How did they correlate their sonic interaction with the visual response?

4.2 Findings

Once they spotted a microphone in the interface, it was clear to all participants that they needed to produce sound to interact with the artwork. At a glance, they were not sure what kind of sonic input and what output they could expect. However, after they made an analogy between the animated road projection and the microphone stand made of car parts, they were pretty confident that they should mimic car engine sound.

They were pleasantly surprised when they discovered that they could control their speed with voice tone modulation. The first-person perspective had an essential role in recalling memories from childhood and keeping users engaged with car engine sound. Some of the participants did not relate their actions with early childhood memories and considered sound only as a tool to control the output from the system. This group of users experimented with the volume and type of sound they produced despite the participants who found a strong relationship between cognitive and type of sound they produced as a reflection to that. The visual narrative made of road line and arrows had importance and took their attention for interpretation. Another group that used sound as a tool focused on the system's response to speed and the correlation between audio input and digital output. They did not consider road signs of any importance (Table 4).

Table 4. User experience research interview results

Gendre	Age	Intuition	Interpretation	Correlation
Female	21	High	Cognitive/Tool	Yes
Male	12	High	Tool	Yes
Male	14	High	Tool	Moderate
Male	20	Medium	Cognitive/Tool	Yes
Female	34	Medium	Tool	Moderate
Male	35	Medium	Tool	Moderate
Male	19	High	Cognitive/Tool	Yes
Female	20	High	Cognitive/Tool	Yes
Male	22	High	Cognitive/Tool	Yes

5 Sensynesthetic Sculptures

In the experimental installation Sensynesthetic Sculptures, we used magnetic frictions and contextual sonic metaphors as a creative medium. The multisensory approach to user experience design in the last decade tended to enrich visual reality by adding sound, texture, gesture, haptic sensations, and engaging more than one sense. Nevertheless, our idea was to extend and overcome visual reality limitations by applying an artistic/design process of sensory immobilization. By excluding certain senses from perception, we tried to reveal universal realities and develop experience beyond sensory limitations. For example, proprioceptive is a related phenomenon where one way of improving proprioceptive efficiency is to diminish or block input from other sensory systems such as the eyes [20]. In the broader social context, we are used mixed experiential reality to diminish body limitations and deliver similar multisensory experiences to everybody. The essential phenomenon regarding user experience design involves a relationship between unconscious processes and perception of objects, dreams and fantasies. That is the foundation upon which Sensynesthetic Sculptures are trying to build collective experiences and start the processes between participants and participants and the author. Sensynesthetic Sculptures are completely non-material energy-based artefacts and, as such, purely experiential, capable of responding with energy-based immobilized sensory feedback to visitors' actions or stimulating emotions upon given meanings by engaged individuals.

With Sensynesthetic Sculptures, we tend to explore and introduce new existing realities significantly beyond visual perception. Our creative tendency is to communicate purely through the sound and tactile language and avoid visual expressive forms such as colours, lines, patterns and forms. By doing that, we are trying to move experiences from dominantly semiotic to more heuristic, oriented toward new qualities of meanings. Accordingly, we are trying to expand the field of expressive, creative mediums choices toward new frontiers where the focus will be on abstract multisensory experiential rather than physical reality, more emotionally than technologically-based (Fig. 6).

Fig. 6. Magnetic friction and sound as new creative medium (© Predrag K. Nikolic. Photo: Predrag K. Nikolic)

In our design language, we are using creative vocabulary based on audio-haptic modality made of:

- Vibrations
- Collapses
- Collisions
- Elevations
- Repulsions

Sounds corresponding to listed phenomena are based on adequate sonic metaphors. Within the human-spatial interactions, we are designing experiences using interaction techniques that use haptic gloves in combination with a tower of electromagnets. The electromagnets are arranged throughout the tower to provide dynamic magnetic frictions while the participant explores the space around the tower and getting sonic and frictional feedback. The electromagnets are hidden from view, and the frictions are created in mid-air (Fig. 7).

Fig. 7. Haptic gloves in combination with a tower of electromagnets. The electromagnets are arranged throughout the tower to provide dynamic magnetic frictions. (© Predrag K. Nikolic. Photo: Predrag K. Nikolic)

The Sensynesthetic Sculptures are made of magnetic energy, which is abstract and experiential. The Sculptures are placed on a magnetic field holder and approachable only through special magnetic gloves. The design process is based on iterative audio-haptic practice. All parts of the sculpture are organized through repetition, contrast, or absence of constitutive elements (vibrations, collapses, collisions, elevations, repulsions) we are using to achieve the desired experience. We are using a cylindrical tower that hides electromagnets, and users are interacting with the tower while wearing a set of gloves that contain permanent magnets at the fingertips. Previously, others have proposed the use of arrays of electromagnets to produce interactions [21, 22, 23]. However, in our sculptures, we enable both a volumetric sense of space and a time-varying interaction to create new experiences for the users during each pass. Rather than feeling a predefined surface, participants will interact with a dynamic volume that is produced by the electromagnets.

The interactions are produced with a magnetic tower and a glove with a set of five permanent magnets (one located at each fingertip, 2 cm diameter, grade 52). The proposed magnetic tower is a 0.5 m tall cylindrical structure with a diameter of 100 mm. Its outer surface is formed with an array of 1–64 air-coil electromagnets. Dynamic forces are programmed into the tower to produce time-varying interactions. Time-varying forces control at each table with an Arduino. Air-core coils are made with 28-gauge wire and 20–100 mm in diameter. The current supplied to the electromagnets varies from 0–2 A (Fig. 8).

When users move their hands around the magnetic tower's surface while wearing the gloves, they can feel interactions with the dynamic virtual sculpture formed around the magnetic tower and hear the sonic metaphor paired to the specific magnetic energy interactions such as vibrations, collapses, collisions, and elevations.

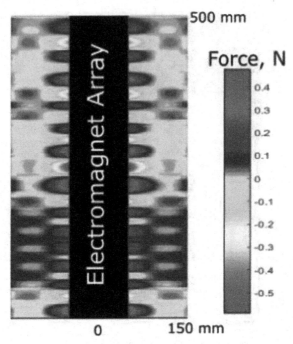

Fig. 8. Sample cross-section of the force felt by a participant's finger when using the electromagnetic array.

5.1 Expert Interview

For the installation Sensynesthetic Sculptures, we interviewed five experts under a controlled laboratory environment with different backgrounds (Table 5).

Table 5. Experts profiles

Gendre	Age	Education	Profession	Experience
Male	37	University	Engineer	Moderate
Male	35	University	Engineer	Expert
Female	28	University	UX designer	Moderate
Male	32	University	Interaction Designer	Expert
Female	51	University	Artist	Expert

We conducted contextual interviews while moving around the magnetic tower with the haptic gloves and defining experienced forms of the sculptures.

5.2 Findings

We were interested in hearing from them opinion about:

- Sufficiency of the used technology
- Detection of the variety of forms
- Sound-Tactile correlation form the UX perspective
- The capability of the medium to communicate inclusive ideas

Considering that it was the prototype of the Sensynesthetic Sculptures technology used, it showed the potential to support the author's idea. The generated magnetic frictions are still tactile sensations rather than 3D forms; we can resemble solid materials such as texture, edge, and surface. Nevertheless, as a new creative medium to offer a new user experience, the experts praised their discrepancies. Under the circumstances where we do not see the material share and feel it under our fingertips, user sonic metaphors attached to specific magnetic friction had a significant role in interacting and engaging with the sculptures and idea they represent.

6 Conclusions and Future Directions

In the Sonic Metaphors projects, we are proposing the use of sounds metaphors in creative practice, which can contribute to user engagement quality during multisensory interactions. Although many questions remain concerning the interfaces proposed, we believe that the suggested design process can deliver genuine user experiences. In the interactive installation Before & Beyond, the sound had an essential role in provoking collaboration between participants' and behavioural changes led by new types of sensory and socio-bodily interactions. Based on sonic features in the installation, user-directed their choices toward establishing new interpersonal and emotional relationships. In the installation Vroom, we invited visitors to interact with the installation by mimicking specific user memories with specific intrinsic values. Relation between the sonic metaphor used and visual respond immersed visitors into unique sensory, narrative and aesthetic experience. Lastly, in Sensynesthetic Sculptures, we use sound to empower magnetic energy as a new creative medium.

We believe sonic metaphors can be used as a creative vocabulary to enrich exiting and novel design practices, significantly when sensory limitations can vastly affect the interaction process and engagement. Hence, our future research directions will be focused on using sound interactions as an integral part of the creative, narrative, and design process within social or personal experiential context toward creating authentic user experiences.

References

1. Keenan, F.: A theatre wind machine as interactive sounding object. Presented at the International Conference on Live Interfaces (ICLI), Doctoral Colloquium, University of Sussex (2016)

2. Franinović, K., Stefania, S.: Sonic Interaction Design. MIT Press (2013)
3. Dourish, P.: Where the Action Is: The Foundations of Embodied Interaction. MIT Press (2001)
4. Hermann, T., Williamson, J., Murray-Smith, R., Visell, Y., Brazil, E.: Sonification for sonic interaction design. In: CHI 2008 Workshop on Sonic Interaction Design: Sound, Information, and Experience, pp. 35–40 (2008)
5. Shusterman, R.: Pragmatist Aesthetics: Living Beauty, Rethinking Art. Blackwell, Oxford (2000)
6. Engeström, Y.: Learning, Working and Imagining: Twelve Studies in Activity Theory. Orienta-Konsultit Oy, Helsinki (1990)
7. Merleau-Ponty, M.: The Phenomenology of Perception, Routledge (2003)
8. Ross, P., Wensveen, S.A.G.: Designing behavior in interaction: using aesthetic experience as a mechanism for design. Int. J. Des. **4**(2), 3–13 (2010)
9. Petersen, M.G., Iversen, O.S., Krogh, P.G., Ludvigsen, M.: Aesthetic interaction: a pragmatist's aesthetics of interactive systems. In: Benyon, D., Moody, P., Gruen, D., McAra-McWilliam, I. (eds.) Proceedings of the 5th Conference on Designing Interactive Systems, pp. 269–276. ACM Press, New York (2004)
10. Murray, R., Caulier-Grice, J., Mulgan, G.: The Open Book of Social Innovation. The Young Foundation & NESTA, London (2010)
11. Bjögvinsson, E., Ehn, P., Hillgren, P.: Design things and design thinking: contemporary participatory design challenges. Des. Issues **28**(3), 101–116 (2012)
12. Design Council: What's Dott? http://www.dottcornwall.com/aboutdott/whats-dott. Accessed 27 Oct 2021
13. Niedderer, K., et al.: Joining forces: investigating the influence of design for behaviour change on sustainable innovation (2014)
14. O'Modhrain, S., Essl, G.: PebbleBox and CrumbleBag: tactile interfaces for granular synthesis. In: Jensenius, A.R., Lyons, M.J. (eds.) A NIME Reader. CRSM, vol. 3, pp. 165–180. Springer, Cham (2017). https://doi.org/10.1007/978-3-319-47214-0_11
15. Barrass, S.: ZiZi: the affectionate couch and the interactive affect design diagram, sonic interaction design, p. 235 (2013)
16. Tanaka, A., Bau, O., Mackay, W.: The A20: interactive instrument techniques for sonic design exploration, sonic interaction design, p. 255 (2013)
17. Quanta Magazine. http://bit.ly/1ShK1tR. Accessed 24 Feb 2021
18. California Department of Education. http://bit.ly/2b7boUm. Accessed 24 Feb 2021
19. Cohen, J., et al.: Helping Young Children Succeed: Strategies to Promote Early Childhood Social and Emotional Development Washington DC, National Conference of State Legislatures and Zero to Three (2005)
20. Fischer, P.T., Zollner, C., Hoffmann, T., Piazza, S., Hornecker, E.: Beyond information and utility: transforming public spaces with media facades. IEEE Comput. Graphics Appl. **33**(2), 38–46 (2013)
21. Dickinson, J.: Proprioceptive Control of Human Movement. Princeton Book Company (1976)
22. Moskowitz, C.: What's 96 percent of the universe made of? Astronomers don't know. http://www.space.com/11642-dark-matter-dark-energy-4-percent-universe-panek.html. Accessed 24 Feb 2021
23. Zhang, Q., et al.: Magnetic Field Control for Haptic Display: System Design and Simulation. IEEE Access (2016)
24. Weiss, M., et al.: FingerFlux: near-surface haptic feedback on tabletops. In: UIST (2011)

Artificial Intelligence, Virtual Reality and Augmented Reality in Learning

Artificial Intelligence, Virtual Reality and Augmented Reality in Learning

Eva Brooks[1] and Jeanette Sjöberg[2]

[1] Aalborg University, Kroghstræde 3, 9220 Aalborg, Denmark
eb@hum.aau.dk
[2] Halmstad University, Kristian IVs väg 3, 30118 Halmstad, Sweden
jeanette.sjoberg@hh.se

Abstract. In this chapter, contributions from EAI DLI 2021 proceedings explore potentials in new technologies suggesting that this requires novel and speculative approaches to inspire users to imagine future perspectives and opportunities. Furthermore, the outcomes from the different contributions show that designing technologies targeting complex content and interactions require carefully designed and coordinated procedures, and involvement of end users. Finally, it is revealed that playful and bodily approaches to interaction with emergent technology such as virtual reality and robotics open up for learning opportunities.

Keywords: Augmented reality · Artificial Intelligence · Creativity · Learning · Presence and immersion · Speculative design · Visual expression and animation · Virtual reality

1 Introduction

1.1 Scope

The emergence of digital technology is becoming increasingly prevalent in a wide variety of areas and even accelerating at such a pace that current technology hype, such as augmented and virtual technology, soon might become outdated. This section explores potentials in innovative technologies involving various disciplines and stakeholders across different learning practices. Accordingly, the different contributions demonstrate that the intended transformation that new technology should contribute with should not be taken for granted. Technology is not in itself an inclusive or learning phenomenon, which is why its use needs to be studied in the context where it is intended to be implemented. When a combination of users' capabilities and conditions is considered, emergent technology can offer a more accessible dimension and allow the benefits it can confer to be enjoyed more widely [1]. The contributions further acknowledge that development of new technology solutions that are accessible and designed for exploration as well as developed by means of innovative methods can influence aspects of presence and immersion, creativity, playfulness and enjoyment in learning. Accessibility is considered as one of the most critical aspects in technological progress and considered to comprise a combination of availability, affordability, awareness, and ability for effective use [2]. Visualisation of complexity is acknowledged as opportunities to describe and communicate content and connect design/technology issues and opportunities [3]. Altogether, the chapters within this part of the EAI DLI 2021 proceedings show a rich variety of emerging technology applied in different learning practices. We hope that these examples will inspire continuous discussions and efforts to contribute to inclusive technology solutions innovating learning environments.

The first contribution investigates how Augmented Reality can enhance motivation and learning among museum visitors. The second contribution presents a study where the authors argue that creativity and emotions most often are not explicitly included in a design process when investigating how technology can be used to supply new learning options. The third contribution describes the development and evaluation of a virtual scenario designed as a journey to the cell scale. The fourth contribution addresses the questions of what kind of learning potentials that Augmented Reality (AR) can offer as well as why, when, and how such learning potentials can be studied. The final and fifth contribution applies a designer perspective and explores the impact of specific elements on visual expressions of 3D narrative animations, primarily focusing on characters, scene, cinematography, and post-processing.

The following text snippets elaborate from each contribution to further assist readership.

2   Towards Mobile Holographic Storytelling at Historic Sites

The paper is authored by Jessica Bitter and Ulrike Spierling and titled Towards Mobile Holographic Storytelling at Historic Sites and focused on how Augmented Reality (AR) can enhance motivation and learning of museum visitors. The authors assess whether head-mounted displays (HMD) would provide an enhanced sense of presence and immersion compared to handheld devices (HHD). The paper describes how the authors transferred an existing concept and AR storytelling content from a tablet to the HoloLens 2. The assessment was based on a prototypical test and involved 16 subjects. The first evaluation approach required the subjects to follow the ongoing story on the tablet, and in the second one, the continuation of the story was dependent on the subject's to trigger the continuance step-by-step. After testing the two alternatives, the subjects filled in a questionnaire with closed and open questions. The findings showed that when placed in a 3D environment, 2D videos hold potentials for the experience of immersion and presence. Here, spatial audio seemed to be important for the orientation in the story and for locating relevant actions in the real environment. However, the authors underline that these outcomes need to be further investigated in future studies. The main contribution of this paper clarifies that 2D videos from tablets, which is an inexpensive solution compared to full 3D (e.g. by volumetric filming), puts forward a sense of presence and immersion and thus can provide new learning environments in museums.

3   Could Playful AI Prototypes Support Creativity and Emotions in Learning?

The paper, Could Playful AI Prototypes Support Creativity and Emotions in Learning by Martin Cooney and Jeanette Sjöberg discusses the broad question of what learning would look like in future. In this regard, the authors argue that creativity and emotions most often are not explicitly included in a design process when investigating how technology can be used to supply new learning options. Hence, the authors report on an ongoing study to explore the integration of AI and education to foster creativity and emotions, following a paradigm of playful learning. The authors acknowledge this as being a highly complex design space and that the research activities related to how AI will contribute to the future of education is still scarce. The study explores three different cases focusing on freedom, ease, and engagement in learning respectively. For each of these cases, a prototype is designed aligned with the principles of playful design and prototyping. The authors suggest that playful design can be a stimulating approach to foster experiential learning, which as such encourages creativity and emotions such as enjoyment. The three prototypes were tested during a period of three years in an engineering course about design of embedded and intelligent systems within a university setting, and further discussed in various workshop settings involving over a hundred university educators. Observations showed that positive emotions were supported via the prototype's positive but logical responses, for example by allowing emotional contagion, and the potential to build trust via humour. Speech recognition accuracy and delays from having to download large files were some of the challenges that the study identified. The contribution of this work-in-progress paper lies in the discussion about computational creativity and emotions in relation to educational AI tools by suggesting some solutions and challenges. This can contribute to initial theoretical and methodical considerations when designing for future learning.

4   Sea of Cells: Learn Biology through Virtual Reality

Ricardo Monteiro, Nuno F. Rodrigues, João Martinho, and Eva Oliveira are the authors of the paper titled Sea of Cells: Learn Biology through Virtual Reality (VR), which investigates whether implementation of VR experiences in an educational context (k10th-grade Biology class) promotes improved long-term knowledge retention. The paper describes the development and evaluation of a virtual scenario designed as a journey to the cell scale, where the students can learn about cells and by touching and tearing cells apart they can see what they look like from inside. Based on related work, this VR journey design targets a hands-on approach intervention, feedback after each session to provide conceptual understanding among the students, as well as opportunities to explore, to fail and try again. Moreover, the study strives to design accurate and artistic representations of the cell to improve students' understanding of the behaviour of the cell, e.g. by observing Prokaryotic cells on a microscopic scale. Due to the pandemic situation, a study with 10th grade students was not possible to perform. Instead, a pilot study with six biology teachers, where the virtual environment was demonstrated to which the teachers could ask questions and, finally, were asked to fill in a questionnaire, which should give input if the VR tool was appropriately designed to be used in an educational setting. The results revealed that VR allowed for a bodily interaction, which indicates a relevance of educational usage, in particular when it comes to approaching complex subjects by means of gamification.

5 Exploring the Learning Potentials of Augmented Reality through Speculative Design

In this contribution, Sara Paasch Knudsen, Helene Husted Hansen, and Rikke Ørngreen, addresses the questions of what kind of learning potentials that Augmented Reality (AR) can offer as well as why, when, and how such learning potentials can be studied. Due to the study's futuristic perspective, the research was based on a speculative design approach applied within five online workshops including 2–6 participants from a K1-12 teacher education programme per workshop. Theoretically, the paper is based on John Dewey's pragmatism. The empirical data included audio recordings of each workshop session, 20 visual storyboards created by the K1-12 teacher education students as well as their written documentation of five creative exercises during the workshops. Further, observation and field notes were noted by the authors after the workshops. By means of a thematic analysis, the findings reveal that AR learning potentials lie in its possibilities to bridge physical and virtual experiences, offering different interaction modalities, supporting social practices, and extending communication, for example across locations. Even though learning potentials of augmented reality were speculative, the findings of the study indicate that a speculative design approach can inform both current situations and direct future investigations in a specific field. However, the paper points out that it is not a guarantee that participants in such a futuristic workshop design bring innovative insights, which relates to the fact that participants often are occupied by their own existing knowledge and attitudes.

6 Visual Expression in 3D Narrative Animation

The last paper in this section of the EAI DLI 2021 proceedings by Yutong Shi, explores the impact of specific elements on the visual expression of 3D narrative animations, primarily focusing on characters, scene, cinematography, and post-processing. The author argues that visual expression most often is addressed as an abstract concept and scarcely applied accurately and systematically to the field of arts. More specifically, the author points out the lack of research, which can guide animators' in specific types of animation activities. The focus of the paper emerged from the author's design of a narrative animation, Tele-Radio, where the author experienced that the roles of being a technician and being an artist had to merge, which resulted in the author becoming responsible for storyline, modelling, audio design as well as programming, character animation, and FX composition. The author carried out a literature review on the specific elements related to visual expression of 3D narrative animations based on an animation designer perspective. This was done relative to the author's introduction of the Tele-Radio design, systematically describing the character visual design as well as scene art design, montage and cinematography of the animation, and post-processing activities using different tools. The author concludes that this procedure, i.e. designing visual expression of 3D animation, requires coordination of the various elements mentioned. Furthermore, the author argues that when animation is designed from the perspective of visual expression, the quality may be improved. However, further research is needed to explore this and other animation research topics.

7 Epilogue and Acknowledgements

This third section, Artificial Intelligence, Virtual Reality and Augmented Reality in Learning, introduced five contributions to promote readership of each full paper that are presented in the following chapters. In doing so, the authors of this chapter acknowledge the contributions from each author whose original work was presented in the EAI DLI 2021 online conference events on December 2nd, 2021.

References

1. OECD: Innovating Education and Educating for Innovation: The Power of Digital Technologies and Skills. OECD Publishing, Paris (2016). http://dx.doi.org/10.1787/9789264265097-en
2. United Nations. Technology and Innovation Report. Catching Technology Waves. Innovation with Equity. United Nations Conference on Trade and Development. UNCTAD (2021)
3. Bolton, S.: The visual thinking method. tools and approaches for rapidly decoding design research data. In: Rodgers, P.A., Yee, J. (eds.) The Routledge Companion to Design Research, pp. 277–291. Routledge Taylor & Francis Group (2015)

Towards Mobile Holographic Storytelling at Historic Sites

Jessica L. Bitter and Ulrike Spierling[✉]

Hochschule RheinMain, Unter den Eichen 5, 65195 Wiesbaden, Germany
{jessicalaura.bitter,ulrike.spierling}@hs-rm.de

Abstract. Augmented Reality (AR) promises to enhance motivation and learning of museum visitors, whereby head-mounted displays (HMD) provide a greater presence and immersion than handheld devices (HHD). To assess this, we transferred interactive AR stories from an existing HHD prototype to the MS HoloLens 2. The app lets museum visitors of a Roman fort 'meet' video ghosts to learn about life at their historic location. We compared two alternative ways to trigger spatial videos. The evaluation shows that, while limitations occur when reusing media once produced for 2D screens on HMDs, the approach is worth focusing on. The HMD enhances the immersion even with 2D videos placed in space, thus granting virtual ghosts more 'presence' in the user experience.

Keywords: Augmented reality · Head-mounted display · Presence · Immersion

1 Introduction

Museums are places for learning. They exhibit cultural artefacts, or natural and fossil finds, thus conveying factual heritage knowledge. In addition, they enable real-life experiences, because exposed objects and sites appear as present 'witnesses' of the past. In the last several years, museums have begun to use emerging technologies such as Augmented Reality (AR) to enhance physical exhibits with virtual information, or to provide pure virtual realities with storytelling.

We focus on AR not only for its possibilities to add digital information, but mainly for its features to enrich an otherwise non-interactive site with human lifelike experiences, displaying dramatic storytelling in real space. Also, with this goal in mind, the related project "Spirit", which preceded this study, presented a prototype of complex location-based and spatial interactive drama in a Roman fort with hand-held devices (HHD) like off-the-shelf tablets [1]. This app allowed to meet the 'ghosts' of roman soldiers and historic inhabitants of the site and to witness an exemplary drama of typical conflicts and life right on the spot within the mural remains. When combined GPS and tablet camera recognized a building (by image comparison with a prepared reference), filmed characters appeared as silhouette videos in front of the sighted backdrop (Fig. 1). The app addressed the human desire to imagine life right within the visited area, thus connecting with the past. The project evaluation looked at the influence of several design aspects

E. Brooks et al. (Eds.): DLI 2021, LNICST 435, pp. 119–128, 2022.
https://doi.org/10.1007/978-3-031-06675-7_9

that would increase this aspired feeling of 'presence' [2]. One supporting aspect for presence was a kind of spatial staging of virtual scenes in the real environment, by letting filmed characters appear at different angles around the user. These were triggered by the gyroscopic sensor of the handheld device, which recognized rotations like panning to the left and right. Meanwhile, presence and immersion as a means for experiential learning are expected to move a big step forward with novel hardware, such as head-mounted displays (HMD) with integrated stereo vision and improved tracking features to recognize the spatial surroundings of users. In this regard, the Microsoft "HoloLens 2" serves as a precursor for future more consumer-accessible devices.

In this paper, we present the result of our first attempt to transfer the existing content of the "Spirit" project to being experienced on a HoloLens 2. We partly build upon theoretical elaborations expressed by Liu et al. [3], concerning the impact of using general interaction patterns from HHD-kinds of devices on an HMD. Therefore, we reuse (with permission) the previous given HHD media content and its basic concept for the HoloLens 2, with the initial goal to reach a most similar interaction pattern and experience on the HMD. Previously, due to the limitations of the handheld hardware, single video actions in a complex spatial scene could only be triggered separately by the gyroscope for appearing on the tablet screen in succession at different recognized orientations. The HoloLens instead – with its tracking option of spatial anchors – allows to place video objects directly into the environment. With these improved possibilities, we also looked at the general problem of how to best perceive linear filmic content in 3D space and compared two ways to trigger the ghost videos. Further, we are interested in the prospects of using 2D videos in 3D space. In the following, after discussing related work, we first explain these concepts, followed by core findings of the qualitative evaluation of the user experience.

2   State of the Art

In the field of AR in museums, most reported projects focus on either HHD or HMD. Geronikolakis and Papagiannakis noticed the lack of multiplatform applications. They tried to close that gap by providing a plugin for Unity3D with which the loading of an SDK and preparing of an approach can be sped up [4].

Handheld AR devices like a smartphone are currently the first choice to establish AR in a museum, as users are familiar with these and can bring their own. Usability is a main design issue to enhance the overall experience [5]. Along these lines, Choi et al. perceive HMDs as disadvantageous and not yet mature enough [6]. They argue that poor accessibility, insufficient image quality, inconvenient form factors and basic usability are reasons why HMDs (and in this case the HoloLens) are not yet ready to compete with handheld AR devices like a Smartphone.

On the contrary, Hou [7] and Sugiura et al. [8] perceive the usability of HMD devices (the HoloLens) as good. In their view, HMD seems to be a promising technology to enhance the visitor's experience in a museum or exhibition, especially encouraging the learning in a museum environment. An innovative example is provided by Kim et al. [9], who developed a mobile tour guide that indicates points of interest on a HMD, while using a connected HHD to display a map with GPS and keywords.

Liu et al. [3] argued that there are not enough experiences of creating "same" content for both kinds of devices at once. They compared different features of tablets and the HoloLens 2, proposing how the HoloLens could partially adopt interaction patterns of a tablet. They hypothesized how the same AR app [1] would be transferable to the HoloLens under the prerequisites of the hardware constraints and possibilities.

O'Dwyer et al. [10] implemented a volumetric filmed actor in an AR museum narrative app that could be perceived on either a tablet or a HoloLens 1. While the evaluation compared the immersive effects of both devices, the linear presentation of one minute length could only be watched at one stationary location. Users could walk around the virtual actor during his monologue, with no further interaction or navigation.

It is not yet fully explored how to best use time-based media such as film storytelling together with 3D immersive technologies. Especially for learning apps, it is essential that users can perceive the content in time, while interacting in space. Hence, previous work in 360-degree filming can be relevant here. Pillai et al. [11] state that it is necessary to implement visual cues to guide users through filmic experiences on an HMD. Especially when the experience is also the first contact with a VR/AR HMD device, it is to be expected that users are more focused on exploring the new technology than following a story, according to Syrett et al. [12]. Gödde et al. [13] add that especially first-time users need an orientation phase, before they can focus on the video content. In addition, after every cut in the filmed story, they need to orient themselves anew to find the location of the action. Visual cues like waving do not always work when users look in an opposite direction.

3 Transferring an AR Storytelling Experience from Tablet to HoloLens 2

We followed a 'design research' approach [14] in the sense of building a prototype to understand the principles of a concept. We implemented the previously existing content of the tablet museum app into a new app for the MS HoloLens 2. Following Liu et al. [3], the goal was to try to keep as much of the "original" as possible, with the hypothesis that already only by using the HMD, there would be an increase in the feeling of 'presence' as part of the user experience. The original app already tried to implement a pseudo-spatial experience by letting the user explore the environment around the main point of view. While this was expected to be greatly enhanced with the HMD that enables 'real' spatial coordinate recognition, there was doubt concerning the believability of the 2-dimensional videos displaying the ghosts (as discussed in [3]).

3.1 Interaction Pattern of the Given Tablet App

The given HHD AR app aimed at creating an educational interactive drama experience in an outdoor museum. Visitors should be able to find locations at which lifelike 'ghosts from the past' appear around the user's position, enacting scenes that represent their life back in 233 AD at the Roman fort that is now the museum [2]. GPS was used for pre-selecting an area, and image marker recognition could compare current camera images with a dataset of prepared views to trigger a first video scene that displayed a recorded film scene. The whole story was divided into snippets that could then subsequently be triggered by the user through turning to the left or to the right, following UI arrows used as hints (Fig. 1). By means of the gyroscope of the hand-held device, these turns triggered the following scenes that were staged around the user. The result was an impression of a pseudo 3D world in which the user could look around. Technically, there was no spatial model underlying, as all videos were triggered in relation to the screen. After triggering, the cut-out video characters stayed within their initially captured image section of the depicted site to create the illusion of keeping their position in the environment, viewed through the metaphorical window of the tablet screen.

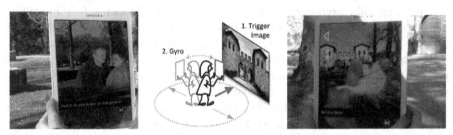

Fig. 1. AR storytelling tablet app, "Encounter/AR" mode. After triggering the first scene (right image), arrows indicated that turning left revealed the next scene (triggered by the gyroscope).

The story was a fictional re-enactment of possible actions within the buildings of the Roman fort. Apart from this "Encounter" mode providing the dramatic story in AR, there were two more interaction modes, without AR, that helped users navigate between the different locations and read some meta-information (Fig. 2). For a complete experience, these modes are also necessary between the AR locations, in order to be usable. The "Search" mode provided a GPS-enhanced map navigation and a possibility to search for buildings with a given stencil outline. The "Read" mode added factual information that fitted the dramatic storyline. For reading and GPS navigation, the tablet could be held horizontally in a relaxed pose.

Fig. 2. AR storytelling tablet app. Left and middle: "Search" mode with map and stencil. Right: "Read" mode, opened via the bar menu at the bottom [2].

The design of the "Encounter" mode was optimized for adjusting the aspired spatial user experience to the limitations of the tablet hardware used at this time. For example, the cut-out video characters were presented in mono vision on top of the camera image of the tablet. There was no depth of field and no stereo vision possible. There was no occlusion feature that would allow video characters to be placed behind real objects. To see characters 'around' the user, these had to be triggered as a new video scene at any updated viewing angle to appear on the screen coordinates, as there was no 3D world model. Accordingly, as the HoloLens 2 would offer to program improved adapted features without many of those restrictions, the question was whether the feeling of presence would be increased in spite of this initial 2D design.

3.2 Transfer to HoloLens 2

The same media material produced for the tablet app was also used in the HoloLens application. However, to keep the initial steps simple and to mainly focus on the multi-direction interaction pattern of the "Encounter" (without "Search" and "Read"), we aimed at an office-only prototype for user testing. (Also, the COVID-19 pandemic posed project restrictions concerning museums during the research.) We used poster images of the original Roman fort buildings as image targets, which could be recognized by the HoloLens app and then used as a trigger to start the videos (Fig. 3, left).

Following Liu et al. [3], the aim was to stay as true to the original functions as possible while implementing for a different device with different unique interaction styles. In the "Encounter" mode, after finding an image target, the HoloLens triggers the first video of a sequence of several videos that make up the entire scene. The ghost videos are now possible to be placed in a three-dimensional virtual space around the user, instead of only on a screen. To keep the ghosts always facing the user's camera, each video rotates on its y-axis in reaction to user movements ("billboard" behavior).

Fig. 3. Image capture of views through MS HoloLens 2 (left: in the office hallway, triggered by the poster image for evaluation, right: outdoor test).

As it was designed in the tablet app, the ghosts in the HoloLens app should also appear to the left and right of the user's main view direction after the first image target recognition. For user tests with the HoloLens, we prototyped two alternative approaches to trigger the following video scenes:

- *Approach 1, "user follows story"*. All following videos of one scene start in direct succession after their previous video in a given order. In order to see them located to the left and right, the user has to follow the spatial sound of the voices and to turn around accordingly.
- *Approach 2, "user triggers story"*. The second approach uses the head rotation of the user to trigger the following videos only when the user finds them and looks at them. This approach is similar to the tablet version, in which also the turning of the tablet (gyroscope sensor) triggered the next videos. Apart from the necessity to trigger, the order is fixed.

As the videos in this second approach wait for the user to be triggered, the affordance emerged to provide hints where to look for the next video. Whereas on-screen arrows (left/right) have been used in the original tablet app for this purpose (Fig. 1), in our approach we decided to place hints more directly into the spatial environment. We placed 3D particle emitters, which appear as 'dust' or 'mist' vanishing in the air, at the same positions as the ghost videos. The particles match the turquoise fairy dust currently appearing in the beginning of the existing videos. They appear after the preceding video has stopped playing, either to the left or to the right, staying in place and bubbling until the user finds them.

For the remaining modes "Search" and "Read" including their screen menu, the transfer to the HMD was not as adequately possible. We decided to avoid any gaze-based interaction with the typical HoloLens menus, because gaze plays an important role in the AR story part of the app (looking around). However, the hands were still free to conceive a hand menu that offers most of the features of the tablet app (Fig. 4). This menu can be navigated with pointing or voice commands. However, both interaction styles were from the start expected to be less convenient to use than with the tablet. Hence, here is an obvious limitation of the HMD hardware, compared to a handheld device that easily integrates modes of reading in a convenient pose and position. We consider finding alternative solutions for general interaction a necessity in future work.

Fig. 4. The hand menu in the HoloLens 2 app (outdoor test)

4   User Evaluation

The implemented prototype was given to sixteen testers for evaluation. As we have been facing the COVID-19 pandemic for a long time, this evaluation was conducted remotely without a possible supporting or observing researcher. We prepared a package for distribution with hardware and instructions, and asked the subjects to fill a questionnaire. The test users also had to mount prepared image marker printouts as backdrop posters to their walls at home to make it work (compare Fig. 3, left). This way, the setup was also location-independent (in contrast to a real outdoor scenario).

As a first step in iterative design, we aimed at only a few users to get quick results for improvement. According to Jakob Nielsen, only five users are enough to find 85% of the usability problems in a first prototype [15]. Naturally, this is not a quantitative evaluation, however, to show some distribution of opinions within the group of 16, we present lists of their results in numbers below.

For the purpose to present the effect of the transfer on the presence experience, we focus on the following guiding questions for the result presentation:

- Which of the two approaches contributes more to the understanding and experience?
- How is the presence and immersion perceived, if 2D videos are used with an HMD?

Out of 16 users, 10 subjects were female and 6 were male, the average age amounted to 33.25 years. 7 of them have watched online video presentations of the previous tablet AR app before; 3 have even used it. A majority of 12 testers have never used the MS HoloLens 2 or other HMD devices before.

The questionnaire has both a Likert scale, as well as freeform text input space. Here, the testers were asked to explain their ratings, which is at this point of development the most important part of the survey. The idea was to identify possible variations or consensus in their opinions (Table 1).

Table 1. Likert scale score. 1 = strongly disagree, 2 = disagree, 3 = neutral, 4 = agree, 5 = strongly agree.

Category	1	2	3	4	5	x̄
After understanding how to interact, approach 1 was easy to use			1	4	11	4.6
The overall experience in approach 1 is good		1	1	9	5	4.1
After understanding how to interact, approach 2 was easy to use		1	2	6	7	4.2
The overall experience in approach 2 is good		1	1	8	6	4.2
Approach 1 is easier to use than approach 2	1	1	5	7	2	3.5
The distance between user and ghosts is good		4	4	2	6	3.6
The places and angles where the ghosts appear are appropriate	2	1	4	4	5	3.6
The ghosts seem present with me in space	1	2	3	6	4	3.6

In Table 1, we can see that the usability of approach 1 is slightly better rated (4.6) than its experience (4.1). Thus, the usability of approach 1 ("easy to use") is mostly agreed on as good, with a tendency to "strongly agree", whereas the overall experience is just good. The usability and the experience of approach 2 are mostly agreed as good. In direct comparison with each other, we can see that the mean of 3.5 indicates only a slight tendency that the usability of approach 1 is perceived as superior to approach 2. Five test users answered "neutral", which means that the difference between the approaches is not too big for a rough third of the testers.

Most users commented on their rating that it has felt natural to turn around to search for the ghosts. Thanks to the guiding through spatial sound in approach 1, they found the ghost videos effortlessly. However, the users also pointed out that they missed the beginnings of the videos because these started sequentially, before they had fully turned around. It created a feeling of being pulled through the story like in a movie, which has not given much time to process its content. For the alternative approach, however, in which a video would not start before the users' gaze triggers it, some testers found it irritating having to look around in search for the ghosts. Those mostly had problems hearing the attracting sound, so that they did not have any guiding indicators, before they finally could only spot indicating particles after they turned around far enough. Additionally, three users pointed out that it would have been necessary to explain beforehand how their movements would influence the start of videos.

These findings suggest that the first approach, where the content does not 'wait' for the user, is not perfectly suited for a learning environment, although usability may be slightly easier. Having to rush to the next scene contravenes getting all the available information and remembering it later. Concerning the second approach, the feedback suggests that more importance must be given to guiding the users to minimize irritation and maximize the learning factor through the content. One possible redesign idea is to use the first approach, but add some non-essential footage to the scene beginnings in order to delay the start of each video's core content in a way that enables a good synchronization between the average user reaction times and the storytelling.

Concerning the presence of the ghosts, the Likert scale score shows that the users' tendency points vaguely towards a good presence and placement in the 3D environment, as all three related questions result in a mean of 3.6. This feedback gets more understandable when looking at the qualitative comments. Six users wrote that the ghosts were too close to them. This effect may be a result of the instance that the test has been performed indoors in small private homes. The possible distances have been restricted due to walls and furniture. This would be different in a museum space, but needs further attention. For example, in a different experiment, we tested the app outdoors in front of real walls (Fig. 3 right, and Fig. 4). While this setting offers more space, new challenges occur like bright sunlight affecting the feeling of presence of the ghosts. This will be addressed and evaluated in future work.

The comments about the place and angles of the ghosts confirm that it is of utmost importance to offer a seamless guiding system for the user. Four users did not understand the necessity of the spatial placement of the ghosts. Two of them even had difficulties to understand that they needed to look around at all, an effect that was also reported for the original tablet app [2]. This shows that the learning process can only take place if the functions of the app are clear to users.

Lastly, all of the users stated that it was clear to them that the videos are 2-dimensional, without complaining about this. One user explicitly emphasized that it did not disturb the impression of ghosts. Moreover, two users mentioned they found the presence and immersion of the ghosts higher than on a screen, regardless that the videos were only 2D. We conclude that even 2D videos hold great potential for a presence experience, if placed in a 3D environment, contradicting the hypothetical concern of Liu et al. [3] that the videos could potentially be discarded as a "fake" impression. Still, we expect that the presence and immersion would even be enhanced greatly when using novel approaches such as volumetric filming in the future.

5 Conclusion

In this paper, we described a prototypical test to enhance AR presence experiences for increasing learning and motivation in a museum, through displaying AR stories of fictional contemporary witnesses in a more holographic way. We described the transfer of an existing concept and AR storytelling content from a tablet to the HoloLens 2. We conclude that it would indeed be advised to develop some new more specific interaction patterns for the HoloLens to ideally match the novel features of the HMD hardware. Still, it saved time that the videos and texts were already produced in a previous app, but for future content creation, assets could be made adaptable to better fit each 3D medium. While the original tablet app always waited for users to trigger videos in a complex scene, we implemented two approaches on the HoloLens. In the first approach, users follow the ongoing story, and in the second, the story continuation depends on the user triggering every step. Both approaches deserve further investigation as both have their specific advantages, given that identified small usability issues would be fixed for both. Lastly, spatial audio appeared to be an important feature for orientation and for locating the relevant action in the real environment, which must be further explored in future design studies.

We see the potential of these approaches for a new learning environment in museums through present and immersive characters or contemporary witnesses. Considering the fact that a full 3D impression – for example by volumetric filming – would be expensive, we found that the aspired feeling of presence and immersion was better than anticipated with only the 2D videos from the tablet app. In the future, we will work on overcoming the restrictions found in the current app, as well as on investigating the limitations faced in our first outdoor test.

Acknowledgements. This work has been funded (in part) by the German Federal Ministry of Education and Research (BMBF), funding program Forschung an Fachhochschulen, contract number 13FH181PX8. We would like to thank Yu Liu and Linda Rau for their inspiration and implementation advice. All video assets were produced within the project "Spirit" [2].

References

1. Kampa, A., Spierling, U.: Smart Authoring for location-based augmented reality story-telling applications. In: Eibl, M., Gaedke, M. (eds.) INFORMATIK 2017. Gesellschaft für Informatik, Bonn, pp. 915–922 (2017). https://doi.org/10.18420/in2017_93

2. Spierling, U., Winzer, P., Massarczyk, E.: Experiencing the presence of historical stories with location-based augmented reality. In: Nunes, N., Oakley, I., Nisi, V. (eds.) ICIDS 2017. LNCS, vol. 10690, pp. 49–62. Springer, Cham (2017). https://doi.org/10.1007/978-3-319-71027-3_5
3. Liu, Y., Spierling, U., Rau, L., Dörner, R.: Handheld vs. head-mounted ar interaction patterns for museums or guided tours. In: Shaghaghi, N., Lamberti, F., Beams, B., Shariatmadari, R., Amer, A. (eds.) INTETAIN 2020. LNICSSITE, vol. 377, pp. 229–242. Springer, Cham (2021). https://doi.org/10.1007/978-3-030-76426-5_15
4. Geronikolakis, E., Papagiannakis, G.: An XR rapid prototyping framework for interoperability across the reality spectrum, ArXiv, abs/2101.01771 (2021)
5. Chan, B.Y., Ismail, Z.I.B.A., Jack, L.P., Asli, M.F.: Augmented reality mobile application. A feasibility study in a local national museum. J. Phys. Conf. Ser. **1358**. 12th Seminar on Science and Technology 2–3 October 2018, Kota Kinabalu, Sabah, Malaysia, IOP Publishing Ltd. (2019). https://doi.org/10.1088/1742-6596/1358/1/012057
6. Choi, H., Kim, Y.R., Kim, G.J.: Presence, immersion and usability of mobile augmented reality. In: Chen, J.Y.C., Fragomeni, G. (eds.) HCII 2019. LNCS, vol. 11574, pp. 3–15. Springer, Cham (2019). https://doi.org/10.1007/978-3-030-21607-8_1
7. Hou, W.: Augmented reality museum visiting application based on the Microsoft HoloLens. J. Phys. Conf. Ser. **1237**, 052018 (2019). https://doi.org/10.1088/1742-6596/1237/5/052018
8. Sugiura, A., Kitama, T., Toyoura, M., Mao, X.: The use of augmented reality technology in medical specimen museum tours. Anat. Sci. Educ. **12**(5), 561–571 (2018). https://doi.org/10.1002/ase.1822
9. Kim, D., Seo, D., Yoo, B., Ko, H.: Development and evaluation of mobile tour guide using wearable and hand-held devices. In: Kurosu, M. (ed.) HCI 2016. LNCS, vol. 9733, pp. 285–296. Springer, Cham (2016). https://doi.org/10.1007/978-3-319-39513-5_27
10. O'Dwyer, N., Zerman, E., Young, G.W., Smolic, A., Dunne, S., Shenton, H.: Volumetric video in augmented reality applications for museological narratives. J. Comput. Cult. Heritage (JOCCH) **14**, 1–20 (2021). https://doi.org/10.1145/3425400
11. Pillai, J.S., Ismail, A., Charles, H.P.: Grammar of VR storytelling: visual cues. In: Proceedings of the Virtual Reality International Conference-Laval Virtual, pp. 1–4 (2017). https://doi.org/10.1145/3110292.3110300
12. Syrett, H., Calvi, L., van Gisbergen, M.: The oculus rift film experience: a case study on understanding films in a head mounted display. In: Poppe, R., Meyer, J.-J., Veltkamp, R., Dastani, M. (eds.) INTETAIN 2016 2016. LNICSSITE, vol. 178, pp. 197–208. Springer, Cham (2017). https://doi.org/10.1007/978-3-319-49616-0_19
13. Gödde, M., Gabler, F., Siegmund, D., Braun, A.: Cinematic narration in VR – rethinking film conventions for 360 degrees. In: Chen, J.Y.C., Fragomeni, G. (eds.) VAMR 2018. LNCS, vol. 10910, pp. 184–201. Springer, Cham (2018). https://doi.org/10.1007/978-3-319-91584-5_15
14. Hevner, A., Chatterjee, S.: Design Research in Information Systems: Theory and Practice. Springer, New York (2010). https://doi.org/10.1007/978-1-4419-5653-8
15. Nielsen, J., Landauer, T.K.: A mathematical model of the finding of usability problems. In: Proceedings of ACM INTERCHI'93 Conference, Amsterdam, The Netherlands, pp. 206–213 (1993). https://doi.org/10.1145/169059.169166

Playful AI Prototypes to Support Creativity and Emotions in Learning

Martin Cooney$^{(\boxtimes)}$ and Jeanette Sjöberg

Halmstad University, 301 18 Halmstad, Sweden
martin.daniel.cooney@gmail.com
https://www.hh.se/english.html

Abstract. How will learning "look" in the future? Everyone learns–and we do so in a creative and emotional way. However, learners' creativity and emotions are often not explicitly included in the design process when exploring how technology can be used to provide new learning opportunities, which could result in shallow learning. One way to support such learning with technology could be playfulness. The current paper reports on some of our ongoing experiences in recent years using a playful design perspective to develop three educational Artificial Intelligence (AI) prototypes. Tackling applications intended to facilitate freedom, ease, and engagement in learning, the prototypes comprise an intelligent tutoring system, an automatic display tool, and a hand-waving detector. In closing, some lessons learned are shared to inform subsequent designs.

Keywords: Educational AI · AI prototyping · Computational creativity · Artificial emotions · Playful learning · EdTech

1 Introduction

Education is a crucial human right linked to benefits such as reducing poverty[1] and promoting health and well-being [16]. Everyone learns–and we do so in a creative and emotional manner:

For example, constructivist learning theory, embraced by many teachers, contends that students actively and creatively construct their own knowledge, sparking intrinsic motivation [9]. As well, creativity is a fundamental cornerstone of advanced learning, as the basis for the "extended abstract" and "creating" categories in the Structure of Observed Learning Outcomes (SOLO) and revised BLOOM taxonomies [2,10]. Likewise, it is known that positive autotelic emotions like enjoyment, engagement, and curiosity are crucial, and from the balance of skill and challenge suggested by Flow Theory and the Zone of Proximal Development (ZPD) [8,17], that it is normal for learners to experience some degree

---

[1] https://en.unesco.org/news/what-you-need-know-about-right-education.

Thank you to all who helped!.

E. Brooks et al. (Eds.): DLI 2021, LNICST 435, pp. 129–140, 2022.
https://doi.org/10.1007/978-3-031-06675-7_10

also of negative emotions like confusion and frustration. Interest in such emotions is increasing, in parallel with a trend in design to consider the wider picture of a learner's experience (UX), rather than only if an educational artifact is usable or not.

At the same time, educators are looking for new ways to offer improved learning opportunities. Gone are the days when we need to remember every detail of an abstruse formulation, or buy and lug around expensive, heavy books filled with answers to questions we never had, in the hopes that they might one day be partly useful. Now we search and communicate nearly instantly, like "cyborgs" that retain a crucial part of our knowledge in our flesh brains while delegating the remainder to our digital brains in the cloud. In the face of continuous challenge–such as a two hundred billion dollar gap in annual education funding related to the UN's Sustainable Development Goals[2]–one "beacon of hope" for further innovation is Artificial Intelligence (AI), which (despite some hype) could reduce teacher workload and improve student learning: Recent plans from the US, China, and Europe for increased investment in AI are in the billions of dollars, which in recent years has resulted in some exciting breakthroughs in game-playing and science (e.g., Jeopardy, Chess, Go, and protein folding) [4]. The dream is that this kind of development will lead us to new heights in our ability to learn and apply knowledge.

Yet, engineers developing AI technologies often do not explicitly design for creativity and emotions. Some general challenges with designing for creativity in education include overloaded curricula and lack of time, unclear assessment, and mismatched expectations and perceptions [1]. Likewise, emotion is a highly complex psycho-physical phenomenon involving cognitive appraisals, subjective feelings, somatic symptoms, and affect displays, related to sentiment and mood, that defies simplistic modeling (the so-called "affective gap"). The main challenge here is that we don't understand these constructs well ourselves, let alone how to embed them into digital functionality; as such, artificial emotions and computational creativity have been called "especially challenging" and a "final frontier" in AI [3,6].

Thus, we are faced with a vast, highly complex design space–no one yet knows how AI will shape the future of education. To gain some initial insight, the current short paper describes a number of our ongoing experiences in recent years toward exploring the integration of AI and education in a way that supports creativity and emotions, following the paradigm of *playful learning*:

- First, we narrow the scope based on discussions with our teachers, focusing on applications that could enhance *freedom*, *ease*, and *engagement* in learning. These goals are defined and grounded in the literature in Sect. 2, and used to derive three specific cases to explore.
- Next, for each case, we design a prototype, applying the principles of playful design and prototyping: Playful design suggests that play can be a stimulating approach to support experiential learning also in adults, which encourages

---

[2] https://en.unesco.org/news/unesco-warns-funding-gap-reach-sdg4-poorer-countries-risks-increasing-us-200-billion-annually.

creativity and positive emotions such as enjoyment [15]. Finally insights are reported in exploring the resulting prototypes with users, in Sect. 3.

Thus, the aim of this paper is to share some lessons learned–toward stimulating ideation and discussion that could contribute to developing our theory of computational creativity and emotions in relation to educational AI tools, while also suggesting solutions to some real challenges hindering progress.

2 Related Work

Some specific cases to explore had to be identified, but creativity and emotions could play a role in various learning applications: For example, in the areas of EdTech, Educational Data Mining (EDM), and Learning Analytics (LA), AI is continually and increasingly being incorporated into learning tools, to help with applications ranging from grading and skill assessment, to knowledge/engagement tracing, problem detection (lesson gaps, social isolation), teaching assistance (conversational agents or robots), and recommendations (for courses, programmes, group members, or teachers). Here, to guide our exploration, we focused on our own idea–based on our perception of the needs of our teachers and students–that education should also be characterized by freedom, ease, and engagement:

Freedom. Freedom here means that students and teachers should have autonomy and control over how they learn. One example of how to potentially enhance students' freedom is with Intelligent Tutoring Systems (ITS). Given the merits of flexible, asynchronous learning, as well as the effectiveness of one-on-one classes, and a widespread need for personalization to address gaps in heterogeneous classes, ITS have long been a "bread-and-butter" dream of the educational futurist. In general, this effort has been complicated by high development costs, silo effects, and traditions in the field, that have led to often using simplified learning approaches such as multiple-choice questions which are not optimal for stimulating creative and emotional processes. Although there is continual progress–for example, the importance of inquisitive creativity for agents has been described [18], and eye tracking goggles are being used to assess creativity [11] and detect negative emotions such as boredom when students look away from an ITS [7]–there is still much to be explored. As Ogan et al. describe, current approaches for trust-building are typically limited to simply saying a student's name and smiling, but "a more involved process ... is likely necessary" [12]. Also given that trust and playfulness have been positively linked previously, we believe there is merit in exploring a playful ITS prototype.

Ease. Learning typically requires effort, but not all work associated with learning might be required or helpful; ease here means that bothersome tasks that don't contribute can be automated. One task that requires work from teachers who often have little time is preparing learning materials, which are typically inflexible and resistant to adaptation. For example, in the data age, simulations and visualizations including augmented reality [5] promise to facilitate better under-standing and avoid drowning students in "rigorous" details, but developing such materials takes time; language teachers as well are often interrupted by students who wish to know how a word is spelled. Therefore, we foresaw a potential need for a dynamic display tool that could adaptively generate visualizations such as images or words to describe what a teacher is discussing.

Engagement. Engagement here relates to motivation and attention. It is known that physical activity aids creativity and positive emotions [13], but students especially in STEM subjects can spend much time seated in front of a computer. Furthermore, allowing students to be more active, and in control of their learn-ing, is desired, in line with self-determination theory and autonomy-supportive teaching [14]. Therefore, a program that can facilitate engagement via physical activity and enhanced autonomy could be useful.

3   Methods

Based on the derived cases, three prototypes were designed and implemented, as shown in Fig. 1, 2, and 3 :

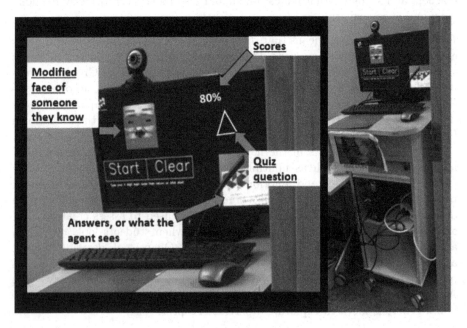

Fig. 1. Questioner. A quiz-giving agent squats upon a wheeled lectern.

Questioner. The basic idea of this prototype was to provide students with a chance to receive asynchronous, continual (weekly) feedback on their progress

Fig. 2. Displayer. A Baxter robot displays words that a teacher speaks during a class on its small display screen.

Fig. 3. Waver. A student waves in the foreground during a class to indicate that they would like to hear more about a topic.

during a course via quizzes, to reduce their stress before exams. We also saw opportunities for personalizing content to students from different backgrounds, who might have gaps in their knowledge. The prototype consisted of a desktop, with a keyboard, mouse, and camera for input, and a monitor and speakers for output, housed on a wheeled lectern to be able to move between classrooms easily. To access appropriate quizzes, students inputted a personal code, then chose from a list of quizzes, and typed in their free answers. To seem engaging, like in an interaction with a person, the prototype agent was set to blink, and to also provide suggestions if students did not quickly answer quiz questions. Response times were logged, although they were not used. Internally, the prototype used OpenCV[3] for face detection and keyboard/mouse event handling, and CMU Pocketsphinx[4] for speech recognition, on top of Robot Operating System (ROS)[5]. Matching with keywords was conducted to determine if answers are correct. Although the main goal of this prototype was to allow students more freedom in being able to choose when they wanted to learn and how they wanted to interact, we also sought to support ease via the familiar interface (humanoid, mouse, and keyboard) and engagement through the prototype's interactivity (not just multiple choice questions).

Playful responses were triggered if the prototype detected behavior from the user that seemed playful, as described in Table 1; for example, the prototype moved its face away slightly in a random direction if a student clicked on it. Furthermore, a familiar face, the face of the main teacher in the course, was also used to be playful, and the prototype was set to increasingly smile as more questions are answered correctly. Thereby, the aim was that a student could feel creative through exploring the prototype's varied and potentially unexpected reactions and suggestions. Positive emotions were supported via the prototype's positive but logical responses (e.g., potentially allowing emotional contagion), and the potential to build trust via humor.

Displayer. The basic idea of this prototype was to continually display what a teacher says during a class. A headset microphone was used to capture the teacher's words. Keywords (nouns) were then displayed, along with an image visualizing them. Images were downloaded via Google, either on the fly, or before class for speed. Images and words to display could be shown on any screen, either a monitor used by a single student, or a large screen for a class. The inspiration for this idea came from the science-fiction movie, Blade Runner[6], in which a detective used voice commands to enhance and manipulate an image to find an escaped android. The closest tool currently to our prototype might be an intelligent speaker like Amazon Alexa[7] or Google Nest[8]–although, to use them, a teacher would constantly have to ask the device to show images, which would not

---

[3] https://opencv.org/.

[4] https://cmusphinx.github.io/.

[5] https://docs.ros.org/.

[6] https://en.wikipedia.org/wiki/Blade_Runner.

[7] https://en.wikipedia.org/wiki/Amazon_Alexa.

[8] https://en.wikipedia.org/wiki/Google_Nest_(smart_speakers).

Table 1. Playful behavior from users and the Questioner.

User action	Agent response
Clicking the agent's eyes	"Hey, that's my eyes!", "Ouch, stop clicking my eyes", "My eyes are very sensitive you know", "Help, help!", "The paiiiin, the paiiiin"
Clicking the agent's face	"Stop slapping me!", "Didn't your mother teach you that it's not nice to touch people's faces", "Are you looking for something to do?", "Oh, that actually felt kind of good"
Waiting after answering	"Good question, eh?", "Do you see why that is the answer?", "Nice weather, huh?"
Calling the agent "cool" or "handsome"	"Thank you!"
Moving face in front of agent	The agent's eyes moved to try to look at the person's face

work for a class. Internally, the prototype was built using speech recognition via CMU PocketSphinx, on top of ROS, in conjunction with web-scraping python code, and OpenCV to display results. Thus, the main goal of this prototype was to make teaching easier by not requiring the production of slides, but the prototype also allows students to freely choose if they want to "see" what is being talked about, and engages via the saliency of the moving display.

The aim was that playful learning could result from the novelty of the prototype, as well as imperfect performance from speech recognition and image searches that might yield odd or humorous results (for example, showing an action figure or power converter instead of a machine learning technique for "Transformer"). Creativity could result from such playfulness by facilitating visualization and providing unexpected stimuli; positive emotions like enjoyment could be supported by the game-like feeling and humor.

Waver. The basic idea of this prototype was to encourage students to wave to decide between two options for how to proceed in a class: for example, if they would like to hear more about a topic, yes or no. The teacher pressed keys to "initialize" the system and quantify the class's response. Internally, the prototype recognized waving via "background subtraction", where it compares the classroom scene before waving and during waving, and finds the sum of the differences in intensities. One potential alternative could be to detect motions via color tracking; the proposed approach however avoids potential problems with colored clothing or backgrounds, or requirements for physical props that students or teachers might have to remember to bring. Although the main goal was to engage students, the prototype could also allow more freedom and ease (a single student can exert a stronger influence over the class than when hands are counted, and not require a teacher to make an assessment themselves).

We expected that playful learning could result from the novelty and physical nature of the prototype, as well as the possibility that students might seek to perform exaggerated motions to compete or outbid one another. Creativity could be supported by new experiences and the physical exercise (better thinking), and enjoyment from the exercise and humor that emerges.

3.1 Lessons Learned

The three prototypes were trialled over three years, mainly in an engineering course called "Design of Embedded and Intelligent Systems", offered to second year master's students at our university in southern Sweden. The prototypes were further reported on and discussed in various workshops, involving over a hundred teachers from universities in southern Sweden. Due to the emergence of COVID-19, work on all three prototypes was temporarily halted, to focus on the large changes required to move from completely campus-based teaching to online teaching; thus, we also provide some thoughts below on how the prototypes could be adapted for post-COVID learning.

Questioner. In 2017, the prototype was brought to the classroom so students could use it in pauses, but we noticed a "Socretian bottleneck" effect in which many students gathered around but few could interact at any given time. In 2018, the prototype was deployed for two weeks at an unnamed but visible location at the university; students were encouraged to search for it, with location-based learning in mind, as well as to give them an opportunity to become familiar with the university. Unfortunately, few students searched for and found the prototype (only one group out of five). In 2019, the prototype was used for three courses (adding "Programming, Data Structures, and Problem-solving" as well as "Artificial Intelligence"). It was co-located with supplemental instruction classes to make it easy for students to find. To encourage regular use, each quiz was set to only appear for a given week. Although not all students experienced the prototype, the changes resulted in somewhat increased usage. To obtain some initial feedback, we sent out a Google form survey, which a few students filled out, as in Table 2. Based on a comment, capital letters were automatically changed to lower case in answers before processing; however, sometimes "close" answers might not be correct, so methods like cosine similarity were deliberately not used. As well, the students that felt the camera seemed suspicious said that they had playfully tried to compliment their teacher in front of the prototype, in the possibility that someone might be listening or watching. (To avoid misunderstandings, the teacher clarified that such functionality would be unethical, and briefly walked them through the code, available publicly on GitHub, so they could see there was no monitoring capabilities.) Some other observations were also made:

- Some students reported playfully "hacking" the accuracy score by repeating questions, despite knowing that the prototype was completely optional for use and had no bearing on their grades. This could be beneficial to help students to learn material through repeated exposure, but could also affect any statistics on response times, where applicable.

- There were social effects: Some students gathered around when the teachers came to turn the prototype on, wanting to see "hidden" features such as logs, etc. Also, groups of students came to use the desktop at the same time, using just one account to see questions. One student mentioned taking photos of the quizzes to share with group members.
- The camera affixed to the monitor had trouble detecting tall students (and on one occasion also froze when pulled, stopping the prototype from tracking faces with its eyes).
- The desktop was heavy, deterring theft, but despite the wheeled lectern it was somewhat irritating to move to different classrooms each time, due to abundant doorway thresholds at our university.
- Some students entered the courses late due to visa problems, and therefore there was always work trying to provide new codes to access the prototype.

Some challenges include the cost in teacher time to prepare quizzes, assuming these do not already exist, and to bring the prototype to the classrooms where it will be used–as well as potential ethical problems with using cameras and microphones and calculating statistics like accuracy scores or average response times. To use the agent in the post-COVID online era, a web interface would be required; challenges would include how to verify that students had cameras and microphones, or that the prototype could yield a playful interaction with various setups.

Table 2. Feedback on the questioner.

Positive characteristics	Suggestions for improvement
Engaging (3) ("A good alternative/help for studying. Helpful for me as I have a hard time keeping my concentration up while Reading." "The human voice of questioner is interesting." "Friendly user interface")	Not enough questions (2) (e.g., "Not having all the questions available. Sometimes you would like to have a session where you could sit down with the stations for more than a couple of minutes.")
Unique	Should be smarter ("The check of answer is not very smart, for example it thinks using capital or not is different.")
	Ethics should be clear ("The camera part of it made it look a bit suspicious, because it was capturing live video.")

Displayer. In 2017, the display screen of a robot "teaching assistant" was used to display concepts, but the screen was small, making it difficult to see well. In 2018, some automatically harvested images were incorporated into course slides. Furthermore, an ability to freeze the dynamic displaying via a key press was added, since a student might not be able to keep up with the display, which could distract rather than help them to know more. Challenges include the speech recognition accuracy, the validity of the image search results (appropriateness of downloaded images), delays from sometimes having to download large files, and licensing of images. To use the prototype post-COVID, a teacher could log in with an extra device onto an online class platform such as Zoom, and adapt the video stream to show the results of the Displayer in one window.

Waver. The first version in 2017 only considered instantaneous motion (in one image frame), thereby potentially missing much of the students' waving. Some students also expressed worry that they might be acting against their peers' interests (which might have also been affected by the fact that the prototype was not anonymous), but noted that they could possibly get used to it. In 2018, motion over a few seconds was calculated, and the response was more enthusiastic: some students waved for both alternatives they were offered (both "yes" and "no"), and asked questions about the underlying algorithm. Challenges included the difficulty of detecting motions from everyone gathered around a camera during workshop demos in small rooms, that small movement of the camera at the wrong time by the teacher could result in large perceived motion, that the teacher is required to press some keys (further automation would be useful), and identifying potential ethical problems with using sensors or detecting student participation. Allowing students more opportunities to select learning topics could also increase a teacher's workload (like in a flipped classroom), and although waving could be democratic (for example, each student could wave for each presentation slide or quiz to indicate that they have understood it), it is unclear if a class should learn at the pace of its slowest member. To avoid seeing people's faces, an overhead camera could be used to detect head motions, or a camera under a desk could record foot movements, although in the latter case occlusions could be problematic. To use the prototype post-COVID, a camera could be set up to view the students in a gallery on an online class platform like Zoom; there, some challenges might be that all students might not be shown in larger classes, and that students often turn off their cameras or claim to not own a working camera (students might also not wish to wave on camera if classes are to be recorded).

4   Conclusion

The current short paper reported on our work-in-progress in designing educational tools that comprise AI:

- We proposed that educational AI designers should explicitly consider creative and emotional processes, for which playful learning could be a useful paradigm.
- We described three playful learning prototypes developed based on our assessment of the literature, and the needs of our teachers and students for freedom,

ease, and engagement in education. Code for the prototypes has also been publicly released[9].

– We described some lessons learned from developing the prototypes, also suggesting future directions for improvement, and adaptation strategies for the post-COVID learning environment.

As we continue to improve the quality of our prototypes and check new possibilities, it is our aim that these ideas could help to stimulate discussion, toward enhancing education experiences.

References

1. Bereczki, E.O., Kárpáti, A.: Teachers' beliefs about creativity and its nurture: a systematic review of the recent research literature. Educ. Res. Rev. **23**, 25–56 (2018)
2. Biggs, J.: Teaching for Quality Learning at University, pp. 165–203, Buckingham: SRhE (1999)
3. Boden, M.A.: AI: Its Nature and Future. Oxford University Press, Oxford (2016)
4. Bouatta, N., Sorger, P., AlQuraishi, M.: Protein structure prediction by AlphaFold2: are attention and symmetries all you need? Acta Crystallogr. Section D Struct. Biol. **77**(8), 982–991 (2021)
5. Challenor, J., Ma, M.: A review of augmented reality applications for history education and heritage visualisation. Multimodal Technol. Interact. **3**(2), 39 (2019)
6. Colton, S., Wiggins, G.A., et al.: Computational creativity: the final frontier? In: ECAI, vol. 12, pp. 21–26. Montpelier (2012)
7. D'Mello, S., Olney, A., Williams, C., Hays, P.: Gaze tutor: a gaze-reactive intelligent tutoring system. Int. J. Hum Comput Stud. **70**(5), 377–398 (2012)
8. Doolittle, P.E.: Understanding cooperative learning through Vygotsky's zone of proximal development. In: Lily National Conference for Excellence in Teaching. ERIC (1995)
9. Jones, M.G., Brader-Araje, L.: The impact of constructivism on education: language, discourse, and meaning. Am. Commun. J. **5**(3), 1–10 (2002)
10. Krathwohl, D.R.: A revision of Bloom's taxonomy: an overview. Theory Pract. **41**(4), 212–218 (2002)
11. Lilienthal, A., Schindler, M.: Conducting dual portable eye-tracking in mathematical creativity research. In: The 41th Conference of the International Group for the Psychology of Mathematics Education, Singapore, 17–22 July 2017, vol. 1, pp. 233–233. PME (2017)
12. Ogan, A., Finkelstein, S., Walker, E., Carlson, R., Cassell, J.: Rudeness and rapport: insults and learning gains in peer tutoring. In: Cerri, S.A., Clancey, W.J., Papadourakis, G., Panourgia, K. (eds.) ITS 2012. LNCS, vol. 7315, pp. 11–21. Springer, Heidelberg (2012). https://doi.org/10.1007/978-3-642-30950-2_2
13. Oppezzo, M., Schwartz, D.L.: Give your ideas some legs: the positive effect of walking on creative thinking. J. Exp. Psychol. Learn. Mem. Cogn. **40**(4), 1142 (2014)
14. Reeve, J.: Teachers as facilitators: what autonomy-supportive teachers do and why their students benefit. Elem. Sch. J. **106**(3), 225–236 (2006)

---

[9] https://github.com/martincooney.

15. Rice, L.: Playful learning. J. Educ. Built Environ. **4**(2), 94–108 (2009)
16. Ryff, C.D., Singer, B.: Psychological well-being: meaning, measurement, and implications for psychotherapy research. Psychother. Psychosom. **65**(1), 14–23 (1996)
17. Shernoff, D.J., Csikszentmihalyi, M., Schneider, B., Shernoff, E.S.: Student engagement in high school classrooms from the perspective of flow theory. In: Applications of Flow in Human Development and Education, pp. 475–494. Springer, Dordrecht (2014). https://doi.org/10.1007/978-94-017-9094-9_24
18. Wahde, M., Virgolin, M.: The five Is: Key principles for interpretable and safe conversational AI (2021)

Sea of Cells: Learn Biology Through Virtual Reality

Ricardo Monteiro[1], Nuno F. Rodrigues[2], João Martinho[1], and Eva Oliveira[1]([⊠])

[1] 2Ai, School of Technology Polytechnic Institute of Cavado and Ave, Barcelos, Portugal
eoliveira@ipca.pt
[2] ALGORITMI Centre/Department of Informatics, University of Minho, Braga, Portugal

Abstract. Driven by the high fidelity and low cost of the latest head-mounted devices reaching the consumer market, Virtual Reality (VR) is a technology upon which rests increased expectations for improving education and training outcomes. The unique capacity of VR to produce experiences with high levels of immersion, presence, and interactivity, opens a series of prospects to improve the learning of declarative, procedural, and practical knowledge through a new modality of educational content. This paper explores some of the most promising opportunities of VR through the development and evaluation of Sea of Cells, an immersive VR interactive experience to enhance the learning of the prokaryotic cell. Methodologies to introduce the VR experience, both inside and outside classes, were also explored by analysing assessments from several Portuguese biology teachers. A test pilot made through video demonstration, shows a promising future for VR in education. Despite the physical limitations of the pilot study, due to Covid, after presenting the project to 7 10th grade Biology teachers, it was concluded that VR might be a relevant and innovative tool for educational settings.

Keywords: Virtual reality · Biology · Education · Cells study

1 Introduction

Education is a complex foundational pillar of a healthy society and, despite the attention and investment it drives, it is never considered complete, leading to a constant quest for improvements in the process of transmitting knowledge more easily, quickly and effectively.

The disruptive technologies brought upon by the digital era provide learners with a rich field of distractions, unfairly competing for the much-needed attention demanded by education systems that many students consider to only provide boring experiences. However, these same distraction technologies also create opportunities for more effective learning methodologies based on digital experiences with an engaging and meaningful power, far beyond current multimedia educational content.

Virtual Reality (VR) is perhaps the most prominent of such technologies due to its unique capacity to create experiences with unprecedented levels of immersion, presence, and interactivity. Combining the latest advances in VR technology offers a realistic

E. Brooks et al. (Eds.): DLI 2021, LNICST 435, pp. 141–155, 2022.
https://doi.org/10.1007/978-3-031-06675-7_11

opportunity to virtually travel to any part of the world, talk to anyone anywhere, and even see what other people see via video chat. Modern VR technologies are also capable of producing unprecedented immersion sensations upon which virtual worlds and scenes can be created to convey embodiment experiences that would be otherwise unreachable. VR proves more and more to be an asset to teach, train and prepare students and professionals in educational contexts such as university and professional scenarios, like the medical world [1, 2].

Traditional education has limitations regarding the representation of complex scientific concepts, even when resorting to multimedia content, like videos, 3D animations, and slideshows. In Biology education, VR has been shown to produce better learning outcomes for cellular structures and microscopic organisms when compared to video and textbook teaching [1]. VR is not a new technology, but its implementation in educational environments studies seems to be more related to performance and usability than the focus on the combination of immersion and teaching methodology to improve knowledge attainment, as highlighted by Jaziar Radianti et al. [3] the systematic review. From 2018, studies using VR as a tool to aid higher education have been increasing, showing a rapidly growing interest in its use in educational settings, certainly driven by the recent improvements in resolution and processing power combined with a sharp price reduction of the VR Head-Mounted Display (HMD) devices.

This work presents the development and evaluation of a pedagogic project aiming to take students of the 10th-grade Biology class on a journey to the cell scale. It seeks to enquire if VR educational experiences implementing proven learning methodologies promote better long-term knowledge retention. This journey takes place in a virtual scenario, where students learn about cells and what they look like from the inside, allowing them to touch, tear apart and see what lies inside the cell.

2   Related Work

A literature review was conducted through searches in scientific databases and an online search engine to identify projects and studies with a similar purpose to our work. Searching in databases like IEEE, PubMed, and ACM, we found a total of 63 studies related to our project, from which we selected 21 to be more relevant and a basis for this project and paper. This chapter highlights, from those 21, the most relevant studies, providing a brief review and critical commentary in relation to our work.

In [1], Onlabs presents a study where a class of 83 undergraduate students from the Department of Primary Education of Patras' university, who were enrolled in "Computers and Education" course, was divided into three cognitively similar groups. Each group knew nothing about the subject and took a test before the experience, after which they were then given learning material in 3 different modalities: watching a video, live presentation, or playing a VR experiment. The groups were retested immediately after being exposed to the content material. The study showed that students who took the VR experience increased 31% on their final score, while students using video and the traditional groups had only 20% and 15%, respectively. This shows the potential of VR technology to combine with traditional methods of teaching, probably because it provides more engaging and immersive experiences to students. In our work we implement a hands-on approach similar to the one adopted in this VR intervention, creating a link between what is expected from the student, what is taught, and what is experienced in practice.

Another study [2] showed that using Da Vinci Surgical Simulator 2019, where students observe an expert surgeon performing surgical procedures, may facilitate the learning of intermediate-level tasks such as basic camera targeting, intermediate energy dissection, energy switching, and advanced suture sponge. In this study, students were asked to identify every step of the expert surgeon before the experience, and after were asked to apply what they had just seen in this VR setting. Although they find that the experience may facilitate the learning of intermediate-level tasks to perform more basic tasks, using this VR context did not prove more or less efficient [2]. For the intermediate-level tasks, at least, this study creates a risk-free learning opportunity. By observing the expert first and then repeating each step with immediate feedback, the students can make mistakes with the notion that they will be corrected and guided by the experience in real-time.

Another study [4] used RobotiX Mentor VR Simulator [4], a training simulator that provides several exercises in the clinical procedures field, used university participants from beginners to advanced university students and practicing professionals. All three groups had to complete tasks controlling a robotic arm via a VR display. They had a checklist to verify if they were completing every task correctly. This study showed the advantages of a VR training curriculum allowing participants to track and monitor their progress, giving them feedback in what areas they made mistakes and what they can improve in the next training session, in a structured and professional manner through five exercises. It was concluded that Robotix Mentor VR Simulator was successful in establishing a benchmark for training in clinical procedures. Even though this study needs to be tested on a larger scale to validate its claims, a teaching method gives feedback to the student after each session, providing a better and direct understanding of the concepts wrongly utilized. This is a learning strategy "Sea of Cells" will also include.

Most of the publications described how VR was important due to its capability of exploring and visualizing concepts not available to the naked eye. LearnDNA [5] was one of the experiments that focused on developing prototypes to help students visualize DNA in a more immersive and realistic way. A total of 20 participants performed a user study in this iteration, out of which 16 were students from Eastfield College. These 16 students also participated in a specialized user study designed to evaluate pre-experiment and post-experiment knowledge. The first students took a written pre-test, then used the Virtual Environment (VE) system. After participating in the experiment, they filled out a survey and took a post-test. The other 4 participants were teachers and therefore did not take the surveys. The subjects that went under the VR experience also answered a survey to help prepare the next prototype. There was not an evaluation on how much they learned but on how much the experience worked efficiently. The students had to build a strand of DNA by placing the right part in the right place. There was a method to count how many times it took them to put the part in the right place for the first time. These results were stored in-game so that, after the experiment, the students could be evaluated. They were graded based on the survey answers they gave [5]. Relating to

"Sea of Cells", we find very important to create a space where the student can fail and try again.

Another work comparing the delivery of the same content through Interactive VR, Non-Interactive VR, or Video, aimed to determine if a more immersive experience would be a better approach to teaching. This study, making use of the "The Body VR, a Journey Inside the Cell", freely available on the Steam repository [6] concluded that not always the most realistic or immersive Virtual Environment (VE) provides the best teaching experience. In other words, the Non-Interactive VR environment proved to be the better of the three tested. Giving the user the 180° of vision to follow what was being described made possible for a better attentive experience, where the user felt more immersed and less distracted. Whereas in the Interactive VR version, the user was free to touch, use and explore more of the world shown, making it harder to sustain attention to the learning content. This study gave important insights to our work, showing how an experience design is more important than what the player can do, and that interaction is not always the best approach for learning purposes as well as the use of VR is more effective than traditional videogames [11].

The VR experience reported in [7] teaches how the cells work in the body by giving the user the point of view of a submarine type transport, allowing him to traverse blood vessels and watch as a narrator describes the function of each visible cell. Once again, it was demonstrated an increased demand for Serious Virtual Reality experiences, supporting the traditional education methods. This argument was also used by [9], where the user ventures inside a cell and touches various cell elements to understand better what each part represents and performs. This study, however, only concluded that the responses to their project were positive and made them look forward to creating even better VR experiences. These studies provide a base for creating a compelling and realistic experience. As [3] points out, realism does not mean that the rendering is as real as possible but might mean that the interaction of each part of the journey experienced in these papers is accurate. Having this type of representation can possibly prove more efficient in an educational setting, regarding the understanding of complex content. Following the conclusions from this study, we aim to create an accurate and artistic representation of the cell to ease the understanding of the organism's behavior.

Beyond the learning contexts, virtual reality has been a special technology used to teleport participants to the micro and the nano space. As examples, the work Noise Aquarium, by Victoria Vesna, recently presented in 2019 at Siggraph, shows vital micro creatures developed with specific 3D scanning techniques in VR environments [7]; and the work Sci-Fi Miners, a virtual reality journey to the nanocluster scale, presented by João Martinho Moura at the European Commission STARTS Science, Technology and Arts event, in 2020, where the author makes a journey to the nanoscale showing reconstructed 3D nano materials observed from advanced microscopy, and presenting simulations of future nanoclusters created at the International Iberian Nanotechnology Laboratory, in VR, on a theatre stage, to a broader audience [8]. Much like the representation of nanoclusters in Sci-Fi Miners and the microorganisms in Noise Aquarium, we focus on creating a VR environment where the student can observe Prokaryotic cells on a microscopic scale. While Sci-Fi Miners presents atoms and their interactions, we point to the cells studied in 10th grade biology class and what constitutes them.

3   Biology 10th Grade Curriculum in Portugal

The main teaching methods in Portugal are very standard. The program is chosen pre-emptively, using a methodology to select a collection of learning material for the students to use. Once the program is developed and revised, teachers may choose their own pedagogic approach. However, the approach is practically the same in every school. PowerPoint presentations and an exercise book accompany the schoolbooks study to help students study at home. The biology program for the 10th grade is divided into 4 units:

a) The first unit approaches the processes of auto and heterotopia in beings of different degrees of complexity;
b) In the second unit, the subject's content puts in perspective the study of vascular systems as evolutive adaptations to the terrestrial field in beings with different levels of organization. The emphasis is placed on function, having the structural aspect referred to as an exemplifying functional solution;
c) The third unit focuses on transforming energy, mainly in utilizing the aerobic and anaerobic processes utilized by living beings. In animals and plants, the structures that allow gas exchange between the external and internal pathways are also studied;
d) On the fourth unit, aspects related to the maintenance of the organisms' internal environment conditions are addressed in the face of fluctuations in the external environment, by studying thermoregulation and osmoregulation in animals' and phytohormones in plants.

This work explores novel content delivery modalities and learning methodologies to the third unit. The traditional teaching methods usually have lab experiments, where the students use microscopes to observe cells and identify its components (Img.1). Some teachers also use the aid of videos where the cells are presented in 3D. Although there are very detailed videos, not every teacher uses them, and the students still cannot see what the cell does and represents.

With this experiment, the aim was to develop a compelling and exciting way to teach, demonstrate and display virtual reality as a tool for enhancing our school's learning methodologies. When learning a new subject or skill, it is important to have a positive attitude towards the taught content—establishing a connection with the presented materials to understand it better and motivate to seek more information about the subject. To this concern, Adrian von Muhlenen and Devon Allcoat depict a comparison case between video, textbook, and VR and how they relate to the student's motivation and want of understanding, concluding that virtual reality provides a better immersive experience in teaching and creating a more incentivizing method to keep the student's focus while learning [10].

Developing this motivational paradigm while learning and making school a more creative and amusing place is one of the main aspects, we are interested in investigating with "Sea of Cells".

4 "Sea of Cells"

In Sea of Cells, the goal is to immerse the students of the 10th grade of a Portuguese Biology class in a guided Virtual experience through an abandoned lab. Led by the imaginary inventor Zacharias Janssen [9], the students trace a series of steps to help the scientist understand where his last lab partner disappeared to, only to discover that students themselves would suffer the same fate. This experiment's primary goal is to take the student to a scale where the microscopic organisms are enormous, comparing to the player, something only achievable through Virtual Reality technology.

4.1 Experience Design

The main goal of this project was to create an immersive environment where the student could focus and stay focused on the taught subjects, and for this purpose, the biology teacher was met with to discuss how to create an entertaining but instructive experience, also to understand all the topics and materials used, and how they were explored in the classroom. The materials provided by the teacher were analysed and lead to the conclusion that the Prokaryotic Cell and the Eukaryotic Cell (Fig. 1) were interesting topics to explore in the experience because they are the basis of understanding how unicellular organism's work. These two cells stay relevant for the study of Biology in the 11th grade as well.

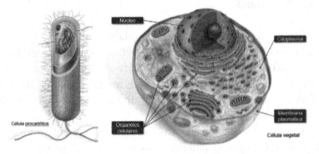

Fig. 1. Prokaryotic and eukaryotic cell. Source: 10th grade teacher material.

From this point, ways to present the cell without making it unrealistic while keeping all its components on display were studied. Starting with the laboratory, the goal was to mimic a biology lab with a satirical twist, a lab where the student could find jars with brains and a blackboard with comical value. The experience focuses on creating a link between the student and the microorganism, presenting them first and then allowing them to dive into the microscale to observe the cell. From interactions with a holographic cell where the student can learn about each part of the cell, the assembly of a microscope is then the bridge between the micro and our world. A space was developed where the student could "walk" freely and explore while still following a storyline, not to feel lost at any moment.

5 Development

5.1 Virtual Environment Considerations

Virtual Reality can be confusing to use the first time if not implemented correctly. When developing any kind of video game there is a need to prepare the player for what he is about to experience. Game design plays a big part in teaching the player how to interact with the world. If the goal is for the player to "jump" in the game, the game must be designed to let the user know what is expected of him. Allowing the player to learn via experimentation is better than telling them exactly what to do [11].

In virtual reality, several things must be considered, the height of the player, the position of objects in the environment, the strength of the lights, and other potentially nausea-inducing elements. There is a need to consider how the users will interact with the world and what can be done to make it easier for them. Virtual reality in an educational context should be clear and straightforward to use.

In the following development points, we point out what was taken into account regarding these game design concerns.

5.2 Virtual Laboratory

Considering the virtual environment design guidelines, the Sea of Cells experience starts outside of the laboratory, in a small room where the student must interact with the doors, providing a basic tutorial for all the VE interactions (Fig. 2). Virtual Reality mimics reality to an extent, so the same laws of physics apply when any force is applied to an object. Therefore, the student controls the speed and pace of the experiment.

Fig. 2. Lab entrance. Source: "Sea of Cells".

Upon entering the lab, the student is presented with the entirety of the space to show the user what could and would be the focus of the experience (Fig. 3). By taking advantage of this point of view, we direct the student to the first step into learning. The lab was created in the Game Engine Unity [12], making use of the Unity asset store, with a few exceptions, as the whiteboard, the prokaryotic cell, the microscope, the desk, the whiteboard pens and eraser, and most interactable items in the experience, that were developed in Autodesk Maya [13]. Each object in the scene has its own texture and reflections made with Unity and Substance Painter [14].

Fig. 3. Inside of the lab. Source: "Sea of Cells".

5.3   Prokaryotic Cell

A first model was developed based on the materials destined to be taught in the 10th grade classes (Fig. 4). Making the connection with the materials, we want to reinforce the teaching methodologies.

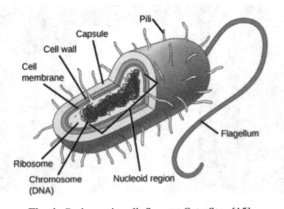

Fig. 4. Prokaryotic cell. Source: OpenStax [15].

A raw low poly mesh with multi-coloured separate sections, represent what each part of the cell contained following the slides provided by the teacher (Fig. 5). Although this corroborates what is explored in class, after consideration and several meetings with the biology teachers, it was determined that this was not optimal. As the goal was to create an immersive and fairly realistic experience, the model seemed out of place, and there was a need to achieve a more detailed model while still maintaining the relevance of each part of the cell. The second iteration of the cell was closer to the desired model, a transparent capsule that showcased its contents while retaining its structure. It was selected a more in-depth version for a more accurate interpretation of how each element behaved with one another (Fig. 5). Finally, it was necessary to create a shader that could provide a more realistic rendering of the cell. Created via Amplify Shader Editor [16], it was developed a texture capable of reflection and transparency, intending to obtain a softer jelly-like feel (Fig. 6) which turned out to be a good way to showcase every part of the cell while keeping a sense of realism.

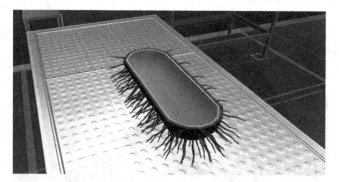

Fig. 5. First prokaryotic model. Source: "Sea of Cells".

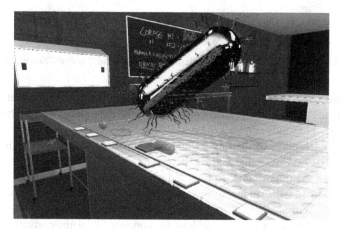

Fig. 6. Final model used in the lab. Source: "Sea of Cells".

5.4   First Interaction with the Cell

The first interaction with the cell must show and distinguish what each piece represents and its purpose. In conversations with the biology team, it was accessed that an interactive but straightforward holographic representation of the cell would be the most efficient form to communicate each element's particularities. To this extent, in one of the laboratory tables, there is a big enticing red button that brings forth the holographic display when pressed, along with several buttons laid out below the main one. Each of these buttons has a small visual display representative of a different part of the cell. When pressed, a voice-over would be heard, relating to a question and a text display in a data pad for the students wanting to read along with the voice-over (Fig. 7).

One of the main goals is to present students to each element before interacting with the cell in the final stage of the experiment.

5.5 Compound Microscope

An extensive and relevant part of biology is the study of cells.

One of the few ways to observe cells in real life is using a compound microscope. Therefore, students from an early age interact with and learn about this instrument, and students in high school must know and identify each part of the microscope.

Fig. 7. Holographic representation, buttons and data pad. Source: "Sea of Cells".

Our meetings with the biology team concluded that it would be an interesting way to allow a hands-on learning experience to explore and manipulate inexpensively. Using Maya software [12] and following the design provided in the materials provided by our expert team, each piece of the microscope was modelled separately to allow then an assembly by the students while in the experience (Fig. 8).

A layout of the microscope is presented to the student. Guided by the instructions of Zacharias Janssen, the student must search for every part of the microscope scattered around the lab. With the help of an image and the witty remarks made by Janssen, the student learns where each part fits and how to pronounce its name correctly.

The purpose of this puzzle is to include a type of learning content much different from the cell, in this case, procedural knowledge about how to mount an artificial device. Moreover, the microscope challenge also explores different pedagogical methods, including game-based and behavioural learning, with students having to find every part of the microscope in order to advance to the next and final part of the experience in a fun learning environment. The expectation is that this way of learning enhances memorization of each piece's name and function.

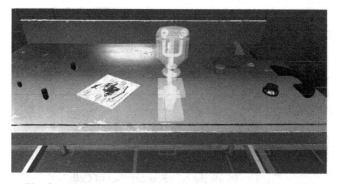

Fig. 8. Microscope layout and pieces. Source: "Sea of Cells".

5.6   Tele-Transportation to the Scale of the Cell

As the main goal of this project was to take the user to the micro-scale, a mechanic was developed to teleport the user to a new area where they can see the cell swimming around them (Fig. 9). A visual effect is triggered by a weary sound effect, giving the students a warning that something is happening around them. After a few seconds, the students are surrounded by prokaryotic cells traversing around them. At this point, the VR experience reaches its climax, having taken the student to the point of view of the cells, where they are enormous, and we are small (Fig. 10).

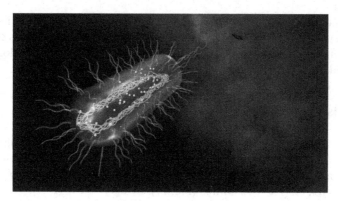

Fig. 9. Sea of cells climax. Source: "Sea of Cells".

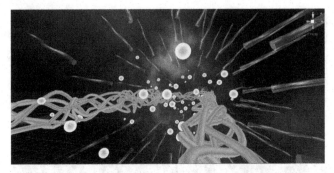

Fig. 10. Inside the cell. Source: "Sea of Cells".

6 Pilot Study

Due to the global pandemic, we could not perform the desired study with the 10th grade class. Instead, we opted to create a demonstration to help assess what other biology teachers thought about the VR experience and what needs to be improved. A meeting was held with six teachers that had never seen the experience. The first author of the paper performed a demonstration of the entire experience, encouraging teachers to ask questions about the VE and how to move and work with it. After presenting the project and its purpose, the teachers were asked to answer a survey to classify the experience, how much they enjoyed it, suggest changes, and point any problems with the devised intervention.

It was interesting to note that none of the teachers had ever used a VR headset, but they felt they would like to use them in class to complement their school's curriculum after the demo. It was also noticed a disconnection with the newer technologies. Most teachers said they do not use many forms of the new media in their classes.

7 Results

The study was conducted with seven 10th grade female biology teachers, with ages ranging from 37 to 60. When asked if the teachers had ever used Virtual Reality technology before, in class or elsewhere, only 1(14.3%) said yes, while the remaining 6 said they had never used it (85.7%) as shown in (Fig. 11).

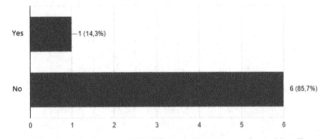

Fig. 11. Question about use of VR. Source: Survey conducted in pilot study.

On a scale of 1 to 5 (1 being very little and 5 being very much), when asked if VR shows a promising approach as a tool to help teachers explain complex topics in class, all seven teachers (100%) agreed that this technology as the potential to be very useful in an educational setting (Fig. 12).

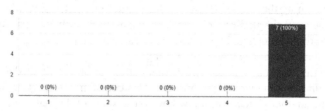

Fig. 12. Question about the relevance of VR in classes. Source: Survey conducted in the pilot study.

The survey also asked about the main mechanics in the VR experience. When asked about the final moment, the teleportation, six of the teachers (85.7%) said they could see it clearly happening, while one of the teachers found it hard to follow (14.3%) (Fig. 13).

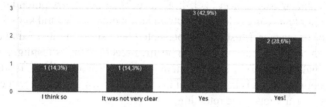

Fig. 13. Question about the teleportation. Source: Survey conducted in the pilot study.

There was a concern in asking about the accuracy of the representation of the cell in the experience. The teachers gave positive feedback about the rendering but alerted us to the importance of defining what prokaryotic cell we were presenting, as these can have many variations. Regarding the storyline and how the student is guided in the experience, when asked if it can be helpful to better prepare the student to understand complex topics: from 1 to 5 (1 being the worst and 5 being the best), one of the teachers (14.3%) answered 4, and the remaining 6 (85.7%) answered 5. (Fig. 14).

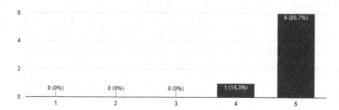

Fig. 14. Can VR prepare the student. Source: Survey conducted in pilot stud.

8 Discussion

Although the answers given by the biology teachers were mainly positive, there is still much work to be done regarding the presentation of the cell and how to better link this VR experience with the teaching methods used in class. The survey shows valuable feedback concerning the use of VR in an educational setting and gives the impression that the teachers would gladly implement this technology in their curriculum. This is a first pilot study that depicts the interest in the use but cannot ascertain how well this project would do in an actual classroom setting.

We found that only one teacher uses 3D animations or other animated technology to explain the dynamic of cells to their students. This corroborates A. Mesquita et.al [17] findings, that even though teachers know how to use some of the newer technologies as tools, most of them stay inside the curriculum and present its content more traditionally. Overall, the pilot study points to a favourable outcome for the application of this project in an educational environment.

9 Conclusions and Future Work

There is a growing interest in VR as a teaching tool, as shown by the systematic review conducted by Jaziar Radianti et al. [3]. This technology shows potential in creating worlds where students can explore subjects and train their procedural knowledge guided by a professor or teacher. Most studies presented here show an interesting approach to the application of VR in education, with positive feedback in its testing. Despite these studies and what appears to be a good outcome using Virtual Reality, it is still needed to create a link between what is being taught in classes and what is taught in the experience for better long-term knowledge retention.

This project was well accepted by the biology teachers that participated in the conducted survey, showing promising results to improve the effectiveness of the understanding of complex topics in biology education. The project was not tested as planned, due to the global pandemic and as such, this study could not ascertain if the VR experience was well implemented as a tool, but rather if the subject and how it was approached, was relevant in an educational setting. Taking the student to a different scale, while showing what cells are made of, shows a promising dive in creating a link between teaching methods and gamification, as also shown in [10] through the use of "The body VR" [6]. Following the answers given in the survey, all teachers agreed that VR might be a relevant tool to adopt in class to approach more demanding subjects.

We look forward to testing this project in 2021 with the students of the 10th grade class, hoping that this VR experience could be an advantage to shed light on the research questions we set to answer. Future work includes a broader coverage of the 10th grade biology curriculum and the assessment of different pedagogical methodologies efficiency in VR to improve long-term knowledge retention and create better learning experiences.

References

1. Paxinou, E., Panagiotakopoulos, C.T., Karatrantou, A., Kalles, D., Sgourou, A.: Implementation and evaluation of a three-dimensional virtual reality biology lab versus conventional

didactic practices in lab experimenting with the photonic microscope. Biochem. Mol. Biol. Educ. **48**(1), 21–27 (2020). https://doi.org/10.1002/bmb.21307

2. Chiu, H.Y., et al.: The role of active engagement of peer observation in the acquisition of surgical skills in virtual reality tasks for novices. J. Surg. Educ. **76**(6), 1655–1662 (2019). https://doi.org/10.1016/j.jsurg.2019.05.004

3. Radianti, J., Majchrzak, T.A., Fromm, J., Wohlgenannt, I.: A systematic review of immersive virtual reality applications for higher education: design elements, lessons learned, and research agenda. Comput. Educ. **147**, 103778 (2020). https://doi.org/10.1016/j.compedu.2019.103778

4. RobotiX Mentor, Simbionix. https://simbionix.com/simulators/robotix-mentor/. Accessed 18 Mar 2021

5. Sharma, L., Prabhakaran, B., Jin, R., Gans, M.: LearnDNA: An interactive VR application for learning DNA structure. In: ACM International Conference Proceeding Series, pp. 80–87, April 2018. https://doi.org/10.1145/3191801.3191810

6. The Body VR, Journey Inside a Cell. http://thebodyvr.com/journey-inside-a-cell/. Accessed 09 Feb 2021

7. Vesna, V., et al.: Noise Aquarium. In: ACM SIGGRAPH 2019 Art Gallery, SIGGRAPH 2019, pp. 1–2, July 2019. https://doi.org/10.1145/3306211.3324024

8. Moura, J.M., Kolen'ko, Y.: Sci-fi Miners: a virtual reality journey to the nanocluster scale. In: ACM International Conference Proceeding Series, pp. 1–10, October 2019. https://doi.org/10.1145/3359852.3359912

9. Davidson, M.W.: Pioneers in optics: Zacharias Janssen and Johannes Kepler. Micros. Today **17**(6), 44–47 (2009). https://doi.org/10.1017/s1551929509991052

10. Allcoat, D., von Mühlenen, A.: Learning in virtual reality: effects on performance, emotion and engagement. Res. Learn. Technol. **26** (2018). https://doi.org/10.25304/rlt.v26.2140

11. Andersen, E., et al.: The impact of tutorials on games of varying complexity. In: Conference on Human Factors in Computing Systems - Proceedings, pp. 59–68 (2012). https://doi.org/10.1145/2207676.2207687

12. Plataforma de desenvolvimento em tempo real do Unity, 3D, 2D VR e Engine AR. https://unity.com/pt. Accessed 05 Mar 2021

13. Maya Software, Computer Animation & Modeling Software, Autodesk. https://www.autodesk.com/products/maya/overview?term=1-YEAR&support=null. Accessed 05 Mar 2021

14. Substance Painter, Substance 3D. https://www.substance3d.com/products/substance-painter/. Accessed 05 Mar 2021

15. 4.2 Prokaryotic Cells – Biology, OpenStax. https://openstax.org/books/biology/pages/4-2-prokaryotic-cells. Accessed 05 Mar 2021

16. Amplify Creations, Amplify Creations » Amplify Shader Editor. http://amplify.pt/unity/amplify-shader-editor/. Accessed 04 Mar 2021

17. Mesquita, A., Peres, P., Moreira, F.: The use of technology in Portuguese higher education: building bridges between teachers and students. In: Rocha, Á., Adeli, H., Reis, L.P., Costanzo, S. (eds.) WorldCIST'18 2018. AISC, vol. 746, pp. 1327–1336. Springer, Cham (2018). https://doi.org/10.1007/978-3-319-77712-2_127

Exploring the Learning Potentials of Augmented Reality Through Speculative Design

Sara Paasch Knudsen(✉) , Helene Husted Hansen , and Rikke Ørngreen

Aalborg University, A.C. Meyers Vænge 15, 2450 Copenhagen, Denmark
{Spk,helenehh,Rior}@hum.aau.dk

Abstract. A state-of-the-art literature review pointed to the need for further investigation of augmented reality to broaden the understanding of the learning potentials of augmented reality. This paper presents an empirical study intended to bring insights into the learning potentials of augmented reality regarding both formal and informal learning using a speculative design process in online workshops with students from a K1–12 teacher education program. The empirical investigation consisted of five online workshops with a duration of 2.5 h and three to six participants per workshop. The theoretical frame of the study was speculative design workshop and John Dewey's theories. The paper explored two research questions: What are the learning potentials of augmented reality when explored by students from a K1–12 teacher education program using speculative design? Why and when is it relevant to explore the learning potentials of augmented reality, in such a way and how can it be done? The findings show that the learning potentials of augmented reality span different categories, such as supporting praxis, bridging the physical and virtual, use of different modalities and activities, supporting social practice, and extending communication e.g. across locations. Our findings further indicate that although speculating on the learning potentials of augmented reality is difficult, it can offer some insights that inform both the current state of a situation or topic and direct future inquiries in the field. However, the user's input does not always bring innovative insights and tends to be dependent on their existing knowledge and attitudes.

Keywords: Augmented reality · Speculative design · Immersive learning

1 Introduction

In the article "Augmented Reality and Virtual Reality in Education. Myth or Reality?," Elmqaddem (2019) argued that augmented reality (AR) has the potential to create change in the form of new teaching and learning methods. According to Garzon et al. (2019) regarding the systematic review of AR in educational settings, researchers should continue to conduct more studies on the inclusion of AR systems in teaching-learning processes. This empirical study materialized to address the clear need for knowledge about the learning potentials of AR, not only in connection with a specific technology but also to inform and guide the development of new technology using AR in learning situations. The research took its point of departure in a speculative design workshop

E. Brooks et al. (Eds.): DLI 2021, LNICST 435, pp. 156–163, 2022.
https://doi.org/10.1007/978-3-031-06675-7_12

(e.g., Auger 2013; Dunne and Raby 2013) in an online format using design tools such as storyboards to investigate and speculate about the learning potentials of AR.

Workshops can function as a research method that allows participants to acquire capabilities in and develop their own practice about that phenomena, as well as enable researchers to investigate the phenomena in question (Ørngreen and Levinsen 2017). In this study, the objective was to engage the participants, students from a K1–12 teacher education program (K1–12 students), in the process of speculating on the use of AR in educational settings for both formal and informal learning. Part of the K1–12 teacher education program is to acquire technological understanding in general and knowledge about the use of new technologies, such as AR. The K1–12 students were a relevant choice as participants because they are used to and able to think about learning situations and develop existing practices, and they could potentially become users of AR in an educational setting in the future. The project had a dual purpose: to investigate the learning potentials of AR in a broad formal/informal setting and to explore speculative design as a method where the participating K1–12 students could gain insight and knowledge on the use of AR in learning situations. This paper focuses on the use of innovative methods when exploring the learning potentials of AR. The aim of the study was to investigate the learning potentials of AR through a series of speculative design workshops that, through the use of reflective, dialogical and explorative design tools, such as storyboards, would engage the participants in a pragmatic exploration-based process. Two research questions guided this aim: What are the learning potentials of AR when explored by students from a K1–12 teacher education program using speculative design? Why and when is it relevant to explore the learning potentials of AR, in such a way and how can it be done?

Below, we provide information about the research design, which includes the definition of AR used in the project, brief theoretical insights, and a presentation of the data (Sects. 2.1, 2.2 and 2.3). These are followed by an analysis of the workshop data, including findings on the learning potentials of AR (Sects. 3 and 4). The paper ends with a discussion and conclusion (in Sects. 5 and 6), where the findings are discussed in relation to the second research question.

2   Research Design

The investigation had a participatory and design-oriented perspective, and the project's knowledge approach stemmed from pragmatism with an overall abductive approach through the research process. Due to the futuristic perspective of wanting to investigate and speculate about the learning potentials of AR, the research design took point of departure in a speculative design workshop (e.g., Auger 2013; Dunne and Raby 2013).

2.1   Definition of Augmented Reality

AR has its origin in 1957, when Morten Heilig invented the machine Sensorama, which was the first example of an immersive and multisensory experience (Sünger and Çankaya 2019). The machine used colors, scents, fans, sound, and a movable chair to create an immersive experience. In 1966, Ivan Sutherland and Bob Sproull created the first head-mounted display, which, despite its limitations, could show the user a virtual layer of information on top of reality. Despite earlier inventions, it was not until 1992 that the concept of AR emerged, and it is attributed to Thomas Caudell and David Mizell at Boeing Company (Sünger and Çankaya 2019). In this period, AR moved from being multisensory to becoming a concept that describes how virtual information is layered on top of reality. The definition of AR used in this project was inspired both by the literature review and Wikipedia - in particular, the definition applied in the Concise Fintech Compendium by Patrick Scheuffel (2017) - expanded with the understanding of AR found in the immersive and multisensory experience that Morton Heilig created with the machine sensorama in 1957 (further described in Sünger and Çankaya 2019). The definition of AR used in this study is as follows:

Augmented reality is an interactive experience of the real and/or augmented world, where the experience of objects found in the real and/or augmented world is enhanced through augmented sensory stimuli. It can be across several sensory modalities, including visual, auditory (sound), haptic (feeling that one is touching or being touched) and somatosensory (experience of touch, pain, temperature, vibration), taste, and smell.

2.2 Speculative Design

According to Mitrović (2015), design has primarily been regarded as a problem-solving practice and is usually aimed at problems detected by professions such as economics and sociology. However, Dunne and Raby (2013) posited that when faced with complex problems, the designer has to act speculatively. Speculative design is an activity in which imagination or speculation is recognized as knowledge, and in which futuristic and alternative scenarios can convey ideas. Speculative design is about allowing all possible possibilities to be discussed and used to jointly define a preferable future for a given group of people, and not about predicting the future (Dunne and Raby 2013). More insights on speculative design as a method, and how it is used in this project, can be found in the article "Speculative Design as a Method of Inquiry in an Online Workshop Setting" (Hansen et al. 2021).

2.3 Data

The empirical data consisted of various data sources over a four-month period in 2020. A state-of-the-art literature review was conducted first to identify the learning potentials of AR. Then, with the intention of gaining deeper knowledge about learning situations and AR, two in-depth interviews were conducted with experts Lise Dissing Møller, Lector at KP, and Lucas Nygaard, Founder of Hololink. Lastly, five workshops with K1–12 students were held, with the purpose of investigating the use of AR in a learning situation, using a speculative method in an online setting. Each of the five workshops was 2.5 h in duration. The data consisted of audio recordings of the workshop sessions, 20 visual storyboards created by the K1–12 students and their written documentation of five creative exercises during the workshops, and observations and field notes written after the workshop. A thematic analysis of the workshops investigated the learning potentials of AR identified by the K1–12 students and visualized through storyboards.

3 Analysis

The analysis of the learning potentials of AR was based on the exercise materials and 20 storyboards created by the 20 K1–12 students in the online speculative design workshops, as well as transcripts and observation/field notes written after the workshop. In this analysis, a learning situation was understood as the framing of one or more tasks that scaffold the learners to achieve a desired knowledge or goal, and where the framing utilizes the different types of interactions that AR offers. The theoretical concepts developed by John Dewey were then discussed and developed into theoretical points of attention for analyzing AR learning situations such as broad activities, social praxis, context, and materials (as presented and discussed in, among others, Brinkmann 2007; Hickman 2016).
Theoretical points of attention in relation to AR:

- Broad activities - The learning situations with AR should be based on broad activities and tasks that incorporate many characteristics and competencies. They must lead to a real and workable result that gives rise to reflection and choices that can be translated and assessed in practice.
- Social practice - Learning situations with AR should be a joint activity or practice where the successes and failures of the joint activity are experienced as one's own.
- Context - Learning situations with AR should connect learning with the "common context" by incorporating everyday context in the form of home, school, community, and business.
- Materials - Learning situations with AR should include physical and augmented materials in the form of raw materials, loose parts, tools (both existing and the production of tools), and finished products. There must be an opportunity for interaction with the artifacts.

The analysis of the learning potentials of AR consisted of a deductive thematic analysis of the transcripts, storyboards, and exercise documents from the workshops. The first round of analysis searched for learning situations in the written empirical data, as it is in the learning situations that the learning potentials emerge.

The learning situations were then categorized based on the theoretical points of attention presented above and further grouped based on similarities. The second round of the analysis focused on the produced visualization from the participants in the form of storyboards. These were also categorized based on the theoretical points of attention presented above. The themes found in the two categorizations were then compiled into seven exemplary learning situations: "race with various tasks," "bridge to surroundings," "project work using the surroundings/city/context," "augmented teacher," "interaction with augmented materials," "use of geographical context," and "use of historical context." In the in-depth analysis, the theoretical points of attention were used to unfold how AR's learning potentials were expressed as they appeared in the teacher students' imagined learning situations.

As an example, the analysis of the storyboard below pointed to the need for an AR help function as well as indicated how AR can be used to provide information about the surroundings, in this case knowledge about physics principles (Fig. 1).

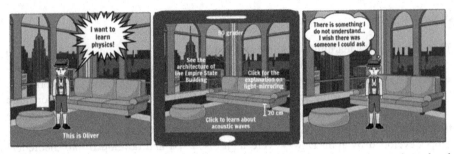

Fig. 1. A storyboard from the workshops (reproduced via www.storyboardthat.com and translated for anonymity)

Analysis of the participants' experience of the workshops showed that some K1–12 students engaged in the speculative process positively, while others were more reluctant. Being innovative in their approach became difficult for the participants due to lack of familiarity with AR and not understanding the technology completely. For example, knowing very little about AR and being critical toward technology in education in general, one participant became quite frustrated by the process but completed the speculative process and, at the end, commented positively on the structure and narrative of the workshop (Hansen et al. 2021).

4   Findings

Analysis of the data from the five speculative design workshops highlighted different categories of learning potentials of AR, which can be utilized in both formal and informal learning situations.

AR can support learning by relating to and supporting praxis

This learning potential is connected to the theoretical points of attention *context and social practice*. AR:

- provides opportunity for trying things out in praxis through a linking of home, school, society, and business.
- allows the learner to place themselves in an augmented context and thereby gain experience with the praxis reflected in that context and learn through praxis in contexts that would not otherwise be accessible due to distance, security issues, or contexts found only in the past.
- supports the learner via a help function in being critically reflective and exploratory.

AR can support learning by bridging the physical and virtual

In connection to the theoretical points of attention *materials and context*, AR:

- bridges the physical and virtual world by placing augmented artifacts in the environment, which adds knowledge to and about the physical context, expanding the interaction potential of the context.

- provides access to the distant and/or historical by creating augmented contexts, which offers the opportunity to explore and interact with the context.

AR can support learning by utilizing different modalities and activities
We associate this learning potential with the theoretical points of attention *context, materials, and broad activities.* In this view, AR can:

- to a greater extent, capture and represent more of life and reality, because placing augmented elements in a context provides increased opportunities and affordances for the use of modalities.
- point to knowledge outside the learning situation, where "online" becomes an extension of "offline," reflecting a greater capacity for facilitation of modalities.
- allow for active use of tools and artifacts.
- be based on "broad activities" that involve a coordination of many factors and combine several learning resources.

AR can support learning by supporting social practice and extending communication
This learning potential is connected to the theoretical points of attention *social practice, context, and materials,* in which AR:

- allows movement between and across locations, out of the classroom and into the immediate community, as AR can be used on mobile handheld devices.
- controls and supports the learning situation when the learning situation takes place in a context other than the school through its help function.
- supports and provides opportunities for social practice and gives learners an experience of being interconnected.
- expands the forms of communication between people due to its expanded ability to use modalities.

The findings do not add innovative insights into the learning potentials of AR; however, the investigation, together with the state-of-the-art literature review, points to a need for further research within the field.

5   Discussion

In the previous section (Sect. 2.2) the first research question was addressed. This section addresses the second research question: Why and when is it relevant to explore the learning potentials of AR in such a way and how can it be done?

In 2019, AR disappeared from Gartner's hype cycle of emerging technologies (Gartner 2019), and the author commented that "while continuing to be an important technology, Augmented Reality is rapidly approaching a much more mature state, which moves it off the emerging technology class of innovation profiles" (Skarredghost 2019). Gartners also predicted that "by 2021, at least one-third of enterprises will have deployed a multiexperience development platform to support mobile, web, conversational and augmented reality development" (Gartner, p. 4, 2020). It becomes important and relevant to continue to explore the learning potentials of AR if the insights on the development of AR are combined with the need for more research on the use of AR in educational settings (Garzon et al. 2019) and the potential that AR has to create change in the form of new teaching and learning methods (Elmqaddem 2019). More studies are needed to demonstrate the effectiveness of the inclusion of AR systems in teaching–learning processes, according to Garzon (2019). Elmqaddem (p. 235, 2019) indicated that an "effective adaption of AR and VR in education and learning will not happen until some technical and social issues are resolved and education programs are more adapted to take full advantage of the potential of these technologies." This points to a need for using innovative approaches such as speculative design when conducting research aimed at informing the development of new technology using AR in educational settings.

This investigation had a participatory and design-oriented perspective that invited K1–12 students to participate in the investigation of the learning potentials of AR in a broad formal/informal setting. The findings from this investigation are not innovative or even new, which points to the fact that even though the K1–12 students were relevant as participants (see Sect. 1), they might not have the capacity to be innovative in the use of AR in educational settings, an exploration that requires continuous critical participation (Spinuzzi 2005). Design methods such as speculative design offer a way of exploring and investigating complex problems (Dunne and Raby 2013) and situations surrounding technology that do not yet exist (Ross 2017); however, the question of who the participants are becomes very important. One way of conducting a speculative design workshop could be with participants spanning different competencies and roles. This can add to the insights, the development of ideas, and perhaps increase the potential for innovation. However, in such a configuration of participants, there is a risk of people with certain knowledge or approaches taking over and dominating the process (Bødker 1998; Spinuzzi 2005; Bødker 2009). Another way is to utilize a longer timeframe so the participants iteratively can develop and expand their own understanding of the technology and the design process. This would allow for a process where the participants can try out and experience different applications of AR technology in educational settings and, based on this experience, further develop their ideas on AR. This approach requires time and resources that are not always available, and not all participants have the same capacity or inclination for creativity.

6   Conclusion

This investigation did not yield innovative new insights on the learning potentials of AR, although features that have not been reported in the state-of-the-art review of current applications were mentioned. Instead, it points to important considerations when using innovative methods in the investigation of the learning potentials of AR. Timeframe as well as choice of participants become essential considerations when choosing such an approach, as it was found that the user's input does not necessarily bring innovative insights, being dependent on their existing knowledge and attitudes. The literature highlights the need for further research in the field of using AR in educational settings, and the technological development of AR is progressing. This supports the need for innovative approaches to explore the learning potentials of AR and to inform and guide the development of new technology using AR in learning situations as well as conducting more research on these topics.

References

Auger, J.: Speculative design: crafting the speculation. Digit. Creativity **24**(1), 11–35 (2013). https://doi.org/10.1080/14626268.2013.767276

Brinkmann, S.: John Dewey. En introduktion, Hans Reitzels Forlag, København (2007)

Bødker, M.: Performative artefacts: users "speaking through" artefacts in collaborative design. In: Proceedings of the 21st Annual Conference of the Australian Computer-Human Interaction Special Interest Group: Design: Open 24/7 (OZCHI 2009). Association for Computing Machinery, New York, pp. 17–24 (2009)

Bødker, S.: Understanding representation in design. Hum. Comput. Interact. **13**(2), 107–125 (1998)

Dunne, A., Raby, F.: Speculative Everything: Design, Fiction, and Social Dreaming. MIT Press, Boston (2013)

Elmqaddem, N.: Augmented reality and virtual reality in education. Myth or reality? Int. J. Emerg. Technol. Learn. (iJET) **14**(03), 234–242 (2019)

Gartner E-book: Top 10 Strategic Technology Trends for 2020 (2020). https://emtemp.gcom.cloud/ngw/globalassets/en/publications/documents/top-tech-trends-2020-ebook.pdf. Cearly, D.W. (ed.) Gartner. Accessed 02 Sep 2021

Gartner Hype Cycle for Emerging Technologies 2019 (2019). https://www.gartner.com/smarterwithgartner/5-trends-appear-on-the-gartner-hype-cycle-for-emerging-technologies-2019. Panetta, K. (ed.) Gartner. Accessed 17 Nov 2021

Garzón, J., Pavón, J., Baldiris, S.: Systematic review and meta-analysis of augmented reality in educational settings. Virtual Reality **23**(4), 447–459 (2019). https://doi.org/10.1007/s10055-019-00379-9

Hansen, H., Knudsen, S., Ørngreen, R.: Speculative design as a method of inquiry in an online workshop setting. In: European Conference on e-Learning, ECEL 2021, pp. 218–226 (2021)

Hickman, L.A.: Educational occupations and classroom technology. Eur. J. Pragmatism Am. Philos. **VIII-1**, 1–14 (2016)

Mitrović, I.: An introduction to speculative design practice. In: Mitrović, I., Golub, M., Šuran, O. (eds.) An Introduction to Speculative Design - Eutropia, a Case Study Practice, Croatian Designers Association Department for Visual Communications Design, Arts Academy, University of Split, pp. 8–23 (2015)

Ross, J.: Speculative method in digital education research. Learn. Media Technol. **42**(2), 214–229 (2017)

Scheuffel, P.: The Concise Fintech Compendium. University of Applied Sciences and Arts Western Switzerland, Schweiz (2017)

Skarredghost, A., Antony, V.: Augmented reality is reaching a mature state according to Gartner (2019). https://skarredghost.com/2019/09/04/augmented-reality-mature-gartner/. Accessed 02 Sep 2021

Spinuzzi, C.: The methodology of participatory design. Tech. Commun. **52**(2), 163–74 (2005)

Sünger, I., Çankaya, S.: Augmented reality: historical development and area of usage. J. Edu. Technol. Online Learn. **2**(3), 118–133 (2019)

Ørngreen, R., Levinsen, K.T.: Workshops as a Research Methodology. Electron. J. E-Learn. **15**(1), 70–81 (2017)

Visual Expression in 3D Narrative Animation

Yutong Shi

University College London, London WC1E 6BT, UK
yutong.shi@ucl.ac.uk

Abstract. According to previous literature references, a large number of researches have been conducted on the expression in animation. However, there is less repetition of attention to visual expression and less literature for animators' operation guidelines in certain types of animation. Therefore, this essay critically explores the impact of specific elements on the visual expression of 3D narrative animation, mainly including the following aspects: characters, the scene, the cinematography and post processing. In addition, A 3D animation called *TeleRadio* has been designing at the same time to support this essay from the perspective of an animation designer.

Keywords: Visual expression · Character · Animation

1 Introduction

The concept of expression or the expressiveness is ubiquitous in the arts, but 'few terms are poorly understood' [1]. Visual expression, an abstract concept, is rarely applied to arts accurately and systematically. Traditionally, animation has been one of the most expressive form of the visual arts, the characteristics of 3D animation are generally in line with this agenda [2]. It can help artists express some abstract creative ideas, and its visual expression are unique compared with other film arts. According to previous literature references, a large number of researches have been conducted on the expression in animation. However, there is less repetition of attention to visual expression and less literature for animators' operation guidelines in certain types of animation.

In order to evaluate the visual expression of some specific aspects and elements in 3D narrative animation, the author began to design a narrative animation called *TeleRadio*. In the development process of this project, technician and artist had to merge into one person due to small number of team members, and the author was mainly responsible for the storyline, models and audio design, as well as programming, character animation and FX composition. Consequently, this essay will use the research methods of systematic and literature review to figure out the research issues from the perspective of an animation designer. Therefore, the research question has been put forward: How to improve the visual expression of 3D narrative animation from the specific aspects of the characters, the scene, the cinematography and post processing.

This paper was submitted to fulfill the requirements for the degree Digital Media: Production in University College London, May 29, 2020.

E. Brooks et al. (Eds.): DLI 2021, LNICST 435, pp. 164–176, 2022.
https://doi.org/10.1007/978-3-031-06675-7_13

2 Brief Illustration of Animation 'TeleRadio'[1]

TeleRadio is a fantasy and low-poly style 3D narrative animation (see Fig. 1), developed on Unity3D engine, coordinated by Maya in the designing process of models, materials and textures, then adjusted the details and composed by After Effects and Premiere. The whole animation consists of 31 shots and lasts roughly 4 min. In addition, inspired by the TV robot model made by David Zhang in Sketchfab.com, this unrealistic style and lovely outline inspired me to develop an animation about TV robot and radio robot. The story tells that, in the X-Star, a tv robot tried to help a radio robot, with a broken antenna wire to satisfy her desire to listen to music again. However, the process was difficult and funny. Playing the correct music for the third time, the tv robot was urgently called back to the camp. At the end of the story flow, the tv robot took down his antenna wire and gave it to radio robot. This is a simple story, beginning by accident but ending in warmth.

Fig. 1. Short animation *TeleRadio*

---

3   Character Visual Design

The visual expression of characters in 3D animation is reflected in its vivid expression, personalized movement and the appearance of the characters themselves. Torre [3] proposed several key steps in the process of role development: firstly, a character is modelled – which defines its form – and is then rigged with a skeletal support structure. This form is given a surface, then a colour, finally a texture or material. Atmospheric conditions may be added, such as lights, which can further significantly alter the appearance of the previous layers.

3.1   Modelling

In animation *TeleRadio*, the development of two characters also followed this form. In order to personify the characters, the author designed the TV and the radio as their heads and matched them with robotic bodies. The proportion of the heads was magnified exaggeratively, referring to the Pixar animation, to improve the overall aesthetic of the animation and to make the audience focus on the characters' face (see Fig. 2). After that, the characters were rigged quickly in Mixamo because of the anthropomorphic bodies. Meanwhile, the movements benefited from the motion capture database of Adobe Mixamo and CMU Graphics Lab, which greatly saved creation effort and time.

Fig. 2. Character draft

The design of colour and textures needs to be based on the story plot and the character itself. Of course, it also needs to form a harmonious and consistent aesthetic feeling with the scene art. The tv robot, a male character, uses light green as his main colour and uses dark grey in some necessary line drawing to make the outline more obvious. The radio robot, a female character, uses light pink which is the complementary colour of green to create the feeling of a little, cute and caring girl. Both displays are orange, a bold colour, allowing the audience focus on the vivid facial expression of the characters- after all, the displays are crucial to the plots (see Fig. 3).

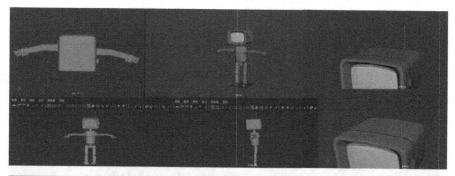

Fig. 3. Modelling and painting of tv robot

3.2 Movement

In addition, movement can add important epistemological dimension to animation – it can give life to the character [3], and audience is therefore able to identify with the world view and the narrative significance of the characters themselves in the animation. Jacobs [4] wrote in his book Framing Pictures: at a specific moment of the development of the storytelling, movement is frozen at a point of heightened meaning, at which the actor's actions are especially capable of expressing the full significance and all the implications of the story. In human experience, we have to admit that language expression through sound alone is more boring than visual expression combining movements and emotions, which is also the main reason why televisions can replace radios. Benefited from Adobe Mixamo and CMU's motion capture database, some of the action animations were suitably complemented at specific moments in the narrative development. For instance, with the relationship warming up, the tv robot performed Michael Jackson's moonwalk while playing the music video of Billie Jean (see Fig. 4), which is the radio robot's favourite song. Movement adds meaning to these abstract plots, increasing or even completely changing our interpretation of the animation [3]. During more than 20 s of camera motion on tv robot's dance, the attitudes of the characters were changed and the plots of the storytelling were subtly advanced.

Fig. 4. Dancing animation of character

3.3 Expression and Emotion

Similarly, more important aspect of supporting the emotions of characters than the movement is the expression on their face [2], and the expressive qualities of artwork are ultimately 'qualities that can be grasped through the emotions they arouse' [1]. As an important part of three-dimensional animation, facial expression animation affects the character and personality performance of animated characters [5]. Each character's external expression of emotions is mainly achieved through physical movements and facial expressions. Through the subtle changes in the character's expression, the audience can measure her emotions, even personality, values, world view and so on. In the *TeleRadio*, both of characters have their own emotional change, which I call flow. For example, the tv robot, from the confusion at the beginning, to the confidence to help the radio robot, to the embarrassment caused by the mistakes, to the joy when he played the right song, to the sadness and helplessness when he had to leave, all these emotions were dynamically pixelated as the 2D animations into the display of his head (see Fig. 5). These are not only designed for the world outlook or the flow of the animation, but also the real reflection of human life.

Fig. 5. Emotional animation design in after effects

As an important part of three-dimensional animation, facial expression animation affects the character and personality performance of animated characters [6]. Each character's external expression of emotions is mainly achieved through physical movements and facial expression. Through the subtle changes in the character's expression, the audience can measure her emotions, even personality, values, world view and so on. In order to show the style of a real television screen, The author added some special effect plug-ins such as TVPixel, Dot Pixels, Bad TV and Glow in After Effect. The final look is more pixelated and grainier, with occasionally shaking to emulate the effect of bad signal.

These 2D expression and effects were designed by AfterEffects, and exported in the form of 2D image sequences. In the process of practice, a more convenient application method of expression animation had been found, which made it easier for designers to make expression move on characters' faces. Rather than applying facial expression animation in Maya, 3DMax and so on, then editing and composing in Unity3D in the traditional process, designers can directly compose 2D animation in Unity3D. This is done by giving the character's face texture a render script in Unity3D:

```
{
    public Texture[] textures;
    public float changeInterval = 0.33F;
    public Renderer rend;

    void Start()
    {
        rend = GetComponent();
    }

    void Update()
    {
        if (textures.Length == 0)
            return;

        int index = Mathf.FloorToInt(Time.time / change-
Interval);
        index = index % textures.Length;
        rend.material.mainTexture = textures[index];
    }
}
```

However, this will lead to the uncontrolled playing time of the characters' facial expression. The actions of animated characters are interactive, and the designers need to accurately arrange the appearance time of each expression of the characters, which often requires the coordination of body movements and words. Therefore, a script to start playing was also added to the facial texture component, and the designer can control the functions of playing and stopping of different 2D expression with one or more buttons.

```
{
        private textureS_TEST Switcher;

    void Start()
    {
        Switcher = GetComponent();
    }

     void Update()
    {
        if (Input .GetKeyUp (KeyCode.Space))
        {
            Switcher.enabled = !Switcher.enabled;
        }
    }
}
```

4 Scene Art Design

Most of the scenes in animation do not exist in the real world and their production depends on the rich imagination of the designer. The animation *TeleRadio* is based on the low poly style (see Fig. 6), which emerged around late 2013 as a specific style [7]. This seeks to highlight the idea that the world can be represented by a composition of shapes, which makes it a self-aware style that is intentionally vague. Hence, in the unrealistic world of X-star, the low poly style is undoubtedly the best choice to achieve the visual expression and easy operation. Thanks to the Unity Assets resource base, after obtaining the license, the author began to consider how to arrange and combine these low-poly models appropriately. In the story, X-star is an unrealistic polar planet. Therefore, snow-capped mountains, crystals and ice rocks were added to the scene. In addition, a large sea was designed outside the characters' acting area to make the scene look less closed and broaden the visual range.

Fig. 6. Low-poly scene and bonfire

All of the above are cool tone, in other words, it will give the audience a cold feeling, but the plots of the story are warm. Consequently, a continuous bonfire was designed in the central area, and the contrast between cold tone and warm tone in the scene is the thematic concept that *TeleRadio* is trying to convey: there is also warmth even in the coldest places.

5 Montage and Cinematography of Animation

Animation is also the same visual art as film. In addition to its own unique artistic expression, it also needs the addition and evolution of cinematography in animation. The cinematography is of great significance for improving visual expression. Some animators only consider composition design rather than cinematographic design, just using plain shots to tell the story, plots or movements, which makes the picture boring. Therefore, in short animation *TeleRadio*, the composition and camera motion were carefully designed and combined together in a rule of montage.

Montage is a major narrative and expression method in movie art. As an artistic technique of connecting the shots and giving new meaning to them, it is also an important way of animation narration. Through the montage method, different scenes and objects of animation shots are connected together to generate different visual expression.

Even though part of the montage theory of traditional films is mature enough and suitable for direct application in the field of animation, the technology of shot switching of animation is completely different form that of traditional films. There is no real shooting scene in the production process of 2D animation. All cameras are put into the virtual scene of animation software as components. In the process of using Unity3D to create 2D animation, the camera movement and the switching between the shots are achieved using C# script. This allows multiple sets of shots to be switched on a timeline:

```
{
    public GameObject Cam1;
    public GameObject Cam2;
    public GameObject Cam3;

    void Start()
    {
        StartCoroutine(TheSequences());
    }

    IEnumerator TheSequences()
    {
        yield return new WaitForSeconds(10);
        Cam2.SetActive(true);
        Cam1.SetActive(false);
        yield return new WaitForSeconds(4);
        Cam3.SetActive(true);
        Cam2.SetActive(false);
    }
}
```

The traditional main shot pattern in Hollywood is composed of 'positioning shot – panoramic shot – medium shot – close shot or close up shot', which is a typical forward montage language. It is usually used at the beginning of a story or narrative passage. The large perspective shot is used to describe the environment or to exaggerate the atmosphere, while a close- up shot is used to describe the process of the characters' action. This is also one of most common opening methods used by animation directors. *TeleRadio* also begins with this theory (see Fig. 7):

Shot 1: distant, describes an empty shot of the polar landscape of X-star;
Shot 2: panorama, the tv robot comes in and sees the radio robot;
Shot 3: close up (insert), describes the expression of tv robot;

Shot 4: close, describes that the radio robot is near the fire;
Shot 5: close up, describes the sad emotion of radio robot;

Fig. 7. Forward montage in *TeleRadio*

Obviously, the main characteristic of forward montage is straight and concise. Meanwhile, many animation directors will use a kind of shot switching mode of reversal shooting cycle for dealing with the scene of two-person conversation. This theory was applied in *TeleRadio* while the robots talked to each other, in which the reversal shot alternate to enrich the visual expression of these shots (see Fig. 8).

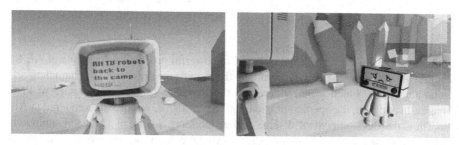

Fig. 8. Reversal shot in conversation scene

6   Post Processing with Diverse Digital Tools

In terms of post-processing of shots and clips, the cooperation of various digital tools has improved visual expression of animation. *TeleRadio* used the Unity Post Processing plug-in to conduct advanced adjustment for image saturation, brightness, hue, shadow as well as depth of field (see Fig. 9), then saved them as LUT for subsequent use and adjustment. In addition, *TeleRadio* used the Unity Recorder plug-in to real-time render each shot of the animation in 4K resolution, then connected with post-processing software such as After Effects (AE) and Premiere (PR), which provided a powerful workflow to create

Fig. 9. Contrast between BEFORE and AFTER

animated videos for a high visual effect. The powerful processing functions of AE for 2D graphic animation helped me complete the high frame rate output of characters' 2D facial animation, which were rendered on the character's face as a sequence of PNG images. In addition, the opening title animation was also developed and rendered in AE.

Thus, the development of diverse digital tools provides a platform for animators to achieve their creative ideas and plays a crucial role in the improvement of visual expression of animation (see Fig. 10).

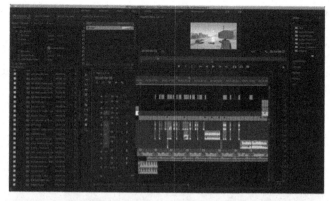

Fig. 10. Diverse digital tools supported the production of *TeleRadio*

7   Conclusion

In this research, the author found that the visual expression of 3D animation requires the coordination of various elements, including but not limited to the visual design of characters, scenes art, cinematography of animation and post processing. As an animator, if the animation is designed from the perspective of visual expression, the quality will be improved. Next, we hope to improve and enhance this animation content in the future work, and actively explore other valuable research topics.

References

1. Robinson, J.: Deeper than Reason: Emotion and its Role in Literature, Music, and Art. Oxford University Press on Demand, Oxford (2007)
2. Power, P.: Animated expressions: expressive style in 3D computer graphic narrative animation. Animation **4**(2), 107–129 (2009)
3. Torre, D.: Cognitive animation theory: a process-based reading of animation and human cognition. Animation **9**(1), 47–64 (2014)
4. Jacobs, S.: Framing Pictures: Film and the Visual Arts: Film and the Visual Arts. Edinburgh University Press, Edinburgh (2011)

5. Butler, M., Joschko, L.: Final fantasy or the incredibles. Animation Stud. **4**(55), 9780429450716-1 (2009)
6. Terzidis, K.: Expressive form: a conceptual approach to computational design. Spon Press, London (2003)
7. Ng, J.: Seeing movement: on motion capture animation and James Cameron's Avatar. Animation **7**(3), 273–286 (2012)

Innovative Designs and Learning

Innovative Designs and Learning

Eva Brooks[1] and Jeanette Sjöberg[2]

[1] Aalborg University, Kroghstræde 3, 9220 Aalborg, Denmark
eb@hum.aau.dk
[2] Halmstad University, Kristian IVs väg 3, 30118 Halmstad, Sweden
jeanette.sjoberg@hh.se

Abstract. In this chapter, contributions from EAI DLI 2021 show that innovative designs and learning can be considered as a bricolage allowing designers and researchers to deploy available strategies and methods to create new approaches and techniques. It further puts forward participatory design perspectives by emphasising innovative designs and learning as social activities opening up for new potential to organise learning environments. The contributions show how this connects exploration to innovative designs and learning by opening to questioning, ideas, and intentions to imagine things differently.

Keywords: Curiosity · Digital game-based learning · Innovative designs · Learning processes · Pedagogy · Programming · Questions and questioning · Virtual environment

1 Introduction

1.1 Scope

Where should innovative designs and learning come from? The contributions in the final part of the EAI DLI 2021 Proceedings elaborate on different ways in which innovation can frame design and learning and, thereby, they are all focusing on innovation but from different angles. A common thread among the contributions relate to their study of the role of prototypes and frameworks for fostering learning through design. In this regard and inspired by the work of Levi-Strauss, Louridas [1] emphasises that design, based on its pragmatic, adaptive, and pluralistic nature of its practice, is a kind of bricolage. Aligned, Yee [2:464] states that research that is based on the concept of bricolage allows researchers to "deploy available and established strategies and methods", and "grant them licence to create new tools and techniques". The author continues by arguing that "multi-perspectival and interdisciplinary characteristics of bricolage lend itself well to the nature of design questions" [2:464]. The contributions also put an emphasis on various moments of interaction and questioning between artefacts and learners/users, hence actively involving them as key stakeholders in the creation of concepts. This builds on a participatory design perspective, where the contributions highlight innovative designs and learning as social activities and as such having potentials to organise new collaborative learning environments [3]. Design has for several years taken the form of participatory design and in Scandinavia, there is a strong tradition of working with design in close collaboration with stakeholders [cf. 4].

The contributions in this part of the proceedings show that participatory design processes constitute fruitful ways to foster exploration by means of different technology and techniques, connecting exploration closely to innovative learning in the form of questioning as acts of making and breaking. Such acts are characterised by being open to existing ideas and a willingness to imagine ways in which things could be done differently (i.e. considering what if) [5].

The first contribution in this section addresses the questions of how to investigate, approach, or act on contemporary challenges in a constantly evolving society. The second contribution focuses on how a pedagogical integration of digital game-based learning (DGBL) can be designed to facilitate learning including a consideration of classroom settings and barriers. The third contribution discusses different kinds of questions and the ways they can be distinguished by their intentions - generic generative questions, consequent questions, and pointed questions. Finally, the fourth contribution targets an understanding of whether students were motivated to learn how to programme and model 3D objects immersed in a virtual environment.

The following text snippets elaborate from each contribution to further assist readership.

2   Perspectives on Innovative Designs and Learning

The paper by Eva Brooks, Susanne Dau, and Staffan Selander, presents three different perspectives on how to approach learning and design in innovative ways. All perspectives address the questions of how to investigate, approach, or act on contemporary challenges in a constant evolving society. The authors argue that this demands for learners' generic and lifelong learning skills. The first perspective introduces an epistemological framing of design and learning across shifting boundaries. Here, the authors discuss a macro level of people's engagement in the world and thus in design and learning processes, where they emphasise the connection between wayfinding and design and point to that learning is embedded in the process and interconnection between entities such as people, artefacts, and spaces. According to the authors, this contributes to creative exploration in wayfinding offering possibilities to capture complexities in learning and design processes. The second perspective focuses on design and play processes including teachers and children engaged in exploratory activities, where sensitivity to material and immaterial resources are central in the interaction between the participants in the study. More specifically, the authors argue that exploration through 'making and breaking' as well as material (prototyping) and immaterial (imagination) interactions have an essential impact on children's innovative design and learning. In addition, the paper underlines the importance of enabling sufficient space for the children's exploration and breaking of boundaries. The third perspective is positioned within a collaborative design framework in educational settings. Here, the authors emphasise context and sequences, framing and fixing points, and choice of material and semiotic resources as essential to express or represent knowledge. In this way, they understand learning as a collaborative and creative process, where sketches and pattern designs contribute to the development of meaning and understanding. Although these three perspectives acknowledge different aspects of innovative design and learning, together they illustrate how different approaches reflect different points of departure for researchers working within the areas of design and play for learning.

3 Pedagogical Integration of Digital Game-Based Learning: Processes Involved

The contribution by Eva Brooks and Jeanette Sjöberg, presents a study of a pedagogical integration of digital game-based learning (DGBL); how it can be designed to facilitate learning including a consideration of classroom settings and barriers. The paper is based on Yrjö Engeström's activity system framework focusing on pedagogical functions and opportunities of DGBL as a teaching method, and the interplay between resistance as an obstruction or as an opportunity. Methodically, the study is based on a qualitative approach, where the authors have investigated two separate workshops including twelve teachers and one toy- and game designer. These workshops were designed to provide a framework for early childhood teachers to evaluate potentials and challenges of DGBL. Based on the outcomes of the study, the authors argue that for teachers to implement DGBL in teaching activities, they need to have knowledge about games to reason about and assess issues of game design mechanics in relation to pedagogy. By learning about games in terms of their design and mechanics, the participants became confident, which according to the outcomes of the study contributed to their interest and motivation to understand how this influenced a game's subject specific value. Hence, the authors further state that the workshop structure functioned as a support of the participants' professional learning through processes of assessing digital games designed for learning.

4 Questions and Appraisal of Curiosity

Questions, not answers, push innovative thinking. This statement constitutes the core of the paper by Melvin Freestone and Jon Mason. The paper discusses different kinds of questions and the ways they can be distinguished by their intentions - generic generative questions, consequent questions, and pointed questions. The authors illustrate this in the form of a three-folded model identifying processes of and circumstances for applying these questions. The authors further emphasise this model as a question-led learning dynamics within a "big ideas" frame of mind, where the three kinds of questions strive towards an action orientation embracing a design orientation, strategic questioning, and tactical questioning respectively. The paper describes questions as an entrance to curiosity, where specific curious relations, which counterpoint related concepts for exploration, for example showing that 'what is it like' questions relate to form, and 'how does it work' questions to function. In this regard, the authors underline that such relations increase complexity within certain kinds of questioning. Furthermore, the paper shows how appraisal of inquiries navigated by curious questions should be articulated by common educational concepts and practices and as such having implications for innovation and creativity.

5 Students' Perceptions Exploring a WebXR Learning Environment

This paper by Bárbra Cleto, Ricardo Carvalho, and Maria Ferreira is based on a case study targeting an understanding of whether students were motivated to learn how to programme and model 3D objects immersed in a virtual environment. The study involved three computer science teachers and 29 first-year students from three different high schools participating in information management and programming courses. The authors assume that immersive web environments can be ideal for schools to explore and investigate potentials of such tools in distance education particularly when it comes to experiential learning. Methodically, the case study is based on a combination of quantitative and qualitative data in the form of questionnaires, video recordings, and field notes. As a framework for the data collection, the authors designed a pedagogical intervention, where the students were challenged to programme their own 3D objects to develop programming skills required by the curriculum. The paper thoroughly describes the intervention and data collection procedures. The authors point to results showing the students' interaction and collaborative learning together with their peers. Despite the fact that the students from the start had high expectations regarding the opportunity to use the immersive web environment for learning about programming, they showed motivation and enjoyment in the activity, which is aligned with related research.

6 Epilogue and Acknowledgements

This final section, Innovative Designs and Learning, presents four contributions to promote readership of each paper presented in the following chapters. In doing so, the authors of the present chapter acknowledge the authors of each contribution, whose original work was presented at the EAI DLI 2021 online conference events on December 2nd, 2021.

References

1. Louridas, P.: Design as bricolage: anthropology meets design thinking. Des. Stud. **20**(6), 517–535 (1999)
2. Yee, J.: Implications for research training and examination for design PhDs. In: Andrews, R., Borg, E., Davis, S. B., Domingo, M., England, J. (eds.), The SAGE Handbook of Digital Dissertations and Theses, pp. 166–184. Routledge (2012).
3. Knutsson, O., Ramberg, R., Selander, S.: Designs for learning and knowledge representations in collaborative settings. In: Brooks, E., Dau, S., Selanders, S. (eds.) Digital Learning and Collaborative Practices. Lessons from Inclusive and Empowering Participation with Emerging Technologies, pp. 12–20. Routledge (2021)

4. Ehn, P.: Scandinavian Design: on participation and skill. In Schuler, D., Namioka, A. (eds.) Participatory Design. Principles and Practices. CRC Press, Taylor & Francis Group. https://doi.org/10.1201/9780203744338
5. Brooks, E.: Designing as play. In: Brooks, E., Dau, S., Selanders, S. (eds.) Digital Learning and Collaborative Practices. Lessons from Inclusive and Empowering Participation with Emerging Technologies, pp. 4–11. Routledge (2021)

Perspectives on Innovative Designs and Learning

Eva Brooks[1]([⊠]) [iD], Susanne Dau[2] [iD], and Staffan Selander[3] [iD]

[1] Aalborg University, Kroghstræde 3, 9220 Aalborg, Denmark
eb@hum.aau.dk
[2] University College North, Mylius Erichsens Vej 137, 9210 Aalborg, Denmark
sud@ucn.dk
[3] Stockholm University, Postbox 7003, 16407 Kista, Sweden
staffan.selander@dsv.su.dk

Abstract. Digitalization has changed ways of learning as well as challenged conditions for creativity in different landscapes of learning. This raises questions about how to approach learning and design in new ways. To address these queries, this conceptual symposium paper presents three perspectives on how innovative designs and learning in analogue and digital activities can promote new metaphors, theories, and methodologies to study these kinds of processes. The first perspective adds a focus on the environment and spaces based on ecological understanding of design and learning with a pivot point on boundaries and people's wayfinding. The second perspective adds a focus on activities with artifacts and people's engagement in creative and playful processes of making and breaking as part of a design and learning process. The third perspective takes the position of collaborative design in educational settings, with a focus on context and sequences, framing and fixing points, and on the choice of material and semiotic resources to express/represent knowledge. Despite differences in these perspectives, they can be used in different educational practices to understand people's engagement in design and learning. The paper shows that differences in perspectives not necessarily represent division or disagreement, but rather exploratory routes that can generate new learning, understanding and resources to approach societal and educational challenges.

Keywords: Innovative designs · Learning · Knowledge representations · Learning ecology · Wayfinding · Play · Exploration · Material interaction

1 Introduction

Digitalization changes people's everyday life, not the least what concerns information seeking, patterns of communication and ways of learning. This change therefore affects and challenges education (and traditional instructional learning) as well as the conditions for creative development in different areas. Given these challenges and the growing complexity of learning and design, there is increased interest from both researchers and practitioners in finding new ways of understanding and fostering people's engagement in learning and design activities. Accordingly, our purpose is to address this issue by

© ICST Institute for Computer Sciences, Social Informatics and Telecommunications Engineering 2022
Published by Springer Nature Switzerland AG 2022. All Rights Reserved
E. Brooks et al. (Eds.): DLI 2021, LNICST 435, pp. 183–194, 2022.
https://doi.org/10.1007/978-3-031-06675-7_14

suggesting three distinct but overlapping perspective of applying and understanding innovative designs and designs for learning, with a focus on (1) conditional framings for learning and design; (2) design as play; and (3) designs for learning. To assemble these three perspectives, we begin with introducing essential conceptualizations of each of them, including an identification of their commonalities. We next elaborate on the three perspectives and propositions illustrating aspects that are likely to elucidate innovative learning and design processes. It is our hope that these clarifications eventually can contribute to identifying opportunities for future work within these three lines of understanding people's engagement in learning and design. A conclusive discussion ends the paper by synthesizing the three perspectives and their propositions of studying, approaching, or acting on contemporary challenges in a continuously changing world.

Importantly, we do not intend to be exhaustive with our explorations, rather the constructs we chose are intended to exemplify possibilities for researchers and practitioners in the field of designs for learning. Implicitly, this is intended to highlight directions for future inquiry.

2 Towards a Turn in Educational Thinking

The above-mentioned changes put a new, overall interest on lifelong learning – in terms of creativity, reflection, collaboration, problem solving, adaptability and communication [1]. In the educational sector, this has been discussed by OECD in term of 21st Century Skills (or Competences) to prepare the younger generations to handle messy problems, uncertainty, and divergent interests. Interesting enough, this also calls for a new interest in Bildung (and *fronesis*), not only in new skills. Play *and* learning are no longer opposites, rather aspects of engagement [2–6]. These are examples of propositions that are issued in the contemporary debate on digitalization, learning and design in educational and design-oriented research and practices. The three perspectives proposed in the present paper put forth such propositions and statement by introducing learning ecologies to understand and analyze complex learning processes. Furthermore, to discuss how creativity and play can act as tools to support practitioner as well as researchers in designing for and researching play experiences. Finally, to elaborate on designs for learning as material and semiotic resources that can be used during the study and performance of different learning sequences. Thus, all three perspectives address the processes of learning and design from an epistemological, to a practical and analytic viewpoint.

2.1 Innovative Designs and Learning

The first perspective describes on a general level the epistemological framing of design and learning across shifting boundaries, characterized by *wayfinding across evolving contextual settings*, blurred boundaries, and ecotones (where people and environment are interrelated). In this section, a learning ecology approach is applied to understand the complexities of design and learning processes related to spaces and places. It is stressed that the understanding of the complexity of learning and design processes are afforded by wayfinding, and people's individual and collective knowledge creation within continuous evolving learning environments. Thus, the frame of an ecological understanding is argued to capture the complexity in design and learning processes at an epistemological level.

The second perspective describes *design as play*. It takes another approach to innovative learning and design framed around the actions of people as designers. This part addresses how design, learning and play are connected processes creating powerful learning opportunities across different areas of development. It is stressed that a design process involves explorative actions and hands-on activities with artefacts. It is also stressed that this is a social process, where not only materiality talks back to the designers but also other people participating in the design process. The idea of *making and breaking* seem to be an essential part in the design process allowing the participant to create, re-design and gain new knowledge through iterative cycles of inquiry.

Finally, the third perspective focus on *designs for learning* and knowledge representations, performative and collaborative learning settings, and virtual cases.

All the three presented perspectives on design and learning offer a way to apply and understand people's engagement in learning and design. Despite the differences between these approaches, they share a mutual understanding of design and learning, which goes beyond the idea of fixed processes and certain steps. Design and learning are seen as situated and complex activities, where people, spaces, places and artefacts are influenced by and affect each other.

3 Epistemological Framing of Design and Learning Across Shifting Boundaries

Emerging technologies and people's use of these technologies are continually under development. These technologies are created to afford people's needs and to meet existing challenges. Many emerging technologies seem to be crossing borders between different professions, e.g., from the leisure industry to educational settings. For instance, games and game principles are developed and redesigned to game-based learning design and virtual reality is changed to accommodate educational purposes. The border crossing of people's use of technologies calls for theoretical perspectives on design, learning and innovation inspired by ecological thinking. Ecological thinking offers a frame for understanding the complexity of design in learning and a frame for design for learning, as it provides an understanding of knowledge creation in a complex and interconnected world where emerging technologies, networks and knowledge modes are under continuous change and development. Learning ecology perspectives contribute to a conceptual frame embracing existing challenges of navigating a technology-rich and continuously developing society. Working from a learning ecology perspective contributes to a language for people's interactions and activities across different environments. The ecological approach accommodates circumstances under which people can gain lifelong learning skills [7]. For instance, Siemens [8:54] stresses that a learning ecology frames the space in which learning occurs in a way where knowledge is shared, co-created, and recreated and in a mode where experimentation and failure are recognized as a part of a learning process. Thus, a learning ecology approach offers a dynamic perspective on learning as ubiquitous, dynamic, and flexible.

3.1 Between Boundaries

Moreover, a learning ecology approach gives researchers an epistemological frame for investigating people's interaction across settings and agencies [7]. From a learning ecology perspective, it is also recognized that boundaries are permeable, blurred, and multiple and that the environment and people mutually influence each other [9]. The concepts of ecotones and ecoclines are in this paper suggested for the conceptualizing of these permeable and blurred boundaries. Ecotones and ecoclines are border zones where there is a rich diversity and emerging of new "species". In these spaces between borders, the concept of species can be understood broadly and metaphorically as both technologies, learning design, people, and other entities. The people's border crossing design and learning processes are here framed by the metaphor of "wayfinding".

Ecotones and ecoclines are concepts derived from biology. Ecotones are characterized as the zones where two ecosystems meet and are in tension. These zones might have vastly different forms. For instance, such zones can be blurry, sharp, or even mixed in different ways [10]. Ecotones are generally defined as ecological transition zones with gradients and diverse vegetation between two relatively but homogeneous ecological communities. However, van der Maarel [11] has stressed a need to distinguish between ecotones and ecoclines. According to van der Maarel [11], the difference is that ecotones represent a stressful zone of coincidence contrary to ecoclines which are characterized to be more stable but still heterogeneous.

3.2 Humans' Wayfinding in Learning and Design

Wayfinding is a concept that has been used in social anthropology, psychology, and geography [12–14]. Golledge [13] represents the psychological understanding and describes it as people's travel or search for different purposes, where environmental knowledge is acquired. Simonsen connects wayfinding to practice, spatiality and embodiment in her approach based on social analysis/human geography: "Active bodies, using their acquired schemes and habits, position their world around themselves and constitute that world as "ready-to-hand", to use Heidegger's [15:107] expression. These are moving bodies "measuring" space in their active construction of a meaningful world. In taking up or inhabiting space, bodies move through it and are affected by the "where" of that movement. It is through this movement that space as well as bodies take shape. Inhabiting space is about "finding our way" and how we come to "feel at home". It, therefore, involves a continuous negotiation between what is familiar and unfamiliar, making space habitable but also receiving new impression" [15:153].

Ingold [12] is working within the field of social anthropology, and he describes wayfinding as the process where: "...people 'feel their way through a world that is itself in motion, continually coming into being through the combined action of human and non-human agencies" [12:155]. The difference between Ingold and Simonsen's understanding of wayfinding is that Ingold acknowledges that wayfinding is a matter of people traversing a fixed environment and the interaction between the human and the environment, e.g., as when peoples are placing their footprint in nature. Ingold´s understanding of wayfinding has been found to accommodate contemporary understandings of learning as wayfinding [16, 17] and learning ecology designs [7]. Learning as wayfinding is here argued to be a metaphor capturing human's knowledge- and identity development here understood as learning. It is not a pre-fixed goal-oriented approach to learning. Instead, it is a process of mapping the learning landscape and finding paths in movements, either physical or mental. It is also a process of interconnections between people and other entities crossing borders and finding their way through new knowledge, understanding and development of oneself or new ideas and knowledge in the ecotones. Sometimes this process might be stressful and flourish in these kinds of ecotones, as in the case in accommodative cognitive processes and when learners are traversing previously gained knowledge. Sometimes the process might be more smoothly but still adding new knowledge, just as in ecoclines and assimilative cognitive processes. An example of how the landscape forms people's journeys is, when people are hiking in the Norwegian mountains, they search for and try to follow the paths of previous peoples walking and might be lost and have to find their way, but sometimes they are supported in their pathfinding by the cains placed by ancestors. This example can be transferred to educational settings, e.g., when students try to find their way and gain new knowledge through experimentation supported by previous learning experiences and knowledge. However, people are often not alone in their learning journey and besides the learning environment supporting their knowledge development, peers, teachers, and artefacts such as books, technologies, and smartphones at hand scaffold learners' journey.

Thus, an ecological approach to learning as wayfinding seems to offer a frame for understanding the process of design in learning and development, as the movement in design processes. These are characterized by abductive processes of research, ideation, sketching and generating design patterns embedded within a particular environmental zone, is stressed to be a process of wayfinding, and thus mapping and mapmaking just as Ingold [12] described it. In this sense, it is argued that the ecological metaphor of learning as wayfinding can deepen our understanding of the learning process and the learners involved [17], particularly with respect to understanding learners as knowledge landscape designers and way finders embedded in contextual settings navigating, mapping and mapmaking ecotones and ecoclines.

The connection between wayfinding and design as learning lies in the process and the interconnections between entities, e.g. people, artefacts, and spaces (mental, physical, and digital). In this way, the creative exploration in wayfinding can be equated with a design process in modern learning activities within the ontological framework of ecological thinking. By extending the understanding of design processes to a frame of ecological understanding of learning as wayfinding, the complexity of learning and design processes are captured, acknowledging the learning trajectories of people's individual and collective mapmaking and thus their knowledge creation across continuously evolving spaces, places, and ecotones.

4   Designing as Play

This section explores another perspective on innovative designs and learning by focusing on design and play situations and processes where educators and children are, or attempt to be, explorative and sensitive to material and immaterial resources when designing and playing together. Design and play can be seen as being at odds with each other, yet they share similarities. On the one hand, both promote curiosity and exploration, which supports interest and acquisition of knowledge. On the other hand, design typically leads to solutions of problems, whereas play is considered as an open-ended asset encouraging imagination. Similarly, designers curiously ask the question "how" in order to get to a desired solution, while playing humans imaginarily ask the question "what if". Still, both questions reflect a wonder about the creation of a possible future.

From a design perspective, Stappers [18] refers to an act of designing as the locus where new ideas become alive when they are confronted with the world. Such confrontations lead to an instantiation of a designed idea in the form of *prototypes*. Zimmerman et al. [19:493] state that this is a way for designers to create "a product that transforms the world from its current state to a preferred state". Sutton-Smith [20], a recognized play researcher, emphasizes the variability of play, where he acknowledges its quirkiness, redundancy, and flexibility. He states that play is not any trivial activity, but a powerful human asset for explorative interactions between people and the environment. This puts forward the concept of play as a somewhat disruptive activity that can foster novel idea generation by processes of *making and breaking* novel and traditional ways of interacting with the world.

In relation to the focus of the present paper, we argue that it is in this contradictory as well as overlapping crossroad between design and play where innovative designs and learning situations can emerge. In addition, we emphasize that such making and breaking processes are pivotal to nurture innovative design and learning. This by reinforcing and enabling us to ask questions of *how* and *what if* to support actions of connecting, decoupling and re-connecting ideas and hypotheses, i.e. making and breaking in prototyping-like activities. As such, both material and immaterial interactions are highlighted. Next, we will unfold designing as playing in terms of exploration through a material lens.

4.1 Exploration Through Making and Breaking

Explorative actions can be sparked by imagination and hands-on doings. In his book, Linnell [21] illustrates how people involved in explorative activities orient themselves in material, sensational and symbolic ways. In this way, the author describes the matter of exploration as a complex and often unexpected chain of expressions. In the design domain. Such expressive processes might be described as emergent, while in the field of play they could be described as social forms of imagination. Vygotsky [22:11] stated that "A child's play is not simply a reproduction of what he has experienced, but a creative reworking of the impressions he has acquired." Understanding exploration in this way means that what a child does is combining prior experiences to create a new concrete situation. This is the essence of imagination. Thus, the significance of exploration has to do with being motivated to follow one's interest and imaginary experimentation with ideas. By opening space for design as play processes, designers and educators must constantly explore the interests, ideas, and motives of children. This would imply that perspectives of children themselves come into play [23], which would have important implications for adult-child relationships. This, in turn, would nurture innovative designs and learning. Design has taken the form of co-design [24]. In the Nordic countries there is a tradition of working with design in close collaboration with stakeholders; participatory design [25].

Participatory design and co-creation are fruitful ways to foster exploration, in particular when mediated by digital and analogue tools connecting exploration closely to acts of making and breaking [26–28]. These kinds of acts correspond to both design and play by proceeding through iterative and imaginative cycles considering the wonder of *what could be* as well as perceived fuzziness [19, 29, 30]. Our previous studies including a combination of analogue (foam clay, LEGO, paper, cardboard boxes, foam bricks) and digital (robotics, Mindstorms, VR and digital games) resources in children's early years' education [26, 27, 31, 32] have shown that this combination promote children to explore boundaries, negotiated strategies to sustain their imaginative exploration. They were increasingly inspired by testing their ideas by making them in, for example clay, LEGO or Mindstorms and then, breaking them apart and trying new things. Thus, we argue that material interactions and *what if* spaces for children to become inspired and experience both contradictions and desired outcomes.

4.2   Material Interaction Through Prototyping

Material properties can help in envisioning innovative designs as well as learning about boundaries of the material itself. *Texture*, on the other hand, can communicate material properties through its material appearance. Attention to *details* can add value to material interaction in terms of their aesthetic quality and offer insights into how they can be used to give form to a design. Focusing on *wholeness* has to do with an overall composition [33]. Considering Wiberg's [33] approach, we claim that prototyping becomes a central anchor when it comes to bringing material interaction to life. Furthermore, acts of prototyping frame ideas and imaginary wonders that are in play, which also force people to discuss, critique and reflect. Prototyping as an activity constitutes an unfinished work and hence open for experimentation and sensing of future situations [34]. In this way, material interaction becomes more than a conversation with the material and more than a representation of concepts or ideas. As such, it extends Schön's [35] statement that materials talk back to designers. We would argue that material interaction through prototyping brings inspiration and sensation, which in turn have an important impact on innovation, design, and learning.

To exemplify, when children in our studies should transform a centicube-model of a house to natural size by means of cardboard boxes, the centicube-model and cardboard boxes provided an in-depth understanding about mathematical concepts as well as of the materials' constraints, possibilities, and textures. The children were concerned about how they should communicate the details of the full-size house of cardboard boxes so that their intended centicube design could be properly understood by the others. This clearly spurred, directed, and inspired their prototyping activity.

To sum up, it was not only the environment and the material resources that offered making and breaking as well as prototyping experiences, but also the way in which the facilitators stood back and enabled sufficient space for the children to explore and to break boundaries. Following the children's ideas and interests meant that the facilitators were not only flexible in their support of the children's actions, but also that they themselves explored possibilities to support the children's experiences in the pursuit of continuous learning. Hence, we emphasize the impact of material (prototyping) and immaterial (imagination) interactions as this, when melded together, contributes to change and diversity. Expressed differently, such interactions have a sustained impact on children's innovative designs and learning.

5   Designs for Learning

The concept of design can be given many different meanings. It is both a verb and a noun, and it can denote a process as well as a product. It could further denote a field of research as well as a theoretic approach or a method that is used for doing research [36]. Design could be understood as a way to construct a prototype for mass production of a specific artefact, but it could also be the very process of investigating a phenomenon anew, and to build up a new theoretic understanding – design (practice) as the prerequisite for theory-building [37].

The traditional idea of design as "giving the thought a form" focused on *form and function*, and on the aesthetics and usability of a product. Contemporary, collaborative and process-oriented perspectives challenge this view, with a focus on *function and meaning* [38].

In designs for learning [39–41], the focus is both on material and semiotic resources, and how these are used during different learning sequences. We cannot "see" learning as such, only the traces of learning and new knowledge in terms of new representation – how the learners are able to show what they have learnt and how they have understood a phenomenon or a field of knowledge [42]. This is also a question of understanding how knowledge can be represented multimodally in different ways, and an understanding of learning as a fundamentally dialogical process (epistemologically as well as ontologically) [43].

To study learning from this point of view is to focus on context and sequences, framing and fixing points, and on the choice of material and semiotic resources to express/represent knowledge. Designs for learning thus also highlight existing "cultures of recognition": i.e. what is "seen as", and "recognized as", learning and knowledge [44]. Representations and representational artefacts can be used to relieve or reinforce cognitive processes, and also to coordinate different information units. This leads us further to the idea of sketching and the construction of new design patterns.

5.1   Sketching

From a design-oriented perspective on learning, as shortly outlined above, learning can only be studied in terms of sign-making and how knowledge has been transformed (or re-designed) into a new representation. Thus, learning can be conceptualized in terms of the (time-based) difference between someone's capability to express things anew, to do new kinds of analysis, to use new techniques or to use established techniques in a new way. A way to study how someone conceptualizes, shows, and finalizes something learnt (or a new idea) is by collecting information from the very process itself, highlighting which elements that have been of most importance, which decisions that have been made, as well as which expressions that are most sufficient for (relevant) others to understand the new idea (or what was learnt) [41].

In shared and collaborative design work, design representations aid to express thoughts and ideas, and there is something shared and inspectable to critique and collaboratively develop further [45]. Moreover, in communication with stakeholders, to communicate and present ideas of future systems and artefacts, their functionality and future use. Hence, the process of creating design representations as well as the results from it serve many complementary purposes.

5.2 Design Patterns

The concept of design pattern as originally introduced by architect Christopher Alexander, consists of a three-part rule, which expresses a relation between a context, a problem, and a solution [46]. In his work on design patterns, Alexander attempted to document collective knowledge about urban design at different scales ranging from regions and cities, to buildings, rooms and even to the detailed level of doorknobs. The idea of using design patterns to share good examples of solutions to recurring problems has been picked up in several and different fields of research and practice, e.g. within the fields of interaction design, technology enhanced learning and education.

When design patterns have been used within the field of interaction design, design patterns as a resource in the design work have proven to work both as a starting point for design by providing examples, as well as an inspiration for the design of certain products or processes. This could also be expressed in terms of going beyond the individual to integrate social networks and digital tools in a networked society [47] which redirects attention from tools to communities.

5.3 Participatory Pattern Design

Participatory pattern design, as rooted in the Scandinavian school of participatory design, views (in this case) teachers as domain experts on teaching, who are invited into a design process of developing a common resource of solutions to teaching problems. Into this process, teachers bring their design problems or solutions having their origin in their own teaching practice. Work and research within participatory design use a range of techniques, methods and practices including different types of workshops, design games, multimodal narratives, and constructions. By interacting and learning in each other's contexts, a mutual understanding between designers and participants is developed. In addition to this, the patterns could improve design performance as well as educate the designer/teacher. Accordingly, this includes not only practical gains of capturing teaching experience in the format of design patterns, but also of the designing of "learning places" (i.e. learning environments that are wanted by teachers and students and constitute a coherent whole) for both teachers and learners.

6 Conclusive Discussion

In this paper, we have presented three overlapping perspectives on how to approach learning and design in innovative ways, but from different points of view. All perspectives address the questions of how to investigate, approach or act on the contemporary challenges in a continuously evolving society with demands for generic and lifelong learning skills. Together, these approaches illustrate how different innovative approaches reflect different ways of departure for researchers working within the fields of design and play as well as design for learning.

The first perspective adds a focus on the environment and spaces based on ecological understanding of design and learning with a pivot point on boundaries and people's wayfinding. The perspective addresses a macro level of people's engagement in the world and thus in design and learning processes. The perspective offers a deepened understanding of learners' learning process in and across spaces and places and in the intersection between.

The second perspective adds a focus on activities with artifacts and people's engagement in creative and playful processes of making and breaking as part of a design and learning process. This perspective expands the first by adding a meso and micro level looking into how concrete playful designs can afford children's and other people's exploration, problems solving and creation of new knowledge.

The third perspective takes the position of collaborative design in educational settings from a meso perspective, with a focus on context and sequences, framing and fixing points, and on the choice of material and semiotic resources to express/represent knowledge. Learning is thus understood as a collaborative, creative process of developing meaning and understanding by way of sketches and pattern designs.

To conclude, we started out by saying that digitalization not only changes ways of learning, but it also challenges conditions for creativity in different landscapes of learning, where a making and creating culture can expand on people's knowledge acquisition. Through the three different perspectives, we illustrated how innovative designs and learning in analogue and digital activities can promote new metaphors, theories, and methodologies to study these kinds of processes. Despite their differences, the three perspectives on design, learning and innovation presented in this paper can be used in different educational practices to understand people's engagement in design and learning. Expressed differently, these perspectives share similarities by moving beyond an understanding of design and learning as fixed processes.

References

1. Epale Homepage, Ten most useful lifelong skills in Learning. EU (2020). Accessed 01 Sep 21. https://epale.ec.europa.eu/en/blog/deset-najkorisnijih-cjelozivotnih-vjestina-u-ucenju
2. Collins, A., Halverson, R.: (2009). Rethinking Education in the Age of Technology. The Digital Revolution and Schooling in America. Teachers College Press, New York (2009)
3. Kress, G., Selander, S., Säljö. R., Wulf, C. (eds.). Learning as Social Practice. Beyond Education as an Individual Enterprise. Routledge, London (2021)
4. Morin, E.: On Complexity. Hampton Press, Cresskill (2008)
5. Selander, S.: Designs for learning and ludic engagement. Digital Creativity **19**(3), 199–208 (2008)
6. Samuelsson, I.P., Carlsson, M.A.: The playing learning child: towards a pedagogy of early childhood. Scand. J. Educ. Res. **52**(6), 623–641 (2008). https://doi.org/10.1080/003138308 02497265

7. Dau, S.: A learning ecology design. In: Brooks, E., Dau, S., Selander, S. (eds.) Digital Learning and Collaborative Practices: Lessons from Inclusive and Empowering Participation with Emerging Technologies, p. 21. Routledge, Milton Park (2021)

8. Siemens, G.: Connectivism: creating a learning ecology in distributed environments. In: Hug, T. (ed.) Didactics of Microlearning, pp. 53–68 (2007)

9. Barron, B.: Learning ecologies for technological fluency: gender and experience differences. J. Educ. Comput. Res. 31(1), 1–36 (2004)

10. Dau, S., Ryberg, T.: Disruptions and disturbance as challenges in a blended learning (BL) environment and the role of embodied habit orientation. In: European Conference on E-Learning, p. 156. Academic Conferences International Limited (2014)

11. van der Maarel, E.: Ecotones and ecolines are different. J. Veg. Sci. 1(1), 135–138 (1990)

12. Ingold, T.: The Perception of the Environment – Essays on Livelihood and Skill. Routledge, Milton Park (2000)

13. Golledge, R.G.: Human wayfinding and cognitive maps. In: Rockman, M., Steele, J. (eds.) The Colonization of Unfamiliar Landscapes, pp. 49–54. Routledge, Milton Park (2003)

14. Simonsen, K.: Practice, spatiality and embodied emotions: an outline of a geography of practice. Hum. Aff. 2, 168–181 (2007)

15. Heidegger, M.: Being and Time. Basil Blackwell, Oxford, Oxford (1988)

16. Dau, S.: Studerendes orientering i fleksible professionsuddannelsers læringsrum: Et narrativt casestudie af vidensudviklingens veje og afveje. Aalborg Universitetsforlag (2015)

17. Woods, C.T., Rudd, J., Robertson, S., Davids, K.: Wayfinding: how ecological perspectives of navigating dynamic environments can enrich our understanding of the learner and the learning process in sport. Sports Med Open 6(1), 1–11 (2020)

18. Stappers, P.J.: Doing design as a part of doing research. In: Michel, R. (ed.) Design research now. Board of International Research in Design, pp. 81–91, (2007). https://doi.org/10.1007/978-3-7643-8472-2_6

19. Zimmerman, J., Forlizzi, J., Evenson. S.: Research through design as a method for interaction design research in HCI In: Proceedings of the SIGGCHI Conferences on Human Factors in Computing Systems, pp. 493–501. ACM (2007). https://doi.org/10.1145/1240624.1240704

20. Sutton-Smith, B.: The Ambiguity of Play. Harvard University Press, Cambridge (1997)

21. Linell, P.: Rethinking Language, Mind and World, Dialogically: Interactional and Contextual Theories of Human Sense-Making, Information Age Publishing, Charlotte (2009)

22. Vygotsky, L.S.: Mind and Society. Harvard University Press, Cambridge (1978)

23. Sommer, D., Pramling Samuelsson, I., Hundeide, K.: Early childhood care and education: a child perspective paradigm. Eur. Early Child. Educ. Res. J. 21(4), 459–475 (2010). https://doi.org/10.1080/1350293X.2013.845436

24. Sanders, N., Stappers, P.J.: Co-creation and the new landscapes of design. Co-design 4(1), 5–18 (2008)

25. Ehn, P.: Scandinavian design: on participation and skills. In: Schuler, D., Namioka, A. (eds.) Participatory Design. Principles and Practices. Routledge, Milton Park (1993). https://doi.org/10.1201/9780203744338

26. Brooks, E., Sjöberg, J.: A designerly approach as a foundation for school children's computational thinking skills while developing digital games. IDC '20: Proceedings of the Interaction Design and Children Conference, 87–95. Association for Computing Machinery (ACM) (2020)

27. Sjöberg, J., Brooks, E.: Problem solving and collaboration when school children develop game designs. In: Brooks, A., Brooks, E.I. (eds.) Interactivity, Game Creation, Design, Learning, and Innovation. ArtsIT 2019/DLI 2019, LNICST (Lecture Notes of the Institute for Computer Sciences, Social Informatics and Telecommunications Engineering), vol. 328, pp. 683–698. Springer, Switzerland (2020). https://doi.org/10.1007/978-3-030-53294-9

28. Catala, A., Sylla, C., Theune, M., Brooks, E., Read, J.C.: Rethinking children's co-creation processes beyond the design of TUIs. In: IDC 2018 Interaction Design and Children. Association for Computing Machinery (ACM), pp. 733–740 (2018)

29. Fleer, M.: Conceptual playworlds: the role of imagination in play and learning. Early Years **41**(4), 353–364 (2018)

30. Parker-Rees, R.: Learning from play: design and technology, imagination and playful thinking. In: IDATER Conference, pp. 20–25. Loughborough University, Loughborough (1997)

31. Brooks, E.: Designing as play. In: Brooks, E., Dau, S., Selander, S. (eds.). Digital Learning and Collaborative Practices. Lessons from Inclusive and Empowering Participation with Emerging Technologies, pp. 4–11. Routledge, Milton Park (2021)

32. Sylla, C., Brooks, E., Tümmler, L.: Blocks as symbolic tools for children's playful collaboration. In: Brooks, A.L., Brooks, E., Vidakis, N. (eds.) ArtsIT/DLI -2017. LNICSSITE, vol. 229, pp. 413–423. Springer, Cham (2018). https://doi.org/10.1007/978-3-319-76908-0_40

33. Wiberg, M.: Methodology for materiality: interaction design research through a material lens. Pers. Ubiquit. Comput. **18**(3), 625–636 (2013). https://doi.org/10.1007/s00779-013-0686-7

34. Stappers, P. J.: Prototypes as central vein for knowledge development. In: Valentine, L (ed.) Prototyping: Design and Craft in the 21st Century, pp. 85–97. Bloomsbury, London (2013)

35. Schön, D.: The reflective practitioner: How professionals think in action. Basic Books, New York (1983)

36. Bannon, L.J., Ehn, P.: Design matters in participatory design. In: Simonsen, J., Robertson, T. (eds.) Routledge International Handbook of Participatory Design, pp. 37–63. Routledge, New York (2013)

37. Redström, J.: Making Design Theory. The MIT Press, Cambridge (2017)

38. Dorst, K.: Frame Innovation: Create New Thinking by Design. The MIT Press, Cambridge (2015)

39. Ramberg, R., Artman, H., Karlgren, K.: Designing learning opportunities in interaction design: Interactionaries as a means to study and teach student design processes. Des. Learn. **6**(1–2), 30–57 (2013)

40. Selander, S.: Designs for learning – a theoretical perspective. Des. Learn. **1**(1), 10–24 (2008)

41. Selander, S.: Transformation and sign-making. The principles of sketching in designs for learning. In: Böck, M., Pachler, N. (eds.) Multimodality and Social Semiotics, pp. 121–130. Routledge, New York (2013)

42. Laurillard, D.: Teaching as a Design Science. Building Pedagogical Patterns for Learning and Technology. Routledge, New York (2012)

43. Selander, S.: Can a sign reveal its meaning? On the question of interpretation and epistemic contexts. In: Zhao, S., Djonov, E., Björkvall, A., Boeriis, M. (eds.) Advancing Multimodal and Critical Discourse Studies, pp. 67–79. Routledge, New Yourk (2018)

44. Kress, G., Selander, S.: Multimodal design, learning and cultures of recognition. Internet High Educ. **15**(4), 265–268 (2012)

45. Ramberg, R., Artman, H., Karlgren, K.: Designing learning opportunities in interaction design: interactionaries as a means to study and teach student design processes. Des. Learn. **6**(1–2), 30–57 (2013)

46. Alexander, C., Ishikawa, S., Silverstein, M.: A pattern language. Towns, Buildings, Construction. Oxford University Press, New York (1977)

47. Kafai, Y.: Seeking to reframe computational thinking as computational participation. Commun. ACM **59**(8), 26–27 (2016)

Pedagogical Integration of Digital Game-Based Learning - Processes Involved

Eva Brooks[1,2(✉)] and Jeanette Sjöberg[1,2]

[1] Aalborg University, Kroghstæde 3, 9220 Aalborg, Denmark
eb@hum.aau.dk
[2] Halmstad University, Kristian IVs väg 3, 30118 Halmstad, Sweden
jeanette.sjoberg@hh.se

Abstract. Aligned with the digital development in society, the use of digital game-based learning (DGBL) as a pedagogical enhancement has increased markedly in schools recently. However, due to various reasons, teachers are not always as enthusiastic to adopt the new technology in their classroom. In this paper we apply Engeströms activity system as an analytical approach to understand teachers' considerations of opportunities, resistance or barriers and pedagogical functions of digital game-based learning as a teaching method. As related research has shown, there is a lack of research answering the question of how DGBL could be designed to structure and facilitate learning as well as of considering the classroom settings and barriers of implementing DGBL. We attempt to contribute to these problems by applying the activity system framework in the context of digital game-based learning (DGBL), in particular the interplay between resistance as an obstruction or opportunity and design of teaching activities by means of digital games. The research questions posed in the study are: 1) How do teachers evaluate the designs of digital games in relation to how they support or hinder learning? and 2) What kind of constraints do teachers identify while translating educational games? The study applies a qualitative approach and includes cases of two separate workshops with a total of twelve participating teachers and one toy- and game designer. The workshops were designed to provide a framework for preschool- and primary school teachers to evaluate challenges and potentials of DGBL. Findings show, among other things, that when a game does not offer exploration or encourage curiosity, a game's design becomes simplistic and children lose their interest, revealing a gap between game mechanics and a game's pedagogical relevance and usefulness. Furthermore, by starting to question the relevance of games, the teachers were able to appropriate digital educational games while assessing the game's value in relation to a subject-specific area.

Keywords: Activity theory · Digital game-based learning (DGBL) · Educational game apps · School teachers · Teaching method

E. Brooks et al. (Eds.): DLI 2021, LNICST 435, pp. 195–212, 2022.
https://doi.org/10.1007/978-3-031-06675-7_15

1   Introduction

Arguments that are often posed in the literature of Digital Game-based Learning (DGBL) indicate that digital games can offer enriched learning experiences compared to traditional teaching methods. It is still unclear though how this actually happens [1]. In an attempt to elucidate this matter, researchers have investigated the use of educational digital games in different subject areas as well as developed models and frameworks for analysing games [1–3]. Besides providing explanations about digital games' educational possibilities and constraints, their motivational and social components to learning, they do not fully offer an answer to how the games should be designed and structured to facilitate learning. This is in line with a study by Kickmeier-Rust and Albert [4] which questions the actual impact of DGBL and suggests that poor game design can influence learning processes and outcomes.

Considering the arguments acknowledging DGBL in positive terms, the barriers that teachers face when they try to optimise DGBL in their teaching are rarely conveyed [5]. Hence, understanding of these resistance and constraints is important to understand how teachers translate digital games into their educational settings as well as understanding the classroom practices in which game-based learning processes are intended to be applied [6, 7]. For example, the choices that they make, including pedagogical constraints that they embody [5]. In her article, Kindred [8] suggests that resistance in learning and at work can be considered as having a productive role in learning and self-development. In contrast to traditional views of resistance as a constraint impeding learning, the author proposes that resistance can be seen as a constructive and deconstructive process in which people create bridges between past and present, during which people act as drivers of change. To reveal such processes, we have applied activity system theory, where human activity constitutes a context in which a constant dynamic movement, historically and interactionally, takes place [9].

The present study investigates how 14 teachers in two workshops discuss and argue while evaluating the design of digital game apps and their pedagogical benefits and barriers or constraints and, furthermore, designing a teaching activity including digital game-based learning. The format and content of the workshops were intended to also become a resource to facilitate their further implementation of DGBL. Research questions posed in this study:

- How do teachers evaluate the designs of digital games in relation to how they support or hinder learning?
- What kind of constraints do teachers identify while translating educational games?

The following section outlines related work to the topic of this paper followed by a presentation of the theoretical framework and methodology. Next follows a description of the outcomes of the study followed by a discussion and conclusion.

2   Related Work

The introduction of DGBL in schools has increased markedly in recent years [10], largely as a result of an increasingly digital society. As mentioned above, previous research has pointed to the benefits of DGBL in various subject areas, such as language [e.g. 11], math [e.g. 12] and science [e.g. 13]. The problem-solving and collaborative activities are often highlighted as extra favourable for learning [14]. Despite this, several teachers are hesitant about integrating the use of DGBL in their teaching for various reasons [15]. These are, for example, a lack of technology resources, technological turmoil, cost and the teachers' lack of knowledge to use technology [e.g. 5, 16, 17, 15]. In addition, there is relatively little research that highlights the teachers' views on the integration of DGBL in teaching activities [5].

However, earlier studies have shown that both teacher students (i. e preservice teachers) as well as practicing teachers have an ambiguous stance regarding the use of DGBL in the classroom: on the one hand they believe that there is a great potential in using games in educational settings and they considered games to be important educational tools, but on the other hand they were reluctant to use them themselves in their own teaching because they were unsure of how to incorporate, or if they wanted to bring DGBL into their future classrooms [e.g. 18, 19, 20]. In a study with Danish teachers, with the aim to discover teachers attitudes towards learning games and apps, Marchetti and Valente [21] found three major attitudes emitted from the teachers: (a) designers of content, teachers who were inventive with the technologies; (b) mediators, teachers who see themselves between the content and the chosen tools; and (c) IT-concerned, teachers who feel IT was something they had to learn in addition to their daily labour [21]. According to previous research of technology and/or games as a tool in the classroom, the overall largest determining factor as to whether a teacher would incorporate DGBL in their teaching or not is the teacher's perception of "usefulness" [22, 23].

In a recent systematic review over research between May 2009 and May 2019, Sun, Chen and Ruokamo [10] aim to unveil how digital game-based methods are being implemented in primary education to assess how teachers' pedagogical activities support digital game-based learning in primary education. The results indicate among other things that teachers' most significant concern regarding learning outcomes is knowledge acquisition, followed by attitude and motivation, skill outcomes, and behaviour change. Hebert and Jenson [24] emphasise that it is a critical component of effective DGBL to recognise the teacher's role in designing and facilitating learning environments that support DGBL, including adapting content to suit the needs of diverse learners. They argue that teachers need to be provided with professional development that focuses on cultivation of pedagogical skills, to create effective DGBL environments. Similarly, an Israeli study by Hayak and Avidov Ungar [25], examined 28 elementary school teachers' perceptions of the integration of DGBL into their instruction at different stages of their career. The results show that teachers at different stages of their career express different perceptions regarding the integration of digital game-based learning into their instruction, which can be related to the need for professional development. In addition, they identify key characteristics among teachers regarding patterns of adopting digital game-based learning and implementing digital game-based learning in teaching with relevance to professional development and teacher training [25].

The related work has shown that teachers' understanding and implementation of digital games in teaching activities is a complex endeavour, which requires considerations not only to games as such but also to how they fit to specific subjects and how content and design can support children's learning. To be able to identify these aspects, we have applied Engeström's activity system as an analytical framework, which is introduced in the following section.

3   Theoretical Framework

In this paper, we apply the activity theory as a theoretical framework. Hassan [26] points out that this approach has a focus on different forms of practices and learning processes, providing a model of humans in their social and organisational context [26]. Activity theory originated in the 1920s and 1930s by, among others, Vygotsky and Leontjev [27]. In this original tradition, Vygotsky developed mediated action as a unit of analysis [28, 29]. This was done as a triangular unity including subject, object and mediating tools and signs (Fig. 1).

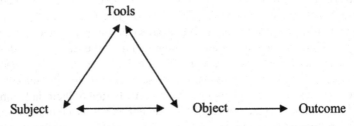

Fig. 1. The activity system as proposed by Vygostsky (1978).

The learning from this unit was the uncovering of the interaction between object and mediating artefact [9]. Activity theory is extensively used in the field of learning, but less used in the study of games [30–32].

Activity as a unit of analysis in activity theory focuses on interactions between subject and object in a process where transformations are achieved. The interaction is mediated by tools, which shape an ongoing interaction [33]. The original activity model proposed by Leontjev (1978) was further elaborated by Engeström [27], where he described an activity as a collective phenomenon conceptualised as *Activity System* in the form of a triangle (Fig. 2). The three sides of the model represent the core elements of the system (subject-object-community) and the corners represent the mediating means to the main elements (tools-social rules-labour division). The activity as such is directed towards the object resulting in an outcome. Engeström has further developed the model to include a diversity of perspectives and interactions between several interacting systems, which is conceptualised as Activity System Network [34]. An activity is not a static unit, but rather a dynamic one. Continuous transformations happen between the parts of the system based on, for example, changes in the subject's motivation or skills or changes in the labour division among the members of a community [9, 31]. Engeström [9] emphasises that it is the object that constitutes a dynamic activity, which is why an activity system is concentrated around its object as well as the contradictions between the different items within the activity system.

Contradictions are central to the dynamics of an activity system as they generate disturbances and conflicts in a team. But they also stimulate innovative thinking and action

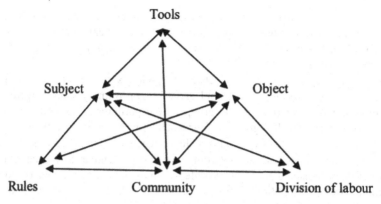

Fig. 2. The activity system as proposed by Engeström (2014).

and, thereby, potentially local changes [35]. Engeström and Pyörälä [36] identified that such situations can be complex and risk becoming fragmented, for example when there is not a common language or understanding between members in a team. This kind of challenge calls for establishing new ways for practitioners to work collaboratively towards the object, which Engeström [37] has conceptualised as acts of knotworking. Knotworking represents a model for overcoming fragmentation of the object, which for example could be through a team's way of seeking ways to negotiate and combine their different viewpoints of expertise. In this way, contradictions "do not speak for themselves", but can be identified when practitioners articulate them in words and actions [38:49]. Expressed differently, contradictions should be identified in their real and historical progression. In her article, Kindred [8] argues that resistance in learning is critical in the implementation of change. She furthermore addresses the engagement of resistance, rather than its repression or avoidance, as essential for cognitive shifts reflecting knowledge integration and thus resistance should be considered as a constructive activity.

This paper applies Engeströms activity system [27] as an analytical approach in order to understand teachers' considerations of opportunities, resistance or barriers and pedagogical functions of digital game-based learning as a teaching method. As related research has shown, there is a lack of research answering the question of how DGBL could be designed to structure and facilitate learning as well as of considering the classroom settings and barriers of implementing DGBL. We attempt to contribute to these problems by applying the activity system framework in the context of digital game-based learning (DGBL), in particular the interplay between resistance as an obstruction or opportunity and design of teaching activities by means of digital games.

4   Methodology

The study applies a qualitative approach [39] and includes cases of two workshops (Case 1 and Case 2). The workshops were designed to provide a framework for preschool- and primary school teachers to evaluate challenges and potentials of DGBL. Hence, different apps were selected within the subjects of math, language, and science. These were introduced to the teachers complemented with an evaluation guide to be used for valuing the apps' learning designs, both regarding their content and form. The teachers were divided into groups and each group should choose one of the game apps that were introduced to evaluate.

Case 1 consisted of nine female teachers from schools in the south-west of Sweden. The nine teachers (three from preschool and six from primary school) were divided into three groups (two participants in group 1; four participants in group 2; and three participants in group 3). The group of four teachers were working in the same school and teacher team. The other two groups included teachers from different schools. Case 2 consisted of three male participants from north-east of Denmark; a preschool teacher, a leader of preschools and an assistant professor in mathematics at a teacher education programme. Moreover, an Indian female toy and game designer participated in Case 2, where all four participants worked together in one group.

Each group had a workstation at their disposal, which was equipped with a fixed camera facing the centre of each table and recorded the activities during the whole workshop. In total, 400 min of video data was gathered. Additional 80 min of video data from Case 2 were lost, which resulted in a follow-up interview after the workshop to capture their further insights from the workshop. The data also includes the groups' final presentations of their game evaluations as well as field notes by the two authors.

4.1 Apparatus

Before starting the workshop, the participants were introduced to some background information and material. To start with, they received a general introduction to game-based learning, for example that using games in education is not a new phenomenon but has been around for decades. Furthermore, the introduction included some general information about game mechanics and their implications in an educational context. For example, that a game-based approach is based on rules, clear goals and includes choices that when applied generate different consequences. Intentions and suppositions related to games designed for learning were discussed, for example that they were supposed to offer students opportunities to collaborate around specific game content and, thereby, add a learning perspective to the gaming experience. Finally, the teachers were introduced to categories of different games and their respective goals, for example collaborating games, explorative games, problem-solving or strategic games and achieving goals games.

4.2 Procedure

After the introduction to the workshop, the participants were divided into groups and started the workshop activities. The workshop was divided into four sections and lasted for three hours. Table 1 illustrates the design of the workshop.

The introduction of the workshop clarified definitions of DGBL and game categories as well as the goal of the workshop. The chosen apps were presented and demonstrated. Based on our previous questionnaire study [15], which was directed to teachers in preschools and primary schools, we identified that teachers primarily used digital games in the subjects of mathematics, language and science. This became the foundation for

Table 1. DGBL workshop design.

Time	Activities
14:00–14:15	Introduction of the workshop and the selected game apps
14:15–14:30	**Workshop section 1**: Exploring and testing the different game apps. Each group chooses which one of the game apps to evaluate
14:30–15:20	**Workshop section 2**: Evaluating the chosen game app including a focus on the game's design and its learning potentials
15:20–16:10	**Workshop section 3**: Development of a teaching activity including the chosen game appl
16:10–17:00	**Workshop section 4**: The groups present their teaching activity to the other groups, including justifications of design choices. Closing and evaluation of the workshop

the choice of including game apps within these subject areas. Tables 2 and 3 illustrate the specific game apps used in Case 1 (Sweden) and Case 2 (Denmark) respectively.

Table 2. Game apps used in case 1 (Sweden).

Swedish language	Mathematics	Science
Spelling game (Stavningslek)	Math bakery 1, 2, 3 (Mattebageriet)	Chemist
School writing (Skrivstil)	Critter Corral	Twitter (Kvitter)
Letter puzzle (Bokstavspussel)	Scratch Jr	Butterflies (Fjärilar)
Yum letters (Yumbokstäver)		

Table 3. Game apps used in case 2 (Denmark).

Danish language	Mathematics	Science
Leo & Mona reading fun (Leo & Mona Læsesjov)	GOZOA - Play & learn mathematics (GOZOA - Leg & lær matematik)	The hero of nature (Naturens helt)
The letter school (Bogstavskolen)	Pixeline - The labyrinth of the number master (Pixeline - Talmesterens labyrint)	

While Case 1 included a mixture of digital games and digital tools (e.g. Scrach Jr.), Case 2 included only digital games. In the workshop Sect. 1, the participants had time to test the different game apps and choose one of them to further evaluate and design a teaching activity including this app. This was followed by a longer session, workshop Sect. 2, where the participants had time to test and evaluate the design of the game to get ideas and reflect upon how the game app could be used for a specific teaching activity. This part of the workshop was assisted by a list of questions to guide the evaluation:

- What is the goal and value of the game app - is it pedagogically clear and convincing? Why or why not? What are the learning goals of the game app?
- The interface of the game app - is it easy and efficient to navigate?
- What are the rules, control and other mechanisms of the game app? How can the player learn and understand those rules and other mechanisms?
- Is the game balanced by for example, offering different game levels? If so, in what way?
- What kind of mechanisms or values would encourage a child to play this game app more than once?
- In what way has the game an aesthetic value?
- What kind of game - is it based on exploration, problem solving, contesting, or a mixture?
- In what way is the game engaging and motivating?
- As a pedagogical expert, would you use this app in your teaching activities? Why or why not?

In Sect. 3 of the workshop, the participants should develop a teaching activity which should be based on the chosen app. They did not receive any guidelines for this activity but were told that they should apply their pedagogical expertise, in particular related to the learning goals that would apply to the chosen game. This was followed by workshop Sect. 4, where the groups presented their digital game-based teaching activity for each other and justified their included choices, game design features and pedagogical benefits.

The participants were informed about the study in writing and agreed to the video recording of the workshop sessions by signing informed consent forms, including approval of using the visuals for academic purposes. In line with ethical guidelines, all names of the participants and their workplaces are anonymised (Fig. 4).

Fig. 3. Some of the participants from the Danish case preparing their DGBL teaching activity (Sect. 3 of the workshop).

Fig. 4. Some of the participants from the Swedish case presenting their DGBL designs (Sect. 4 of the workshop).

4.3 Analytical Approach

Engeström's [27] activity system was applied as an analytical tool when analysing the video recordings. Figure 3 shows how Engeström's activity system model was used to form a tool for the analysis of the participants' evaluation of educational digital game apps and their design of digital game-based teaching and learning activities. By using this as a conceptual model for the analysis, we could unfold complexities of concerns, contradictions, and opportunities (Fig. 5).

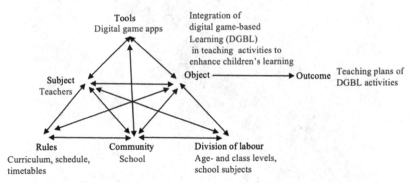

Fig. 5. Teachers' activity system analysis model as implemented in the study (adjusted from Engström [27]).

Teachers' activity system model depicts the participating teachers as *subject* and the school as their *community*. The activity as such targets the *object*, to work with how digital game-based learning (DGBL) can be implemented in their teaching activities in respective schools, which result in concrete teaching plans of digital game-based activities applied in different school subjects as an *outcome* of the activity. The corners of the model are mediating to the subject, object and community and represent the *tools* in terms of different DGBL apps, the *rules* including the curriculum, schedule, and timetables and, finally, *labour division* which represent school subjects and age- and class levels. We did not analyse all elements of the teachers' activity system in detail, but the model allowed us to identify triangulations in relation to the participants' activity (evaluation of a digital game app and design of a teaching activity including this app). We were interested in what in their discussions and game app explorations gave rise to concerns, which we, then, systematically analysed. However, we iteratively considered less examined incidents to avoid missing out on configurations that could have bearing on the overall activity. In particular, we were interested in:

- The subjects' motivations when evaluating the digital game app and designing a teaching activity including this app.
- The subjects' use of the digital game apps.
- The interconnections between the subjects and the mediating game apps, rules (curriculum, schedule, timetable) and labour division (school subjects, age- and class levels).
- The interdependence between the subjects and the school community.
- The potential development of common understanding among the subjects in the group.

This means that we did not analyse each of the elements in depth, but had the subjects in focus when triangulating their motivations, interconnections, interdependencies etc. Our systematic analysis of (i) identifying the incidents that were of concern by the participants and (ii) understanding the meaning of these concerns was inspired by Interaction Analysis (IA) and carried out in x different steps, as described by Jordan and Henderson [40]. Interaction analysis is used for empirical studies of human interaction, between people and with the environment and the objects in it. This includes expressions such as verbal and non-verbal interaction and the use of artefacts and technologies. This is helpful to identify routines, problems and resources used for solving problems [40]. For this, video documentation is crucial, i.e. to have the opportunity to play and replay a series of events. The video recordings were transcribed and analysed according to the principles of IA and presented in Table 4.

Table 4. Analytical steps in the interaction analysis.

Steps	Activities undertaken
Step 1	Overall view of the material
Step 2	Identifying events
Step 3	Transcribing events
Step 4	Analysing events in relation to the activity system model
Step 5	Identifying themes

After the first three steps, as described in Table 4, we related the events to the activity system model (as described in Fig. 3) and finally, based on the analysis of the events, it was possible to identify three emerging themes: (1) *Formation of pedagogical functions of the digital games*; (2) *Discovering gaps in the digital games*; and (3) *Constructive resistance*. These themes are further elaborated in the below sections.

5 Analysis

The analysis unfolded constraints and opportunities while the teachers were evaluating their educational meaning and relevance of the games. Moreover, by focusing on the games' design, the teachers identified how they could support or hinder children's learning. This is described in the following subsections where the themes are unpacked.

5.1 Formation of Pedagogical Functions of the Digital Games

The first theme, *Formation of pedagogical functions of the digital games*, embraces how the teachers considered the digital games as mediating tools in their teaching activities. The design and structure of the games were in focus when the teachers tried to identify their pedagogical functions, with emphasis on how the game designs supported learning. Considering this, the discussions about what a game is or could be in an educational context were necessary for the teachers to clear out before considering their pedagogical functions. The below excerpt describes how teachers explore a game's pedagogical function by translating its content.

Excerpt 1

Case 1, group 3. The three teachers in this group discuss the app 'Scratch Junior', which is more of a programming app than a game app - it is not a game in itself, but it admits people to make and play games with it. They are discussing what the game app is actually about, what is possible to do with it, and whether or not it can be considered as a game.

Teacher 1: It is probably more problem solving… But there are no given problems. It is not the case that you go into the app and have to solve different problems and advance to different levels. That is not the case.

Teacher 2: And you should not collect points or… It is more like an educational tool. Perhaps more that than a game.

In this excerpt, the teachers referred to basic game design criteria while assessing the game that they had chosen. Through this process, they identified that the game perhaps was not a game due to having other pedagogical qualities compared to a game. The latter should include, for example, a clear goal, levels, and rewards. Here, the teachers explored a common language to first understand what a game is and then, consider its pedagogical potentials. Engeström and Pyörälä [36] identified that establishing a common language and understanding between members in a group is essential in order to avoid fragmentation of a topic.

The next excerpt exemplifies how the teachers tried to find out how a game could enhance children's learning. They did this by identifying that the game as such could not stand by itself as a learning tool, but they as teachers needed to take on a mediating role to establish a pedagogical relevance in relation to a specific subject (in the case of this excerpt, the subject refers to mathematics).

Excerpt 2

Case 1, Group 2. The teachers are talking about how to introduce the game app they have chosen to evaluate to their students in a teaching activity. The three of them have tried out the game apps Math bakery 1–3 and are discussing how these apps can be integrated in a learning context.

Teacher 1: For our third graders, we would say that here you have the opportunity to rehearse differently, because here [in math bakery 1] you do not have to go through line-up and such, but if it had been new, you would have had to talk about how to set up … and have a lesson first, or if you have never worked with multiplication before. Then you would have had to go through it. But multiplication is not put in the hands of someone who has not done it before.

Teacher 3: …if you have a lesson and say 2×6 or 6×2, it does not matter because it is the same. I think it's good here [in Math bakery 3], it explains a lot, you can clearly see that it does not matter.

Teacher 1: You need to connect it to a smartboard and show them [the school children], or that you as an adult explain. So they know what they can get out of it. Otherwise it will just be like, now you can play a little, that they focus on the game.

Teacher 2: Here you want them to test, so they can see how to line up.

Teacher1: Yes, but then you have to show them and explain.

In this excerpt, the teachers highlight in what way the game app can be introduced in a meaningful way depending on the previous experiences of the children. In doing so, they put forward the importance of their own mediating role so that the students do not just 'play around'. This is in line with Hebert and Jenson [24] who underline that it is critical for teachers to recognise their role in facilitating DGBL. The excerpts show how the pedagogy of the game design is constructed when teachers act as mediators between the students' learning and the game content [21]. This is in line with previous research stressing that teachers' perception of digital games relate to how they consider its usefulness in a pedagogical context [22, 23].

5.2 Discovering Gaps in the Digital Games

In the second theme, *Discovering gaps in the digital games*, there is a focus on what the teachers are doing when they are "translating" the games. Gaps are types of breaks or holes causing in continuities as well as breaks in understanding what is going on. In the following excerpt, the teachers identified gaps between their own pedagogical beliefs, which are also expressed in the Danish curriculum, and the games' design. They stress that the game cannot be used to enhance children's learning as they represent a completely different pedagogical angle. The curriculum related to early years' education emphasises children's play and exploration of the world, while games directed to this age group do not any of these matters.

Excerpt 3

Case 2, group 1. The teachers discuss game mechanics and state that digital games for young children are based on simple mechanics and, even though the technique is available, they do not offer the needed aesthetics or explorative narratives to be regarded as a 'real' game. They discuss this in relation to game criterias. As detailed in the method section, case 2 teachers participated in a follow-up interview and this excerpt is an extract from this interview.

Teacher 1: It is a challenge to find good games that not only focus on learning, but also have explorative opportunities. Most of what we find includes that the child shall manage a level in a game and if you do not manage it, then, it is just a pity. You have to find something else to do. This creates a bit of an A and a B team of game players. If you cannot manage a level, you are out and not part of the playing team. Beside this, you cannot be curious about something in these kinds of educational games. A game consists of rules, that's how it is, you cannot be curious about something, I mean, on something that you jump into while playing.

Teacher 2: Something that we discuss a lot, in relation to how, that you on the one hand have the necessary technique [to develop games that are more explorative] and, on the other hand this about right or wrong answers or choices when you play this kind of game. And if you transfer this to pedagogical thinking, then we come to that while playing this kind of game the child will do something right or wrong. And the more you make the wrong choice or answer wrong on a question in relation to what is expected from the game design, the less explorative you become. You'll stop exploring. What we lately have talked a lot about in relation to level-based games is what is called sandbox-games. This kind of game offers exploration for you to take your own initiatives towards what you yourself think would be exciting to do or explore. There are no right or wrong answers. Not anything that needs to be solved in a certain way. If you cannot solve it you leave it to another time and move on. Unfortunately, there are not so many games in this genre. They are coming though. But where they are coming is in relation to adult players, not children.

Teacher 1: Yes, that's right. It is like this. In relation to technical issues, there are many high quality, complex game alternatives for adult game players, but if we look at it in relation to children, these games are simple, very simple. Regardless what game you choose. There are no details like in adult games. So, children miss out on this extra dimension, the aesthetics. Adult players can be involved in aesthetically designed games, but not children.

The teachers underline that when a game does not offer exploration or encourage curiosity, a game's design becomes simplistic, and children lose their interest. What they express here is that there is a gap between game mechanics and a game's pedagogical relevance and usefulness. From an activity theory perspective, this excerpt highlights teachers' interpretive repertoire as inflected by regulations and perspectives that inflect on children's interest and curiosity. Thus, this excerpt draws attention to significant gaps between educational game designs and pedagogical regulations expressed in the curriculum topic.

However, earlier studies have shown that both teacher students (i. e preservice teachers) as well as practicing teachers have an ambiguous stance regarding the use of DGBL in the classroom: on the one hand they believe that there is a great potential in using games in educational settings and they considered games to be important educational tools, but on the other hand they were reluctant to use them themselves in their own teaching because they were unsure of how to incorporate, or if they wanted to bring DGBL into their future classrooms [e.g. 18, 19, 20].

5.3 Constructive Resistance

The third theme, *Constructive resistance,* shows how the teachers' initial resistance to the games they have chosen to evaluate changed over time while assessing the games. While resistance often is considered as holding back change in educational activities, Kindred [8] suggests that resistance in learning is not only to be against something, but also an exploratory pathway that can generate learning. In our findings, the unknown territory of appropriating digital educational games was at start in the form of questioning their relevance. By trying out the games, they became more familiar with the content and could identify properties in the games that potentially could be adopted to be used in learning situations. The following excerpt shows how the teachers at first considered a math game as too complex to use, it was hard to identify the tasks and how to progress from one level to another.

Excerpt 4

Case 1, group 2. In this example, the four teachers in this group have individually been trying the game app 'Math bakery' (a math game app) for a while and are now discussing their experiences of that as well as the advantages and disadvantages with the game app in relation to learning. They explore what happens when they move cookies to learn the multiplication table and how their actions are visible on the screen of the game.

Teacher 1: If you move the cookies, you get results that are shown on the number line in a clear way...

Teacher 2: So, yes, it [the game] is not totally dumb...

Teacher 3: Should I show mine too? I think it is clear, to... [she points to the screen]...here we train multiplication, here I choose...different kinds of cookies, so here I can actively choose which Table 1 want to train on. Then it goes on as you also have with stars and so on. And here it's great, here they show the different ways.

Here, their resistance, through a process of exploring, changed from considering the game as nontransparent and closed to becoming transparent and open for making choices. This is in line with Martin et al. [35] stressing that contradictions also offer dynamics in an activity system as they generate disturbances but also initiate innovative thinking and thereby contributing to potential change. The essential turning point within the teachers' discussions emerged through their intense exploration of the games.

In case 2, the resistance was pretty strong and led to productive thoughts about alternative game designs as expressed in their discussions. In case 1, there was resistance when the game did not fit at all, that they were tied to their traditional view of the material used, but still they started redesigning the game and were excited about it. By means of the model of knotworking [38] the teachers could overcome fragmentation of the object by discussing and combining their different viewpoints of expertise.

6 Conclusive Discussion

Since the research focusing on teachers' views on the integration of DGBL in teaching activities is rather scarce [5], we wanted to carry out a study that could contribute to filling this gap. The workshop was approached as an activity where not only the teachers' assessment of the games, but also the processes and context of use were investigated [27]. The workshop structure used in both cases in this study was designed to support professional learning and their processes of evaluating the games were thus captured as processes of learning. The input given to the teachers (i.e. the questions to ask about a game) was intended to be used not only during the workshop but also after. Furthermore, the workshop itself provided the participants greater insight into games, what games could be and how they could be used in teaching, etc. Given the fact that teachers have an ambiguous stance towards DGBL [e.g. 18, 19, 20], we wanted to find out more about the teachers' actual view of why this is, since the teachers' role is crucial for an effective use and support of DGBL [24].

The results show that when the teachers tried to find out how a digital game could enhance children's learning, they uncovered the importance of the teacher as a mediating tool, since the game alone could not stand by itself in the educational situation. Furthermore, when a game does not offer exploration or encourage curiosity, a game's design becomes simplistic and children lose their interest, revealing a gap between game mechanics and a game's pedagogical relevance and usefulness. Additionally, findings show that in order for the teachers to appropriate digital educational games, they needed to start out with questioning their relevance. During the process of trying out the games and hence getting more familiar with them, they were able to identify properties in the games that potentially could be adopted to be used in learning situations. In line with Engeström and Pyörälä [36], they extended their understanding not only about games' pedagogical functions, but also about game design and how it could contribute to a game's value. Their translations of the games thereby went from concerning snippets of a game to a more holistic look at the games, for example in relation to a subject or the curriculum. The key turning point for this to happen emerged from the teachers' joint discussions and exploration of the games. This supports Kindred's [8] and Martin et al.'s [35] suggestions about contradictions as dynamic resources in activity systems, which not only disturb but also generate new ways of thinking.

The contribution to the field is twofold: first, the results have shown that in order for teachers to implement DGBL in teaching activities, they need to have knowledge about games. We could identify this through the teachers' conversations, where they could be more specific about opportunities and challenges the more they explored the games and learned about their design mechanics and pedagogy. This knowledge is of great importance for practitioners in the field when implementing DGBL in classrooms. Second, the workshop design included that teacher should assess a game that was specific to a school subject. The outcomes of the study showed that the teachers were confident in discussing a game's subject-specific value, which enabled them to apply their pedagogical expertise. This seemed to influence their interest and motivation to understand the games' subject specific value.

Acknowledgement. The authors direct their sincere thanks to all the teachers who participated in and contributed to the study. The study was carried out within the project 'Nordic DGBL - Digital Computer Games for Learning in the Nordic Countries', supported by Nordplus Horizontal, NPHS-2016/10071.

References

1. Van Staaduinen, J.-P., de Freitas, S.: A game-based learning framework: linking game design and learning. In: Khine, M.S. (ed.), Learning to play: Exploring the future of education with video games, pp. 29–54. Peter Lang (2011)
2. Amory, A.: Game object model version II: a theoretical framework for educational game development. Educ. Tech. Res. Dev. **55**(1), 51–77 (2007)
3. De Freitas, S., Oliver, M.: How can exploratory learning with games and simulations within the curriculum be most effectively evaluated? Comput. Educ. **46**(3), 249–264 (2006)
4. Kickmeier-Rust, M.D., Albert, D.: Micro-adaptivity: protecting immersion in didactically adaptive digital educational games. J. Comput. Assist. Learn. **26**, 95–105 (2010)
5. Hébert, C., Jenson, J., Terzopoulos, T.: "Access to technology is the major challenge": teacher perspectives on barriers to DGBL in K-12 classrooms. E-Learn. Digit. Media **18**(3), 307–324 (2021). https://doi.org/10.1177/2042753021995315
6. Sung, H.-Y., Hwang, G.-J.: Facilitating effective digital game based learning behaviors and learning performances of students based on collaborative knowledge construction strategy. Interact. Learn. Environ. **26**(1), 118–134 (2018)
7. Marklund, B.B., Taylor, A.-S.A.: Educational games in practice: the challenges involved in conducting a game-based curriculum. Electron. J. E-Learn. **14**(2), 122–135 (2016)

8. Kindred, J.B.: "8/18/97 Bite me": resistance in learning and work. Mind Cult. Act. **6**(3), 196–221 (1999). https://doi.org/10.1080/1074903990952472

9. Engeström, Y.: From learning environments and implementation to activity systems and expansive learning. Actio: Int. J. Hum. Act. Theory **2**, 17–33 (2009)

10. Sun, L., Chen, X., Ruokamo, H.: Digital game-based pedagogical activities in primary education: a review of ten years' studies. Int. J. Technol. Teach. Learn. **16**(2), 78–92 (2020/2021)

11. Hitosugi, C.I., Schmidt, M., Hayashi, K.: Digital game-based learning (DGBL) in the L2 classroom: the impact of the UN's off-the-shelf videogame, food force, on learner affect and vocabulary retention. CALICO J. **31**(1), 19–39 (2014)

12. O'Rourke, J., Main, S., Hill, S.M.: Commercially available digital game technology in the classroom: Improving automaticity in mental-maths in primary-aged students. Aust. J. Teach. Educ. **42**(10), 50–70 (2017). https://doi.org/10.14221/ajte.2017v42n10.4

13. Khan, A., Ahmad, F.H., Malik, M.M.: Use of digital game based learning and gamification in secondary school science: the effect on student engagement, learning and gender difference. Educ. Inf. Technol. **22**(6), 2767–2804 (2017). https://doi.org/10.1007/s10639-017-9622-1

14. Sjöberg, J.. Brooks, E.: Problem solving and collaboration when school children develop game designs. In: Brooks, A., Brooks, E.I. (eds.) Interactivity, Game Creation, Design, Learning, and Innovation. ArtsIT 2019/DLI 2019, LNICST (Lecture Notes of the Institute for Computer Sciences, Social Informatics and Telecommunications Engineering), vol. 328, pp. 683–698. Springer, Switzerland (2020). https://doi.org/10.1007/978-3-030-53294-9

15. Brooks, E., et al.: What prevents teachers from using games and gamification tools in Nordic schools? In: Brooks, A.L., Brooks, E., Sylla, C. (eds.) ArtsIT/DLI -2018. LNICSSITE, vol. 265, pp. 472–484. Springer, Cham (2019). https://doi.org/10.1007/978-3-030-06134-0_50

16. Sjöberg, J., Brooks, E.: Discourses of digital game based learning as a teaching method. In: Brooks, E.I., Brooks, A., Sylla, C., Møller, A.K. (eds.) DLI 2020. LNICSSITE, vol. 366, pp. 120–139. Springer, Cham (2021). https://doi.org/10.1007/978-3-030-78448-5_9

17. Brooks, E., Bengtsson, M., Gustafsson, M.J., Roth, T., Tonnby, L.: To become digitally competent: a study of educators' participation in professional learning. In: Brooks, A., Brooks, E.I. (eds.) ArtsIT/DLI -2019. LNICSSITE, vol. 328, pp. 699–713. Springer, Cham (2020). https://doi.org/10.1007/978-3-030-53294-9_53

18. Ray, B., Coulter, G.A.: Perceptions of the value of digital mini-games: implications for middle school classrooms. J. Digit. Learn. Teach. Edu. **26**(3), 92–100 (2010)

19. Baek, Y.: What hinders teachers in using computer and video games in the classroom? Exploring factors inhibiting the uptake of computer and video games. Cyberpsychol. Behav. **11**(6), 665–671 (2008)

20. Schrader, P., Zheng, D., Young, M.: Teachers' perceptions of video games: MMOGs and the future of preservice teacher education. Innov. J. Online Educ. **2**(3) (2006)

21. Marchetti, E., Valente, A.: It takes three: re-contextualizing game-based learning among teachers, developers and learners. In: Connolly, T., Boyle, L. (eds.), Proceedings of The 10th European Conference on Games Based Learning, pp. 399–406. Academic Conferences and Publishing International (2016)

22. Proctor, M.D., Marks, Y.: A survey of exemplar teachers' perceptions, use, and access of computer-based games and technology for classroom instruction. Comput. Educ. **62**, 171–180 (2013)

23. Stols, G., Kriek, J.: Why don't all math teachers use dynamic geometry software in their classrooms? Australas. J. Educ. Technol. **27**(1), 137–151 (2011)

24. Hébert, C., Jenson, J.: Digital game-based pedagogies: developing teaching strategies for game-based learning. J. Interact. Technol. Pedagogy **15** (2019)

25. Hayak, M., Avidov Ungar, O.: Elementary schools teachers' perceptions of integrating digital games in their teaching at different career stages. In: Graziano, K. (ed.) Proceedings of Society for Information Technology & Teacher Education International Conference, pp. 1850–1856. Las Vegas, United States, Association for the Advancement of Computing in Education (AACE) (2019)
26. Hassan, H.: Integrating IS and HCI using activity theory as a philosophical and theoretical basis. Australas. J. Inf. Syst. **6**(2), 44–55 (1999)
27. Engeström, Y.: Learning by expanding: an activity-theoretical approach to developmental research, 2nd edn. Cambridge University Press, Cambridge (2014)
28. Vygotsky, L.S.: Mind in Society: The Development of Higher Psychological Processes. Harvard University Press, Massachusetts (1978)
29. Wertsch, J.V.: Vygotsky and the Social Formation of Mind. Harvard University Press, Cambridge (1985)
30. Carvalho, M.B., et al.: An activity theory-based model for serious games analysis and conceptual design. Comput. Educ. **87**, 166–181 (2015)
31. Peachey, P.: The application of 'activity theory' in the design of educational simulation games. In: Peachey, P. (ed.), Design and implementation of educational games: theoretical and practicaæ perspectives, pp. 154–167. IGI Global (2010)
32. Zaphiris, P., Wilson, S., Ang, C.S.: Computer games and sociocultural play: an activity theoretical perspective. Games Culture **5**(4), 354–380 (2010)
33. Kaptelinin, V., Nardi, B.A.: Acting with Technology: Activity Theory and Interaction Design. The MIT Press, Cambridge (2006)
34. Engeström, Y.: Expansive learning at work: toward an activity theoretical reconceptualization. J. Educ. Work. **14**(1), 133–156 (2001)
35. Martin, G.P., Kocman, D., Stephens, T., Peden, C.D., Pearse, R.M.: Pathways to professionalism? Quality improvement, care pathways, and the interplay of standardisation and clinical autonomy. Sociol. Health Illn. **39**, 1314–1329 (2017)
36. Engeström, Y., Pyörälä, E.: Using activity theory to transform medical work and learning. Med. Teach. **43**(1), 7–13 (2021). https://doi.org/10.1080/0142159X.2020.1795105
37. Engeström, Y.: From Teams to Knots: Activity-Theoretical Studies of Collaboration and Learning at Work. Cambridge University Press, Cambridge (2008)
38. Sannino, A., Engeström, Y.: Cultural-historical activity theory: founding insights and new challenges. Cult. Hist. Psychol. **14**(3), 43–56 (2018)
39. Denzin, N.K., Lincoln, Y.S.: The SAGE Handbook of Qualitative Research. Sage, New York (2011)
40. Jordan, B., Henderson, A.: Interaction analysis: foundations and practice. J. Learn. Sci. **4**(1), 39–103 (1995). https://doi.org/10.1207/s15327809jls0401_2

Questions and Appraisal of Curiosity

Melvin Freestone[✉] ⓘ and Jon Mason ⓘ

Charles Darwin University, Darwin, NT 0909, Australia
saorcloc45@gmail.com

Abstract. Questions not answers drive innovative thinking. Yet pressure to produce answers often obscures the need to find questions that generate inquiry. To overcome this paradox practicable ways to make questions and questioning central to learning in educational and community settings are explored. A three-fold model for enactment of question-led learning is presented within a 'big ideas' frame of mind. Means for appraisal of inquiries steered by curious questions are articulated by drawing on well-established educational concepts and practices. These means have potential to integrate question-led learning and appraisal as interdependent partners in inquiries as well as in the acquisition and creation of knowledge. Question-led inquiries have profound implications for innovation and creativity as well as for the design, development, and implementation of educational practices.

Keywords: Questions · Curiosity · Appraisal · Pedagogy · Curriculum · Change

1 Introduction

1.1 Educational Context

Questions and curiosity generate knowledge, understanding and capability across the gamut of human endeavour. While the journey embodies a life-long dialogue with experience (Freire 1970; Dewey 1997; Vogt et al. 2003), questions often get lost in a maelstrom of answers. They become swamped with the intention to seek clarity, insight and innovation becoming a supreme irony (Haeleli 2016; Spencer 2017 and 2019). The questions teachers and educators ask are important, but learner questions are key (Chin 2002; Murdoch 2013 and 2018).

Questions and questioning drive thinking and innovation (Ram 1991; Chappel 2008; Thomas and Brown 2011; Project Zero 2015; Doherty 2018; Gregersen 2018; Sanitt 2018; Bouygues 2019; Classroom Nook 2020). TeachThought Staff (2019) put the issue succinctly. *'Questions are more important than answers because they reflect both understanding and curiosity in equal portions. … To ask a great question is to see the conceptual ecology of the thing'.*

Curious questions are the heart of intelligence and key to generating wise answers (Schank 1991). They connect us to phenomena of the life-world (Hood 2018) often provoking creativity and imagination that opens new possibilities or different ways of

E. Brooks et al. (Eds.): DLI 2021, LNICST 435, pp. 213–229, 2022.
https://doi.org/10.1007/978-3-031-06675-7_16

seeing the world. Asking questions enables people to direct their learning and engage in knowledge construction (Chin and Chia 2004; Chin and Osbourne 2008; Scardamalia and Bereiter 2010, Tawfik et al. 2020). The process is integral to sensemaking (Weick 1995).

1.2 Curious Questions

Different kinds of questions can be distinguished by their intention (Fig. 1).

- *Generic generative questions* (GGQs) have the potential to be applied across all areas of human knowledge, experience and endeavour. These questions direct inquiries.
- *Consequent questions* (CQs) emerge when GGQs are translated into the content of specific subject matters. These questions shape agendas capable of investigation
- *Pointed questions* (PQs) are designed to elicit defined responses. These questions address specific contextual issues within inquiries.

The GGQs in Fig. 1 expand those identified in the International Baccalaureate's Primary Years Program (IBO, 2000). Each of them has a label and a brief description which differentiates their strategic direction. The Covid-19 pandemic is used to indicate what translation of three selected GGQs into CQs and PQs might look like. The shaded areas indicate the overall 'movement of thinking' as an inquiry unfolds. Situated challenges together with prior knowledge sharpen the selection of appropriate GGQs. While 'answers' that emerge may address the initial challenge, they also open-up understandings for future application or inquiry. The whole process is iterative, not lock-step.

The unfolding of questions embodies three interdependent processes – a cognitive search to make connections (Chiu and Linn 2013; Manogue et al. 2014; Maloney 2015), an argumentative dialogue to construct and critique explanations (Berland and Reiser 2011; Ford 2012), and framing to synthesise thinking with prior knowledge and extant personal understanding (Danielak et al. 2014; Kapon 2016). A mix of convergent (Sternberg 1986) and divergent thinking (DeBono 2007) as well as metacognition (Wellman 1985; Click 2020) is often in play, with tensions kindling imagination and inventiveness (Bailin 1987; Bolger 2018). The implied dissonance creates a sense of instability that promotes continual internalization of understanding, sometimes producing an 'ah-ha' effect (Conlin 2013).

As an inquiry progresses, initial questions are often revisited. Indeed, these recurrences may have a vexing dimension that keeps sensemaking going (Odden et al. 2019). Addressing the subsequent puzzlement can be self-motivating, analogous to pleasurable discomfort derived from the pursuit of difficult or challenging questions (Jaber and Hammer 2016).

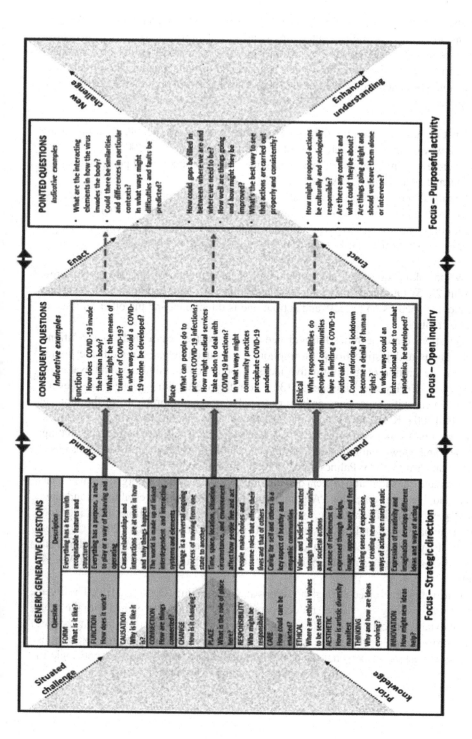

Fig. 1. Different kinds of questions.

The questions in Fig. 1 are open-ended. They provoke interpretations and explanations, ideas and possibilities, alternatives and speculations, and sometimes insightful decisions and actions (Delgado 2019; Goodwin 2019). The process is one of 'sensemaking' through which insights into what has happened or is happening, and possibilities for action, are generated (Weick et al. 2005; Mason 2014; Colville et al. 2016). In so doing, people:

- Construct unique interpretations of experience with no two people so doing in the same way or at the same rate (Fosnot and Perry 1996; Pritchard 2009).
- Generate multiple realities of experience that echo combinations of personal assumptions and aspirations (Lidsky 2016).
- Produce diverse answers to the same question derived from different functioning, structures and perceptions in the brain (Balkenius and Gärdenfors 2016).
- Employ metaphorical images to explain perceptions of experience and explore theories for action (Lakoff 1993; Kosecki 2011).

While asking questions and questioning share semantic roots, they are different (Koshik 2015). Questions are strategic means of directing and shaping inquiries whereas questioning focuses on process and action: one is directional and the other an issue of tactics (Table 1).

Questions direct searches for evidence and perspective, cause and effect relations, explanations and justifications, assumptions, and uncertainties. As well, they guide strategic generation of transformative ideas, hypothetical possibilities, and evaluative procedures (Corley and Rauscher 2013). The reflective thinking evoked goes beyond entanglement with experience or inquiry to solve pragmatic problems of the moment (Turnbull 2004; Klein and Moon 2006; Chater and Loewenstein 2016). In contrast, questioning employs focussed processes like - querying, clarifying, predicting, speculating, synthesising, view-pointing, contradicting, and challenging - to explore questions posed (Lewis and Smith 1993; Palincsar 2011; Peterson and Taylor 2012).

Strategic questions and tactical questioning are typically in a synergistic state of harmony and dynamic contention. 'Argument' between them engages established and alternative perceptions of experience, as well as different conceptualizations, mental images and imaginative possibilities (Donaldson 2010; Brogaard and Gatzia 2017; Gideonse 2019). 'Playful dialogue' does much to help resolve tensions between personal and situated dissonance and generate connections from critical and creative thinking (Wegerif 2007).

Curiosity is energized through questions and questioning (Oppong 2019). The diversity of sensemaking engendered reflects personal perceptions intertwined with the ecology of extant connections formulated from them. Practical problem solving may be part of the process but the whole widens outlooks into the unknown and towards possibilities for the expression of personal talents. With potential to know going beyond logic to create intuitive and imaginative thoughts, and actions (Dalsgaard 2014).

Table 1. Questions and questioning.

Feature	Questions	Questioning
Intention	Determining directions for personal and collective inquiries in real-life contexts	Engaging in processes and actions to explore different aspects of challenges
Concept	Shaping inquiries to focus on issues, ideas, problems, and alternatives	Executing inquiries guided by strategic directions and possibilities for exploration
Emphasis	Focusing on design, purpose, scope, and forward-thinking possibilities for inquiry	Concentrating on performing investigations, tasks, actions, and their practicability
Orientation	Exploring challenges, understandings, contradictions, feasibilities, problems, possibilities, and novelties	Tackling investigations in the context of needs, demands, situations, circumstances, and conditions
Essence	*Strategic intention*	*Tactical action*

Figure 2 represents evolving relationships outlined in Fig. 1. Each of the four elements combine to form a propositional framework for inquiries built around questions. The features identified for each element distinguish their roles and functions. GGQs represent 'starting blocks' with CQs and PQs connecting them with life-world action. Enactment of these questions often benefits from structured processes such as 'action research' (Kemmis and McTaggart 1998), especially if they are appreciative of current conditions yet mindful of future possibilities (Shuayb et al. 2009; Cooperrider 2016).

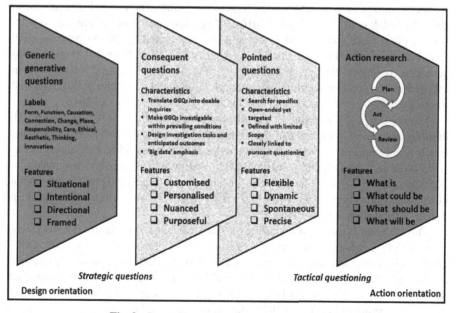

Fig. 2. Strategic questions to tactical questioning.

Assigning a pivotal role to GGQs creates a means to add coherence, consistency, and purpose to inquiries (Freestone 2018). Indeed, the ability to apply them in multiple contexts and for diverse purposes could provide a life-long resource for question-led learning. They create an innovative mindset that promotes design, insight and practicability.

1.3 Intentional Exploration

Establishing an inquiry begins with analysis of the situational features and socio-cultural practices in play. Once a clear picture is to hand two or three GGQs can be selected. A few that best reflect the needs and intentions behind a prospective inquiry is advisable, as too many can become unmanageable. With chosen questions in mind, investigative processes can be devised; although, sometimes disordered thoughts, even confused or messy thinking may instigate inquiries (Gregoire and Kaufman 2015; May-Li Khoe 2016).

A central intent is to perceive and construct connections that have value (Odden and Russ 2018). The inherent complexity is seldom satisfied by investigating narrow or detached sets of variables. Instead, an array of interrelated aspects are involved (Madsjberg 2017).

- Exploring cultures – not just individuals or isolated events
- Investigating in depth – not just thin data or simplistic variables
- Focusing on real life – not just a smorgasbord or issues detached from experience
- Highlighting creativity – not just manufacturing or assembling thinking
- Building vision – not just searching for destinations or reputable endpoints.

Mental images are modified in the light of emerging experience (Frank and Scherr 2012; Danielak et al. 2014; Kapon 2016). Of necessity much of the thinking is imaginative, often tacit, and beyond extant silos of understanding. In the process, subtle combinations of 'wonderment' questions (Aquiar et al. 2010; Perin 2011) and 'vexing' questions are helpful (Odden and Russ 2019). The whole is enhanced when people are engaged in constructive learning communities (Eteläpelto and Lahti 2008), especially where a tenor of improvisation and innovation prevails (Corbett et al. 2016).

Voltaire (1694–1778) posited: *'Judge a man by his questions not by his answers'*. The limitless horizon of questions and questioning bespeaks the enormity of the challenge, which is accentuated by the scope of the indicative 'curious relations' related to each GGQ in Table 2. Each 'curious relation' counterpoints related concepts for exploration (Erickson et al. 2014). Within this milieu, questions around facts and procedures generate little discussion whereas questions that evoke wonder provoke more thoughtful and deeper conversations (Zambrano 2019).

This scenario is too multidimensional to be amenable to standardized testing. Even tests like PISA, which purport to ask questions around concepts (NSTA 2009; OECD 2018), often evoke responses that are based on memory (Bennett 2016). As well, much controversy exists around the capacity of multiple-choice testing to reveal deep learning due to guessing or choices being made on what appears to be 'correct' with little thoughtful consideration (Biggs 1973; Beard and Senior 1980; Entwistle and Entwistle

Table 2. Curious relations. (modified from Freestone 2018).

What is it like? FORM	How does it work? FUNCTION	Why is it like it is? CAUSATION	How is it connected to other things? CONNECTION
Systems/Processes	Designs/Intentions	Consequences/Impacts	Circumstances/Conditions
Mechanisms/Operations	Effectiveness/Efficiency	Contexts/Situations	Initiatives/Opportunities
Materials/Properties	Power/Energy	Motivations/Inspirations	Networks/Relationships
Performance/Functionality	Processes/Mechanisms	Causes/Effects	Powers/Motivations
Structures/Purposes	Roles/Elements	Patterns/Sequences	Intentions/Benefits
Wholes/Parts	Systems/Maintenance	Theories/Explanations	Interoperability/Sustainability
How is it changing? **CHANGE**	**What is the role of place here?** **PLACE**	**Who might be responsible?** **RESPONSIBILITY**	**How could we care for each other?** **CARE**
Adaptability/flexibility	Cultures/Backgrounds	Citizenship/Rights	Empathy/Understanding
Factors/Influences	Features/needs	Justice/Prejudice	Friendship/Compassion
Growth/Development	Histories/Circumstances	Opinions/Decisions	Needs/Support
Movement/Flow	Interactions/Relations	Participation/Exclusion	Teamwork/Collaboration
Cycles/Sequences	Resources/Infrastructures	Individual/Community	Appreciation/Respect
Transformations/adaptations	Sites/Locations	Personalities/Affinities	Rights/Responsibilities
Where is the ethical reasoning? **ETHICAL**	**How is aesthetic sense manifest?** **AESTHETIC**	**How is the thinking evolving?** **THINKING**	**What might innovation add?** **INNOVATION**
Beliefs/Traditions	Appeal/Attraction	Alternatives/Possibilities	Creativity/Improvisation
Outcomes/Benefits	Designs/Structures	Dependent/Independent	Flexibility/Adaptation
Equity/Equality	Images/Messages	Critical/Creative	Innovative/Pragmatic
Justification/Rightness	Perceptions/Interpretations	Imaginative/Inventive	Ideas/Actions
Diversity/Difference	Relationships/Linkages	Issues/Problems	Prototypes/Products
Values/Moralities	Style/Flair	Reflections/Contradictions	Research/Trial

1992; Dulger and Deniz 2017; Weimer 2018). Differences in the values and cultural backgrounds of responders are also overlooked.

Traditional means for assessing knowledge are based on demonstration of increasing conceptual sophistication. Bloom's taxonomy (1956) or variations of it are widely used. Yet the scope and complexity of GGQs and their associated CQs makes dependence on one, or even a few, means for appraisal problematic. Pictures of personal and collective learning often become skewed by the means with important aspects of performance omitted. A more authentic picture might be derived from profiling experience and performance around observed realities, as distinct from a proxy sequence of preordained levels or perceptions of expected performance.

1.4 Continuous Appraisal

In addition to issues of authenticity and reliability, appraisal of inquiries and questions need to be comprehensive. Earl (2013) distinguished three kinds:

- Process orientated appraisal as learning
- Progress orientated appraisal for learning
- Achievement orientated appraisal of learning

A balance between the three is integral to question-led inquiries. A strategic possibility to meet the criteria of authenticity, reliability and comprehensiveness might be to profile questions asked and enacted (Broadfoot 1987a and 1987b). The process could take place in three stages.

Stage 1 – Profiling Possibilities. With the GGQs selected in mind, consider the possibilities embedded within the content and context of inquiries. What opportunities might be available or created to explore – situated, conceptual, hypothetical, known and unknown features? Exploration of these investigative possibilities might also reveal other latent questions nested within those already identified.

Stage 2 – Collecting Evidence. To be authentic, not contrived, evidence needs to be comprehensive and collected over the life of an inquiry. In so doing, it needs to encompass as many aspects of the investigative processes as possible. A diverse repertoire of strategies is available.

- Portfolios of work
- Data from conferencing
- Peer feedback
- Performance results
- Anecdotal records
- Discursive writings
- Conferencing feedback
- Photographic records
- Multimedia presentations
- Metacognitive perceptions
- Talents required
- Story telling or retelling
- Multimedia storyboards
- Self-assessment

Portraits of individual progress gained through an inquiry are enhanced when several of these means are employed. Once a volume of evidence is to hand it can be culled to select the most representative or indicative samples.

Stage 3 – Profiling Performances. Sensemaking performances can be appraised in terms of the depth and breadth of curiosity. Analysis of the evidence collected against specific criteria or backtracking to the goals behind an inquiry would expose:

- the sophistication of thinking, different kinds of thinking, integration across different disciplines of knowledge and experience, and consistency of performance.
- the breadth of thought and action reflected in the organisation of tasks, the diversity experiences encountered, and the opportunities created for cooperative or collaborative activity.

'On balance', judgements across the range of evidence collected tend to provide a more dependable assessment of the knowledge, capability, and innovative thinking exhibited than attempts to identify the best or worst within the material that has been accumulated.

A summary record of development (James et al. 1988) could be distilled from evidence of progress revealed through profiling processes. In so doing, a visual representation (Fig. 3) of the quality of question-led learning could be built around markers like - depth of thinking, scope of subject matter, consistency of performance, collaboration with others, and organisation of investigations. Such visualizations would be enriched by illustrative samples of individual and collective work or annotated snapshots of activity.

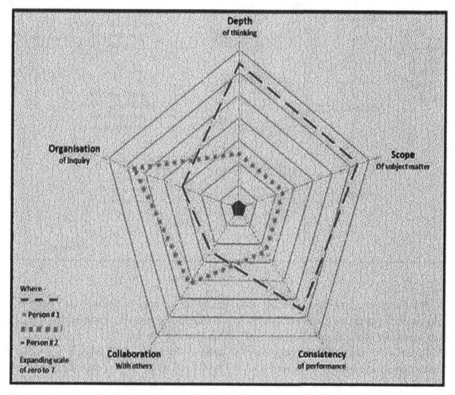

Fig. 3. Visual record of development (indicative example).

If keeping records of development is to be doable, each person or group needs to take responsibility for maintaining, and where necessary culling, their own record of development. This process promotes reflection on the relative worth of ideas developed and achievements accrued.

To gain maximum benefit from profiling a means of interpretation is required. Figure 4 which draws on established theories of learning put forward by Vygotsky (1978), Biggs and Collis (1982), and Bruner (1966) creates a possibility. The cascading movement upwards through zones of proximal development (ZPD) bespeaks internalization of intelligence. Increasing depth of learning through four levels of sophistication labelled – descriptions, explanations, interrelations and extrapolations – can be observed along the lines of the SOLO taxonomy (Biggs and Collis 1982). The horizontal spiral at each level of sophistication describes movement from enactive or action-based to iconic or image-based to symbolic or language-based activity.

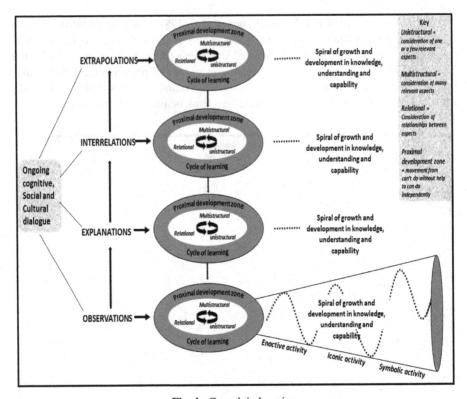

Fig. 4. Growth in learning.

Standards of thinking could be ascribed by observing progress from recall and reproduction, to development of skills and concepts, to growth in strategic thinking, to expansion of imaginative and innovative ideas and practices.

Appraisal of the questions people ask would be informed if the GGQs in Fig. 1 could be articulated in terms of different foci or maybe 'de facto' degrees of sophistication. Table 3 indicates increasing complexity in making observations, seeking explanations, perceiving interrelationships, and extrapolating understandings to unrelated contexts. The patterns are indicative with precise descriptions dependent upon their translation into the content and context of particular inquiries.

Profiling is analogous to telling stories about performance. It provides a means for appraising curiosity and questions posed in complex systems and 'wicked' problems, and the inquiries emanating from them (Ollove and Lteif 2017). Insight into some of the tacit, explorative, reflective and declarative knowledge being developed would likely be gained (O'Toole 2011). Analysis of the language used and imagery evoked in the verbal, written, visual or multimedia aspects of stories told would deepen these insights. (Lakoff and Turner 1989).

When people think about how their thinking has evolved, they come to recognise what they know and what they don't know (Costa 1984 and 2011). The metacognitive insights that emerge do much to inform the 'next' questions bubbling across the template of a persons' consciousness. And when 'next' is juxtaposed against the 'previous' more of

Table 3. Complexity within GGQs.

Generic generative questions	Focus Indicative examples			
	Observation	Explanation	Interrelationship	Extrapolation
FORM What is it like?	Features of things have similar and different properties	Things are made up of parts working together for a purpose	Elements interact, often harmoniously, to form systems	Designs can be adapted or transformed in different contexts
FUNCTION How does it work?	Different features in natural or human built systems work together	How entities interact in a physical or a living system powers its functions	Functions of a system are shaped by the roles and performances of its parts	Design principles on which a system is based informs future advances
CAUSATION Why is it like it is?	Intentions, ideas, and relationships affect the value and impact of actions	Consequences, impacts and benefits of ideas and actions can be predicted	Relations between entities reveals causes and effects, and ways to intervene	Ideas and actions reflect human and ecological values and their implications
CONNECTION How are things connected?	Things have internal links and external interrelationships	Interconnections between entities affect value and performance	Situated impacts and performances reveal needs and future possibilities	Insights into interconnectedness informs action and potential worth
CHANGE How is it changing?	Change in each context has specific causes, effects, and potential value	Context and purpose affect the emerging and latent effects of change	Factors affecting change vary in intent, nature, impact, magnitude...	Application of strategies for change affects intended benefits and impacts
PLACE What is the role of place here?	Places have specific features which vary in nature, role, and significance	The needs of each place incorporate specific purposes, needs, and conditions	Knowing how things work or could work helps refine human practices	Managing places requires balancing needs, intents, effects, and actions
RESPONSIBILITY Who might be responsible?	Actions by people and groups affect how self and others feel, and act	Personal choices have consequences that affect self and other people	Balanced choices combine purposes, principles, and obligations	Criteria and obligations for making choices vary in different contexts
CARE How can care be enacted?	Care for others respects their needs, desires, feelings, and circumstances	Caring people can empathise with diverse personalities and aspirations	Respect for the needs of people and communities creates realistic support	Collaboration creates nuanced ways to support, respect, and help others
ETHICAL Where are the ethical values?	Values behind ideas and actions underpin their worth and effect	Diversity in culture and tradition often underpins how people think and act	Views of worth, dilemma, and merit evolve with time and circumstance	Appreciation builds respect for diversity in values, beliefs, and traditions
AESTHETIC How is artistic value evident?	Different ideas and actions create specific features, images, and effects	Aesthetic concepts echo personal experience, perspectives, and intent	Artistic practices and artefacts reflect cultural, aesthetic, and attractive value	Aesthetic ideas and practices embody imagination and creativity
THINKING Why are ideas evolving?	Values, social practices, feelings, and emotions echo experience	Reasoning and sensemaking evolve as reflections on experience unfolds	Effective responses to challenges often grow from thinking laterally	Tension amid critical and creative thoughts incite inventiveness
INNOVATION How might new ideas help?	Inventiveness requires imaginative application of ideas in a context	Ingenuity searches for new ideas and fresh ways to apply old ideas	Development of innovative ideas and actions is a never-ending process	Original ideas or new ways to apply old ideas can change human practices

the unknown that needs to be explored comes into view. Indeed, metacognitive reflection is a mix of personal appraisal, and growth (Zohar and Barzilai 2013). The process is innovative in tenor as much as it is descriptive.

Much remains hidden within the personal knowledge people develop, which often makes a person's 'next' questions more enlightening than those already addressed. Selected GGQs become refined and different CQs often emerge in response to personal growth or collegial dynamics among people or shifting challenges within an inquiry (Elkins-Tanton 2018). When 'next' is intermeshed with the evolving substance of an inquiry a more profound picture of the sensemaking and the potential for further work comes into view. An agile view of 'where we are' and 'where to next' ensues. Indeed, curious patterns of - what is, what might be, what should be, and what will be – come into being.

1.5 Emerging Pictures

When thinking and dialogical capabilities are illuminated the state of an inquiry is revealed. A means to aid reflection on the maturation of performances from simple to complex understanding and movement of dialogues from certainty to exploration of uncertainty is presented in Fig. 5. The features for each 'condition' provide a lens for analysing the 'state of play'. Maps of the overall 'condition' that emerge may orientate towards technicality, judgement, or complexity. The question is *'where is the emphasis?'*, especially as all three would likely be involved to some degree in most inquiries.

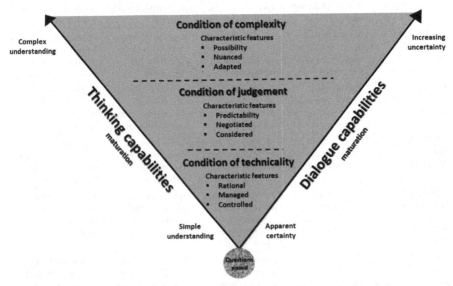

Fig. 5. Thinking and dialogical capabilities (Inspired by Zimmerman 2001)

The appraisal processes argued here are underpinned by a concern to celebrate curiosity, imagination and innovation. They are appreciative borne on 'can do', as distinct from searching for what people cannot do or deficits in what they have done. Judgement is part of the process, but accrued benefits focus on appreciative understanding of the capabilities developed and expressed with an eye to further development.

2 Future Outlook

In this paper questions, curiosity and appraisal are viewed as an integrated whole that provokes innovative thought and action. Encouraging question-led learning would do much to light up curiosity and empower people and communities to deal creatively and imaginatively with life-world challenges as well as address global issues of present and future significance. 'Wicked problems' like the current pandemic, climate change, and population growth will challenge humanity for the foreseeable future.

From a teaching and learning perspective, pedagogical strategies and much curriculum practice would be enhanced if question-led inquiries were to become more prominent. Finding ways to support action among communities of learners across the spectrum of educational settings would be key.

References

Aquiar, O.G., Mortimer, E.F., Scott, P.: Learning from and responding to students' questions: the authoritative and dialogic tension. J. Res. Sci. Teach. **47**(2), 174–193 (2010)

Bailin S.: Critical and creative thinking. Informal Logic **9**(1), 23–300 (1987)

Balkenius, C., Gärdenfors, P.: Spaces in the brain: from neurons to meanings. Front. Psychol. (2016). https://doi.org/10.3389/fpsyg.2016.01820

Beard, R.M., Senior, I.J.: Motivating Students. Routledge & Kegan Paul, Milton Park (1980)

Bennett P.W.: PISA Mathematics Lessons: why zero-in on "Memorization" and minimize teacher-directed instruction? Educhatter, Schoolhouse Consulting (2016). https://educhatter.wordpress.com/2016/10/19/pisa-mathematics-lessons-why-zero-in-on-memorization-and-minimize-teacher-directed-instruction/

Berland, K.K., Reiser, B.J.: Classroom communities adaptations of the practice of scientific argumentation. Sci. Educ. **95**(2), 191–216 (2011)

Biggs, J.B.: Study behaviour and performance in objective and essay formats. Aust. J. Educ. **17**, 157–167 (1973)

Biggs, J.B., Collis, K.F.: Evaluating the Quality of Learning – The SOLO Taxonomy (Structure of the Observed Learning Outcome), Educational Services, Academic Press, Cambridge (1982)

Bloom, B.S.: A Taxonomy of Educational Objectives 1: Cognitive Domain. Longmans (1956)

Bogler, M.: How to improve collaboration, communication, creative and critical thinking in students. Project pals (2018). https://www.projectpals.com/project-based-learning-blog/how-to-improve-collaboration-communication-creative-and-critical-thinking-in-students

Bouygues, H.L.: 3 simple habits to improve your critical thinking. Harvard Business Review (2019). https://hbr.org/2019/05/3-simple-habits-to-improve-your-critical-thinking

Broadfoot, P.: Introducing Profiling. Nelson Thornes (1987a)

Broadfoot, P.: Introducing Profiling: a Practical Manual. Macmillan Education, London (1987b)

Brogaard, B. Gatzia, D.E.: Unconscious imagination and the mental imagery debate. Front. Psychol. (2017). https://doi.org/10.3389/fpsyg.2017.00799

Bruner, J.S.: Towards a Theory of Instruction. Belkap Press of Harvard University (1966)

Chappel, K., Craft, A., Burnard, P., Cremin, T.: Question-posing and question-responding: the heart of 'Possibility Thinking' in the early years. Early Years Int. Res. J. **28**(3), 267–286 (2008). https://www.tandfonline.com/doi/full/10.1080/09575140802224477

Chater, N., Loewenstein, G.: The under-appreciated drive for sense-making. J. Econ. Behav. Organ. **126**, 137–154 (2016). https://doi.org/10.1016/j.jebo.2015.10.016

Chin, C.: Student-generated questions: encouraging inquisitive minds in learning. Sci. Teach. Learn. **23**(1), 59–67 (2002).

Chin, C., Chia, L.G.: Problem-based learning: using students' questions to drive knowledge construction. Sci. Educ. **88**, 707–727 (2004)

Chin, C., Osborne, J.: Students' questions: a potential resource for teaching and learning science. Stud. Sci. Educ. **44**(1), 1–39 (2008). https://doi.org/10.1080/03057260701828101

Chiu, J.L., Linn, M.C.: Supporting knowledge integration in chemistry with a visualization-enhanced inquiry unit. J. Sci. Educ. Technol. **23**(1), 37–58 (2013). https://doi.org/10.1007/s10956-013-9449-5

Classroom Nook. Reading comprehension strategy series: how to teach students to ask questions (2020). https://www.classroomnook.com/blog/reading-strategy-asking-questions

Click, N.: Metacognition: thinking about one's thinking - putting metacognition into practice. Vanderbilt University (2020). https://cft.vanderbilt.edu/guides-sub-pages/metacognition/

Colville, I.D., Pye, A., Brown, A.: Sensemaking processes and Weickarious learning. Manage. Learn. **47**(1), 3–13 (2016)

Conlin, L.D.: Three views of an Aha! moment: Comparing tutorial groups' affective responses to a moment of sudden conceptual insight. Poster Presentation at 2013 Physics Education Research Conference. Portland, OR (2013)

Cooperrider, D.L.: What is Appreciative Inquiry (2016). http://www.davidcooperrider.com/aiprocess/

Corbett, M., Vibert, A., Green, M., Rowe, J.N.: Improvising the Curriculum, Routledge, Milton Park (2016)

Corley, M.A., Rauscher.: Deeper learning through questioning. TEAL Fact Sheet No 12, Teaching Excellence in Adult Literacy (2013)

Costa, A.L.: Mediating the Metacognitive. Education Leadership, pp. 57–64 (1984)

Costa, A.L.: Habits of mind. in developing minds: a resource book for Teaching Thinking, Costa, A.L. (eds.) Association for Supervision and Curriculum Development, ASCD (2011)

Dalsgaard, P.: Pragmatism and design thinking. Int. J. Des. **8**(1), 143–155 (2014)

Danielak, B., Gupta, A., Elby, A.: Marginalized identities of sense-makers: reframing engineering student retention. J. Eng. Educ. **103**(1), 8–44 (2014). https://doi.org/10.1002/jee.20035

DeBono, E.: Lateral Thinking: A Textbook of Creativity. Penguin, London (2007)

Delgado, P.: The key to curiosity? Asking the right questions. Observatory Educ. Innov. (2019). https://observatory.tec.mx/

Dewey, J.: How we think. Dover Publications, New York (1997)

Doherty, J.: Skillful questioning: the beating heart of good pedagogy. Impact J. Chartered Coll. Teach. (2018). https://impact.chartered.college/article/doherty-skilful-questioning-beating-heart-pedagogy/

Donaldson, A.: Cognitive dissonance. Ted Talks (2010). https://www.youtube.com/watch?v=NqONzcNbzh8

Dulger, M., Deniz, H.: Assessing the validity of multiple-choice questions in measuring fourth graders' ability to interpret graphs about motion and temperature. Int. J. Environ. Sci. Educ. **12**(2), 177–193 (2017)

Earl, L.M.: Assessment as Learning: Using Classroom Assessment to Maximize Student Learning. 2nd edn, Corwin Press, Thousand Oaks (2013)

Elkins-Tanton, T.: Turning around question-asking. The Beagle Blog (2018). https://www.beaglelearning.com/blog/question-asking-in-your-class/

Entwistle, A., Entwistle, N.: Experiences of understanding in revising for degree ex-aminations (1992). https://doi.org/10.1016/0959-4752(92)90002-4

Erickson, K.L., Lanning, L.A., French, R.: Concept-Based Curriculum and Instruction for the Thinking Classroom. Corwin Teaching Essentials, Thousand Oaks (2014)

Eteläpelto, A., Lahti, J.: The resources and obstacles of creative collaboration in a long-term learning community. Thinking Skills Creativity **3** (2008). https://doi.org/10.1016/j.tsc.2008. 09.003

Ford, M.J.: A dialogic account of sense-making in scientific argumentation and reasoning. Cogn. Instr. **30**(3), 207–245 (2012). https://doi.org/10.1080/07370008.2012.689383

Fosnot, C.T., Perry, R.S.: Constructivism: a psychological theory of learning. In: Fosnot, C.T. (ed.), Constructivism: Theory, Perspectives, and Practice, pp. 8–33, 2nd ed. Teachers College Press (1996). http://rsperry.com/wp-content/uploads/2015/10/Final-CHAPTER-2.pdf

Frank, B.W., Scherr, R.E.: Interactional processes for stabilizing conceptual coherences in physics. Phys. Rev. Spec. Top. Phys. Educ. Res. **8**(2), 1–9 (2012). https://doi.org/10.1103/PhysRevST PER.8.020101

Freestone, M.: Curriculum improvisation. Aust. Educ. Leader **40**, 35–39 (2018)

Freire, P.: Pedagogy of the oppressed. Herder and Herder (1970)

Gideonse, T.: Cognitive dissonance and my friend Michael (2019). https://www.youtube.com/ watch?v=dr00TrsG_eo

Goodwin, B.: Mystery: Posing curious questions to spark student interest in learning. McRel International (2019). https://www.mcrel.org/mystery-posing-curious-questions/

Gregersen, H.B.: Questions Are the Answer: A Breakthrough Approach to Your Most Vexing Problems at Work and in Life. Harper Collins, New York (2018)

Gregoire, C., Kaufmann, B.K.: A Messy Mind Is Good for Creativity. Time (2015). https://time. com/collection-post/4115669/wired-to-create/

Haeleli, S.: From answers to questions: fostering student creativity and engagement in research and writing. J. Music Hist. Pedagogy **7**(1), 1–17 (2016)

Hood, M.: Questions that Spark Our Students' Curiosity. Heinemann Publishing (2018). https:// medium.com/@heinemann/questions-that-spark-our-students-curiosity-219db80f3b0bJan18

IBO. Making the Primary Years Program (PYP) Happen. International Baccalaureate Organisation (2000)

Jaber, L.Z., Hammer, D.: Learning to feel like a scientist. Sci. Edu. **100**(2), 189–220 (2016). https:// doi.org/10.1002/sce.21202

James, M., Broadfoot, P., Nuttall, D., McMeeking, S.: Records of Achievement – Report of the national Evaluation of pilot Schemes, HMSO (1988)

Kapon, S.: Unpacking sensemaking. Sci. Educ. **101**(1), 165–198 (2016). https://doi.org/10.1002/ sce.21248

Kemmis, S., McTaggart, K., (eds.), The Action Research Planner, Deakin University Press, Melbourne (1998)

Klein, G., Moom, B.: Making sense of sensemaking 1: alternative perspectives. IEEE Comput. Soc. **21**(4), 70–73 (2006). http://perigeantechnologies.com/publications/MakingSenseofSense making1-AlternativePerspectives.pdf

Kosecki (Łódź), K.: Conceptual Metaphors and Concepts of Multiple Reali-ties: Points In Common. Kwartalnik Neofilologiczny, Lviii 3/2011 (2011)

Koshik, I.: Questions and Questioning (2015). https://doi.org/10.1002/9781405186407.wbiecq 005.pub3

Lakoff. G., Ortony, A. (eds). The Contemporary Use of Metaphor, Metaphor and Thought, Cambridge University Press, Cambridge (1993)

Lakoff, G., Turner, G.: More Than Cool Reason - A Field Guide to Poetic Metaphor. University of Chicago Press, Chicago (1989)

Lewis, A., Smith, D.: Defining higher order thinking. Theor. Into Pract. **32**(3), 131–137 (1993)

Lidsky, I.: What reality are you creating for yourself? TED Talks (2016). https://www.youtube.com/watch?v=cmpu58yv8-g

Madsbjerg, C.: Sensemaking: The Power of the Humanities in the Age of the Algorithm. Hachette Books, New York (2017)

Maloney, D.: Teaching critical thinking: sense-making, explanations, language, and habits. Phys. Teach. **53**(7), 409–411 (2015). https://doi.org/10.1119/1.4931008

Manogue, C.A., Gire, E., Roundy, D.J.: Tangible Metaphors. In: Physics Education Research Conference Proceedings, pp. 27–30 (2014). https://doi.org/10.1119/perc.2013.inv.005

Mason, J.: Theorizing why in digital learning. In: Sampson, D., Ifenthaler, D., Spector, M., Isaias, P. (eds.) Digital Systems and Open Access to Formal and Informal Learning. Springer, Cham (2014). https://doi.org/10.1007/978-3-319-02264-2

Khoe, M.L.: Messy thought, neat thought. Khan Academy (2016). https://klr.tumblr.com/post/154784481858/messy-thought-neat-thought

Murdoch, K.: Moving on from the kwl chart: student questions and inquiry. Seastar (2013). https://www.kathmurdoch.com.au/blog/2013/06/08/moving-on-from-the-kwl-chart-student-questions-and-inquiry

Murdoch, K. (2018). Getting the mix right: teacher guidance and inquiry learning. Seastar, September. https://www.kathmurdoch.com.au/blog/2018/9/26/getting-the-mix-right-teacher-guidance-and-inquiry-learning

NSTA. PISA Science 2006 – Implications for science teachers and teach-ing. In: Bybee, R.W., McCrae, B.J. (eds.) National Science teachers Association, NSTA Press, Arlington (2009)

OECD. PisaPISA-Based Test for Schools Sample Test Items (2018). http://www.oecd.org/pisa/aboutpisa/PISA%20for%20Schools%20sample%20test%20items.pdf

Odden, T.O.B., Russ, R.S.: Defining sensemaking: bringing clarity to a fragmented theoretical construct. Sci. Educ. (2018). https://doi.org/10.1002/sce.21452

Odden, T.O.B., Russ, R.S.: Vexing questions that sustain sensemaking. Int. J. Sci. Educ. **41**(8), 1052–1070 (2019). https://doi.org/10.1080/09500693.2019.1589655

Ollove, M., Lteif, D.: Integrating systems thinking and storytelling. FormAkademisk **10**(1), 1–15 (2017). Art 5. https://doi.org/10.7577/formakademisk.874

Oppong, T.: All Knowledge Starts With Curiosity - The importance of speaking up, asking questions, and always staying hungry for more information. Thrive Global, January 3 (2019)

O'Toole, P.: Knowing About Knowledge, Chapter 2 in How Organisations Remember – Retaining Knowledge through Organisational Action. Springer, Cham (2011)

Palincsar, A.M.: Using higher order questions (2011). https://www.youtube.com/watch?v=XZ4LFxGi0mI

Perin, S.: The ways educators address students' wonderment questions. Relating Research to Practice (2011). http://rr2p.org/article/192

Peterson, D.S., Taylor, B.M.: Using higher order questioning to acceler-ate students' growth in reading. Read. Teach. **65**(5), 295 (2012)

Pritchard, A.: Ways of Learning - Learning Theories and Learning Styles in the Classroom. Routledge, Milton Park (2009)

Project Zero. Creative Questions. Harvard Graduate School of Education (2015). https://pz.harvard.edu/resources/creative-questions

Ram, A.: Theory of questions and question asking. J. Learn. Sci. **1**(3 & 4), 273–318 (1991)

Sanitt, N.: Culture, Curiosity and Communication in Scientific Discovery: The Eye in Ideas. Routledge, Milton Park (2018)

Scardamalia, M., Bereiter, C.: A brief history of knowledge building. Canadian J. Learn. Technol/La revue canadienne de l'apprentissage et de la technologie **36**(1), 1–16 (2010)

Schank, R.G.: The Connoisseur's Guide to the Mind: How We Think, How We Learn, and What It Means to Be Intelligent. Pocket Books, New York (1991)

Shuayb, M., Sharp, C.,Judkins M., Hetherington M.: Using Appreciative Inquiry in Educational Research: Possibilities and Limitations. Report, National Foundation for Educational Research (2009). https://www.nfer.ac.uk/publications/aen01/aen01.pdf

Spencer, J.: The Shift from Engaging Students to Empowering Learners (2017). https://www.you tube.com/watch?v=BYBJQ5rIFjA

Spencer, J.: Spark curiosity and help students ask better questions (2019). http://spencerauthor. com/ask-tons-of-questions

Sternberg R.J.: Critical Thinking: Its Nature, Measurement, and Improvement (1986)

ERIC - ED272882 - Critical Thinking: Its Nature, Measurement, and Improvement

Tawfik, A.A., Graesser, A., Gatewood, J., Gishbaugher, J.: Role of questions in inquiry-based instruction: Towards a design taxonomy for question-asking and implications for design. Educ. Technol. Res. Dev. **68**(2), 653–678 (2020). https://doi.org/10.1007/s11423-020-09738-9

TeachThought Staff. A Guide to Questioning in the Classroom. TeachThought (2019). https://www.teachthought.com/critical-thinking/quick-guide-questioning-classroom/

Thomas, D., Brown, J.S.: A new culture of learning: Cultivating the imagination for a world of constant change. CreateSpace (2011)

Turnbull, N.: What is the Status of Questioning in John Dewey's Philosophy. Australian Political Studies Association Conference, University of Adelaide (2004). https://www.academia.edu/2783340/What_is_the_Status_of_Questioning_in_John_Dewey_s_Philosophy

Vogt, E.E., Brown, J., Isaacs, D.: The Art of Powerful Questions. Whole Systems Associates, Pegasus Communications, Inc, Arcadia (2003)

Vygotsky, L.S.: Mind in Society: the Development of Higher Psychological Processes. Harvard University Press, Cambridge (1978)

Wegerif, R.: Creativity: Playful Reflective Dialogue in Classrooms. In: Dialogic Education and Technology. Computer-Supported Collaborative Learning, vol. 7. Springer, Boston (2007). https://doi.org/10.1007/978-0-387-71142-3_5

Weick, K.E.: Sensemaking in organizations. Foundations for Organizational Science. Sage, Thousand Oaks (1995)

Weick, K.E., Sutcliffe, K.M., Obstfeld, D.: Organizing and the process of sensemaking. Organ. Sci. **16**(4), 409–421 (2005)

Weimer, M.: Multiple-Choice Tests: Revisiting the Pros and Cons. Educational Assessment, Faculty Focus, Higher Ed Teaching Strategies from Magna publications (2018). https://www.facultyfocus.com/articles/educational-assessment/multiple-choice-tests-pros-cons/

Wellman, H.M.: The origins of metacognition. Metacognition Cogn. Hum. Perform. **1**, 1–31 (1985)

Zambrano, R.: The "Big Bang" of Motivation Questions That Evoke Wonder in our Students. Teaching and Learning, Faculty Focus, Higher Ed Teaching Strategies From Magna Publications (2019). https://www.facultyfocus.com/articles/teaching-and-learning/the-big-bang-of-motivation-questions-that-evoke-wonder-in-our-students/

Zimmerman, B.J.: Ralph Stacey's Agreement & Certainty Matrix. Schulich School of Business, York University, Canada (2001)

Zohar, A., Barzilai, S.: A review of research on metacognition in science education: current and future directions. Stud. Sci. Educ. **49**(2), 121–169 (2013)

Students' Perceptions Exploring a WebXR Learning Environment

Bárbara Cleto(✉) , Ricardo Carvalho , and Maria Ferreira

Universidade de Aveiro, Aveiro, Portugal
{barbara.cleto,ricardojoc,mariajesusferreira}@ua.pt

Abstract. The work described in this paper is a case study, which involved 3 computer science teachers and 29 students from secondary school programming course, from 3 high schools. Informed consent was obtained from the students (those of legal age and the rest from their Parents and Guardians). In this initial phase of the course, it is important to know if the students are motivated to learn how to program and model objects, on the other hand it is intend that the students have a learning experience immersed in a 3D environment to evaluate the impact of this strategy in their willingness to learn. To carry out this study, the following research question was formulated: What is the student's perception about learning 3D programming and modelling immersed in a virtual environment? Two questionnaires were applied, a pre-test before the intervention and a post-test, immediately after the intervention. The results proved to be promising, having verified that these environments allow students to collaborate and learn in an intuitive and interactive way.

Keywords: Immersive web environments · Programming · 3D object modelling · Collaboration

1 Introduction

The emergence of immersive web environments democratizes the access to these sorts of environments and puts an end to some constraints, since the teacher has access to a simple customization technology [1], any teacher from any area or teaching level is able to design and customize an immersive web environment, adapting it to their teaching practice, without having to know how to handle a programming language. This environment runs on a browser, without the need to connect to any other device so that students and teachers are able to share the virtual space and interact with each other.

Interaction, in an immersive web environment, is one of the most important aspects of the interface, since it is related to the computer's ability to detect the users' actions and react to them, modifying the environment [2, 3]. This allows leveraging some skills, at a creativity level, in the replication of real spaces, or the creation of imaginary worlds, using static or moving objects [2] and collaboration, by interacting with others in the creation of these worlds.

© ICST Institute for Computer Sciences, Social Informatics and Telecommunications Engineering 2022
Published by Springer Nature Switzerland AG 2022. All Rights Reserved
E. Brooks et al. (Eds.): DLI 2021, LNICST 435, pp. 230–241, 2022.
https://doi.org/10.1007/978-3-031-06675-7_17

Engagement is a process that reflects the quality of the user experience, based on the level of cognitive, temporal and/or emotional dedication employed in the interaction with a digital system" [4]. For the author, engagement is a multidimensional concept and is directly related to student participation during didactic activities. The more engaged with the activity, the greater the motivation to develop it, therefore, the greater the learning effectiveness. There is great concern on the part of interaction designers and developers to create immersive web environments that create and keep users engaged in tasks, otherwise, if the immersive environment does not have the ability to maintain attention and improve the user experience, it tends to be abandoned.

Immersive experiences are engaging and create a sense of presence in students, as if they were part of the virtual world. These experiences are useful to stimulate students' interaction with learning activities and foster collaboration among them. In addition, self-creation and interactivity within immersive environments allow the development of activities close to reality, resembling the practices performed in learning labs [2, 5, 6].

A benefit of using these environments in education, is the possibility to manipulate, visualize and explore the objects in real time using their senses and natural body movements [2]. This type of interface allows the transfer of the student's intuitive knowledge with the physical world, to the virtual world. Traditional virtual learning platforms, such as Moodle or Google's classroom, are usually static and do not allow this type of interaction.

Immersive web environments, such as Mozilla Hubs [7], FrameVR [8], Spatial[9], among others, intuitively allow students and teachers to meet in a three-dimensional space, build rich environments with personalised experiences, converse by voice or text, together or separately, as well as enabling students and teachers to bring the constructs of the virtual world into their real environment through augmented reality.

Immersive web environments may present themselves as ideal for schools to begin exploring and researching the potential of these tools in distance education for experiential learning - not as a substitute, but as a complement. This experiment arises from the willingness of authors/teachers to study the potential and limitations of using this technology in learning activities, and whether it brings benefits for students' learning.

The work presented here was carried out by three computer science teachers and twenty-nine first-year students of the Information Systems Management and Programming course, from three secondary schools, located in different places of the country. We intended to understand if students are motivated to learn how to program and model 3D objects but immersed in a virtual environment.

2 Methodology

An investigation always involves a problem, formulated by the researcher, and to which there is no theoretical answer. In qualitative methodology, based on the phenomenological-interpretative paradigm [10], the problem has the important function of focusing the researcher's attention to the phenomenon under analysis, playing a "guide" in the research, because it focuses the research on an area or domain, organises the project by giving it coherence and direction, delimits the study by showing the boundaries, directs the literature review to the central question, provides a reference for the drafting of the project and points to the data that will need to be obtained [11].

For this intervention cycle, the following research question was formulated "What are the student's perceptions regarding the learning of 3D programming and modelling, immersed in a virtual environment?" To answer the question the following specific objectives were defined:

– To assess whether the student is predisposed to learning how to model 3D objects through programming,
– To assess the students' perception of their enthusiasm for programming.
– To assess whether students enjoy learning in immersive virtual environments.

Quantitative data were collected through a survey and qualitative data from the video recordings made during the intervention. Notes were also collected (field diary) from the participating teachers/observers [11, 12].

2.1 Pedagogical Intervention

In this experience we transposed the "traditional" classroom to an immersive web environment (Fig. 1), using the Mozilla Hubs platform.

Fig. 1. Virtual classroom room in the Mozzila Hubs environment

Students were challenged to program their own 3D objects (Fig. 2), using the TinkerCad Platform [13] to develop programming skills required in the curriculum of the Professional Course of Management and Programming of Computer Systems, in the subject of Programming and Information Systems, whose module one "Introduction to Programming and Algorithmics" this module was taught in a distance learning regime, using a learning management platform (Moodle [14]) and the immersive web environment, Hubs by Mozilla, with the following learning objectives:

– Apply instructions and logical sequences in problem solving.
– Learn concepts about programming logic

- Identify the different types of data
- Identify variables and constants
- List and identify arithmetic, relational, and logical operators.

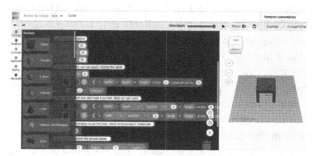

Fig. 2. TinkerCad: 3D programming software

The Mozilla Hubs environment is a collaborative web application that allows people to come together in customisable immersive environments, for example for meetings, for learning or simply for virtual socialising, and in which participants can join using virtual reality glasses or by using a computer with a browser. We chose to create a space in this tool that simulated the face-to-face classroom, as students moved into distance education due to the pandemic. The aim was to make them feel as if they were in a typical physical classroom. In this environment two different spaces were personalised; a large room, decorated with a world map, the periodic table, chairs and two whiteboards. In one of the whiteboards the teacher's computer screen was projected, showing the code and explaining its construction, line by line; in the other, the already programmed 3D object was projected. In the second space it was decided to customise six smaller, collaborative breakout rooms (Fig. 3), reserved for group work. These contained a table, six chairs and three boards, one on each wall. On the boards the students shared the monitors of their computers and discussed the solutions as they were programming the 3D objects.

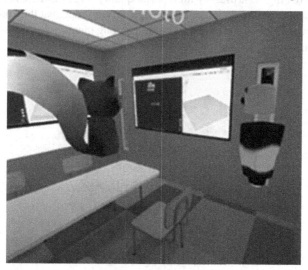

Fig. 3. Breakout rooms

TinkerCad, is a free online platform, provided and maintained by Autodesk, which provides a set of online development tools. It allows you to create 3D objects in a very simple and intuitive way, modeling 3D objects using the Codeblocks programming language.

The students being physically in their homes and virtually in the immersive environment, shared their computer screen in the collaborative room. As shown in Fig. 3, two students are interacting with each other, talking, and simultaneously viewing the two screens, where the TinkerCad software is projected.

The experiment ran for three weeks, one fifty-minute lesson per week. In the first lesson, the students attended, in the large room, a short briefing on navigating the Hubs Mozila environment. They created their avatars and explored for a few minutes all the spaces of the classroom environment. Next, they were invited to sit down to listen to the instructions from the guiding teacher, after settling down and satisfying all their doubts about the environment, the teacher taught the 3D object modelling programming content. For that purpose, he shared his screen inside the 3D immersive environment (most of the students didn't know the block language and had never modelled 3D objects), after the explanation they went to the small rooms to program their objects, in the first class they had to create a table (Fig. 2). On the second lesson, the students showed more mastery and comfort in both navigation and procedures, they questioned less and were more familiar with the environment, so the lesson flowed quite well. In this class, the students entered, immediately went to the large room, and waited for the teacher's words. The teacher presented the lesson objectives, the programming content for the second lesson, demonstrated the code and the modelled object. Then the students went to the collaborative rooms and developed their activity, this time they had to program a rocket. In the third and last class an Easter related activity was proposed, in this class there was no previous explanation, being expected that the students would apply the knowledge acquired previously. The final works exceeded the teachers' expectations, who expected most of the works to be Easter eggs decorated with other geometric shapes, since it would be the easiest approach, however the students used their creativity and ended up creating 3D artifacts with superior quality (Fig. 4), which revealed not only application but also consolidation of knowledge. It was found that they only resorted to the teachers' help, after discussing the solution among themselves and with colleagues from other classrooms.

Fig. 4. 3D object programming - Example of an artifact produced by the students

2.2 Data Collection Instruments and Techniques

To carry out this experiment, the authors chose indirect observation, using video recordings, survey questionnaires and an unstructured grid to record everything they saw and heard within the immersive environment. The interactions between students and teachers were recorded in 30 video recordings of approximately 3 to 5 min each, these videos were transcribed and analytically processed. Two strategies were developed to capture the video recordings. One camera recorded in the common room, recording the interactions in the large room. The other consisted of creating several camera avatars placing them in the various work rooms (breakout rooms).

Two questionnaires were designed, the first (Q1), was applied in the first class, before the students entered the immersive web environment of Hubs Mozilla and focused on the expectations and prior knowledge of students regarding immersive web environments, programming language and 3D modelling, the second (Q2), was applied in the third class, after the conclusion of the experiment. The questions of the questionnaires were similar, in order to allow the comparison of the students' answers, before and after the intervention. The questionnaires were answered online and consisted of six questions. A 5-level Likert scale (1 - Strongly disagree, 2 - Disagree, 3. No opinion, 4- Agree, 5 - Strongly agree) and a non-mandatory open-ended question were used to collect the student's opinion about the experience. A 5-level Likert scale was chosen, to enable the choice between two levels of negative and two levels of positive answers, and a neutral level, for students who have no, or do not intend to give their opinion.

2.3 Results Analysis

Direct and Indirect Observation

First lesson in the Mozilla Hubs Immersive Web Environment: Students explored the environment, configured their avatar, tested navigation, tried out the features available in the environment (Screen sharing, placing 3D objects, images, videos), entered and left the rooms, looked at the information displayed on the walls and talked to each other. They listened to the teacher's instructions about 3D programming, they organised themselves in teams and went to the breakout rooms; they programmed a table in 3 dimensions, in Tinkercad, the students shared the screen inside the environment and talked amongst themselves; A group of students left and entered the environment, the internet connection was very unstable, so students were disconnected and lost workflow.

Second lesson: More dexterity in handling the platform was observed. The students went to the "big" room as soon as they entered, they focused on the teacher's instructions in a more organized way (they sat on the chairs), they interacted with the teacher, asking questions about programming and 3D modeling, more familiarity with teachers and students from other schools, they organized the working groups and the strategies to solve the proposed activity. The internet was more stable which allowed a consistent work since the students were not disconnected. The students programmed a 3D rocket, more complex compared to the table they programmed in the first class.

In the third class on the Immersive Web Environment: the students showed great ease of navigation, they configured new avatars, avatars with webcam, which allowed the students to see each other's faces. They kept the same behavior and interaction of session two and demonstrated acquisition and application of the acquired knowledge, they cooperated amongst themselves and between groups to complete the activity which consisted in programming 3D objects allusive to Easter, the artifacts produced by the students showed great quality.

Analysis of Students' Answers of the Before and After the Experiment Questionnaires

It was of interest to the authors to find the students perceptions about this experience in these immersive environments. To the statement "I like/liked learning programming" (Table 1).

Table 1. I like/liked learning programming

Questions	Q1	Q2
I totally agree	21	20
Agree	7	9
No opinion	1	0
Disagree	0	0
I totally disagree	0	0

In this matter, the differences of opinion before and after the experience are not significant. Only one student, who had no previous opinion, gave a favourable opinion after the experience, stating that he liked learning to program. On the question "I will like/liked learning 3D Modelling" (Table 2).

Table 2. I will like/liked learning 3D modeling

Questions	Q1	Q2
I totally agree	14	17
Agree	8	9
No opinion	5	3
Disagree	2	0
I totally disagree	0	0

It can be inferred that the students enjoyed modelling 3D objects using visual programming, noteworthy that none of these students had programmed 3D objects before. As it can be seen from the table, before the experiment, 5 students had no opinion and 2 students thought that they wouldn't like 3D modeling. After the intervention the students' perception was more favourable. On the question "I will liked/like learning in an immersive web environment." (Table 3).

Table 3. I will liked/like learning in a virtual reality environment

Questions	Q1	Q2
I totally agree	20	18
Agree	5	8
No opinion	3	3
disagree	1	0
I totally disagree	0	0

As can be seen the students had higher expectations regarding the virtual immersion experience, perhaps it is due to the fact that they are used to the immersion of video games and these present components of greater playfulness, when compared to educational immersive environments.

In the questionnaire presented before the experiment the students were asked to answer the following question "Tell in your own words what you expect to find in the classroom in an immersive environment" The following answers were given (Table 4).

Table 4. What you expect to find in the classroom in virtual reality environment (**Q1**)

3D modeling
I would like to learn more about virtual reality since never had experience with it
Entertained
Don't know
More "fun" ways to learn
A new challenge that is very interesting and fun
To have a real life like experience
Many 3D objects
Many interesting and diverging objects I hope it will be good
I honestly have no idea
Real things but in virtual reality
No idea
Learning to use virtual reality
A big space with many possibilities to learn new things in a more creative
New things in more creative ways
I hope to find new ways of learning about
Game programming and programming in general and how to
Create games in virtual reality

(*continued*)

Table 4. (*continued*)

3D modeling
An open space with a menu where you can select objects and make objects, using them to make something creative
A new world where I can be creating whatever I want
I hope to find new ways to learn to program, both in general and in games
A dynamic or different learning
I don't really know
Some virtual reality goggles, and I green background so we can have a better view of the result
To have a healthy environment
The VR glasses
I hope I find something surprising
I hope to find something surprising
To be able to create objects
I hope to find a realistic classroom

Analyzing Table 4, we can see that of the 20 top written words by students (Fig. 5) the words "learn", "hope", "objects" and "Virtual reality" stood out. It should be noted that students had never experienced an educational activity in virtual reality and/or 3D immersive environment. Students were only informed that they would program 3D objects in an immersive environment. Regarding expectations, some students associated this type of environment with video games, others with a creative and fun way of learning, while others had no idea what they were going to find.

Fig. 5. Top 20 words mentioned by students (before the experiment)

After the experience the students were asked to answer the following question "Tell in your own words what you found in the classroom immersive environment". The following responses were given (Table 5).

Table 5. "What you found in the classroom in the virtual reality environment" (**Q2**)

Good
In the virtual reality classroom, you can solve problems with the other people there and "see" each other
3D objects

(*continued*)

Table 5. (*continued*)

Good
Diversity
In the virtual reality classroom, there is not much distraction and I find it better
Very fun and an interesting experience
A classroom
Nothing special, it was just a virtual classroom
I don't know
I found some classrooms, meetings, moved objects, boards etc.
A classroom
I was surprised, because I was not expecting all that
I found the possibility to find objects and different people in which we could create objects
It is very nice because we can feel ourselves in a new environment
My classmates, and others from other schools
A different emersion
Funny objects
Students
I found a good environment where all users could interact freely with each other
I found many things between animals and objects but I made a rocket
I created I blue rocket, many objects that we could interact with
Work, a camera going into the walls, my share flying and going through walls, making a rocket and a table with the scheme that was on the board was interesting, the outside with a house and the rest empty; and people who don't talk coming in and out of the room

The students' answers to the open question "what you found in the classroom in the virtual reality environment" highlighted the words "classroom" and "objects" (Fig. 6) as the most frequently mentioned. The students focused on the activity to be performed (programming 3D objects), collaborating with colleagues from other schools, in a space identical to the traditional classroom, but they refer to this space as less distracting.

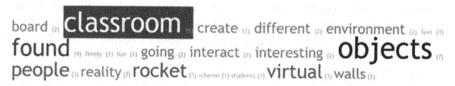

Fig. 6. Top 20 words mentioned by students (after the experiment)

In the questionnaire applied after the intervention, it was also asked if they agreed with the following statement "I was inspired to learn more about programming after this class in immersive environment" they picked the answer from a Likert scale that started on "I totally agree" and ended in "I totally disagree as shown in Table 6.

Table 6. I was inspired to learn more about programming after this lesson in virtual reality environment

Questions	Q2
I totally agree	10
Agree	8
No opinion	3
Disagree	1
I totally disagree	0

Not all students answered this question, only 21 out of 29 and it was found that most enjoyed and felt inspired to learn to program in an immersive web environment.

3   Final Remarks

The results show that the students interacted, collaborated, and learned with their peers, however they had high expectations about using the Immersive Web Environment to learn curricular concepts, on the other hand, the students enjoyed modelling 3D objects using programming. The experience was classified as very positive, and they referred that they would like to have more classes in this sort of environment. Despite the reduced number of classes, only three of 50 min, the results were optimistic, and it is possible to conclude that: i) students like programming, ii) students like modelling 3D objects through programming, iii) students liked the immersion experience. The results allow us to infer those students were motivated to learn programming, in this sense, this research will start the next stage of development of an immersive experience under a theme to be decided by the students, in which they will create the 3D objects to include in the environment and customize it to their liking.

In conclusion, as indicated in the literature review, these environments have the potential to provide a good learning experience, with several benefits for students, and can be used as strategic resources to motivate and engage, as they offer the possibility to collaborate and interact, allowing exploration and discovery. The more involved with the activity, the greater the motivation to develop it, therefore, the greater the effectiveness of learning. It also enables collaboration between students from various institutions and allows interaction between peers, or even, extend to collaborations between teaching institutions [15].

References

1. Schussler, T.: XRC XR Collaboration. https://xrcollaboration.com/wp-content/uploads/2020/05/XR-Collaboration-V4.pdf. Accessed 22 Nov 2021
2. Gomes, M.S., Piovesan, S.D., Wagner, R.: Modelagem do 'sistema imersivo da unipampa' Campus Bagé Modeling of the 'immersive system of unipampa' Campus Bagé. Braz. J. Dev. **5**(6), 5509–5518 (2019)
3. Carolina, A., Queiroz, M.: Ambientes virtuais imersivos e aprendizagem, August 2020
4. de Carvalho, A.: Engajamento e ambientes virtuais imersivos: uma proposta de diretrizes, Feburary 2018. http://lattes.cnpq.br/0973290870837883
5. Cheng, K.H., Tsai, C.C.: A case study of immersive virtual field trips in an elementary classroom: students' learning experience and teacher-student interaction behaviors. Comput. Educ. **140**, 103600 (2019)
6. Dede, C.: Immersive interfaces for engagement and learning. Science **323**(5910), 66–69 (2009)
7. Hubs - Private social VR in your web browser. https://hubs.mozilla.com/. Accessed 29 May 2021
8. FRAME. https://framevr.io/. Accessed 22 Nov 2021
9. Spatial - Virtual Spaces That Bring Us Together. https://spatial.io/. Accessed 22 Nov 2021
10. Amado, J.: Manual de Investigação Qualitativa em Educação, 2ª. (2014)
11. Coutinho, C.P.: Metodologia de Investigação em Ciências Sociais e Humanas, 2ª. (2015)
12. Bogdan, R.C., Biklen, S.K.: Investigação Qualitativa em Educação - Uma Introdução à Teoria e aos Métodos. Porto (2013)
13. Tinkercad, Create 3D digital designs with online CAD, Tinkercad. https://www.tinkercad.com/. Accessed 29 May 2021
14. Moodle - Open-source learning platform, Moodle.org. https://moodle.org/. Accessed 22 Nov 2021
15. Ziker, C., Truman, B., Dodds, H.: Cross reality (XR): challenges and opportunities across the spectrum. In: Ryoo, J., Winkelmann, K. (eds.) Innovative Learning Environments in STEM Higher Education: Opportunities, Challenges, and Looking Forward, pp. 55–77. Springer, Cham (2021). https://doi.org/10.1007/978-3-030-58948-6_4

Author Index

Printed in the United States
by Baker & Taylor Publisher Services